STARING DOWN THE
BEAST

How I Enjoyed Myself Well from a
Brain Tumour Death Sentence

KEITH LIVINGSTONE

BALBOA
PRESS

A DIVISION OF HAY HOUSE

Balboa Press books may be ordered through booksellers or by contacting:

Balboa Press
A Division of Hay House
1663 Liberty Drive
Bloomington, IN 47403
www.balboapress.com.au
1 (877) 407-4847

ISBN: 978-1-5043-1522-7 (sc)
ISBN: 978-1-5043-1523-4 (e)

Print information available on the last page.

Balboa Press rev. date: 11/28/2018

CONTENTS

Grant Vesey, Champion bloke, 1954-2003

On the 16th day of February each year, a large group of surfers gather together in the constant grey swell off Muriwai Beach, northwest of Auckland in New Zealand, for a *sunset surf*–the last surf of the day. They are occasionally watched by a very old lady.

They paddle out into the surf, and gather in a large circle, in remembrance of one of their own whose life was tragically cut short in 2003, by a silent assassin; the lethal brain tumour glioblastoma multiforme.

This book is dedicated to the memory of Grant Vesey, a great bloke who was once a surf-lifesaving champion with Muriwai Surf Lifesaving Club, and an extremely popular Props-Master with Television New Zealand.

Grant's mother, Rose Vesey, passed on recently at 102 years old, and to this day Grant's loss cuts deeply for the whole clan.

Kerrie Walker, Champion Lady, 12th May 1965 - 31st October 2017.

Kerrie, younger sister of my friend and university mate Doctor Michael Troy, passed after an extremely determined battle with glioblastoma multiforme over several years.

Right to the very end, she was willing herself to get back, and took to conversing by facebook when her speech was struck down early on: nevertheless; she painstakingly touch-typed notes as her condition deteriorated around her.

Kerrie passed peacefully, leaving her former husband Andrew, brothers Michael and Simon, and parents Tommy and Gloria, as well as her children Amanda, Daniel, and Andrew.

Rose Vesey, Champion bloke's Mum, 1916-2018

In 1930, when she was only 14 years old, Roseanna Fitzpatrick left her family home in Bunnahow, County Clare, to escape depression-era Ireland for London, where she soon got a job in a hotel as a maid. She followed older siblings to London. Her sheltered upbringing in a large Catholic family didn't prepare her for the seedy side of life in London- especially when she had to prepare a double bed for two gentlemen guests, one of whom she found murdered in the same bed the next morning. Within a few days of moving to London, Rose had been interviewed as a witness in a murder case by detectives from Scotland Yard!

Roseanna later emigrated to New Zealand, marrying Doug Vesey, a nuggety tradesman and *bushman* who had survived polio as a youngster, and had a wicked sense of humour. Together, they had four children; Greg, Anne, Grant and Michele. Grant was our childhood friend, who unfortunately passed on with the same type of tumour that I eventually had, in 2003.

Aunty Rose was a mainstay in my childhood in New Zealand, and we've always kept in contact over the years.

Until her last few weeks, Rose was a *regular* at Sky City Casino in Auckland, where she played *Bingo* with her girlfriends (all about 50 years younger!). Her hundredth birthday made national television news in New Zealand as the Casino gave her a free birthday reception.

FOREWORD

Reflecting on a friendship that has spanned more than fifty years, and sharing the many trials, tribulations and triumphs, the simplest way to describe Dr Keith Livingstone is this: – Tenacity, determination and an unswerving belief in himself. All the reserves that Keith could muster and then a whole reservoir I suspect even he didn't know he possessed, has enabled him to not only face death head on but smash through the limitations that many around him were placing on him.

Through sheer guts and a healthy dose of denial Keith has been able to not only beat the odds but recreate a life not only worth living but worth getting up for each and every day.

Surrounded by a young and growing family and with unwavering support from his loving wife Joanne (Jo), Keith is an inspiration to those who know him and have walked the journey with him.

Read, Reflect and Treasure every day.

Gavin Harris, Auckland.

FOREWORD

Writing an autobiography is a process of reflection. Like most reflections, when someone looks in a mirror, they see an inverted image of themselves from their own point of view. Arguably, this is not the whole perspective or the full picture. With the various blind spots we all have as human beings, it is a hard task to see ourselves without distortion from our own point of view, let alone how others see us. How much harder still, when you have barely survived the swirling blades of the Grim Reaper, several times in a lifetime?

The task is amplified when your cerebral cortex has been invaded by an alien impostor, then opened up in a series of traumatic yet delicate neurological operations. Reviewing your memories would be like trying to find documents in an upside down filing cabinet, in complete darkness, after an earthquake. Where does one start?

To my brother, holding on to life with the slightest ray of light has always been a far better option than dutifully following the script and quietly slipping away. Indeed, there has been nothing dutiful or quiet about Keith over a lifetime, which is probably why he's still here as I write.

Colin Livingstone,

Colin is on the left, with Keith holding the cat.

FOREWORD

I've been involved in Keith's management of his primary brain cancer since the 17th of August 2007. He presented with a right frontal mixed anaplastic astrocytoma. He has had treatment for his cancer including neurosurgery on three occasions, as well as radiotherapy and chemotherapy.

Having spent quite a lot of time with Keith, he is extremely self-motivated and has always strived to optimize his outcomes. He has worked tirelessly to maintain general health through diet, exercise and neuroplastic techniques. A truly remarkable effort.

Dr Robert Blum, Medical Oncologist, Bendigo Health.

INTRODUCTION

My name is Keith Livingstone, and I have managed for the most part to *enjoy myself well* while having a medically-diagnosed *terminal* tumour of the brain that was *supposed* to have killed me outright over a decade ago.

The tumour, *glioblastoma multiforme*, has the reputation of being *unsurviveable*. If that's the case, then I am here to tell you that if you care for your brain's general health, and give it what it really needs, you might find that even the *unsurviveable* can be relatively pleasant to cope with while you choose to outlast it.

So here I am, about 11 years down the track from my first collapse, enjoying a relatively normal life and still planning my future adventures and projects.

I decided to write this book to encourage others in my situation to think differently about what's going on, and to give people advice based on what's definitely worked for me.

In telling my story, you're likely to get confused if I don't clarify the broad overview beforehand. My story spans several countries and eras, starting in Kenya where I was born in 1958, with my twin brother, Colin, arriving 5 minutes after me in a bit of a surprise for my parents at that time. We started school in Kenya, but with all the uncertainties of Kenyan Independence in late 1964, we emigrated to Auckland, New Zealand, in early 1965 with our mother, Valerie Livingstone, who was a highly qualified secondary school teacher. My father, who was bound to contractual work in Kenya, emigrated about 18 months after we had settled in Auckland.

In Auckland, we *grew up Kiwi* and completed our schooling. My brother eventually went on to work for Television New Zealand as a scenic artist and set designer, while I went on to work for Radio New Zealand as firstly a radio cadet in 1977, and then as a copywriting production-writer in Christchurch, Auckland and Wellington between 1978 and 1982.

In the interim, I had become a national-class distance runner, and won a number of titles and races over cross country, track, and road, with the aim of perhaps making it to Olympic level. It was not to be; despite having beaten several people who later did well to make the Olympics, I never did, due to youthful impatience and the untimely injuries or form lapses which resulted.

In 1982 I moved to Melbourne, Australia, to study Chiropractic. I raced at top state level in Victoria for about nine years. I am now married to an Australian girl, Joanne, and have five Aussie kids between 10 and 24 years of age. We live in Bendigo, a large Victorian town that dates back to the Gold Rush era. I'll share my life story as best I can.

CHAPTER 1

How to Make Lemonade: First-You Need Some Lemons

In July 2007 I collapsed suddenly while writing a report in my newly built and heavily-financed chiropractic office in Bendigo, Victoria. I can clearly remember what I was doing up to the moment of my collapse, and how good I felt as I was nearing a *completion* on the task at hand.

Bang! Was all I heard. It was like a shotgun blast inside my head. Then the darkness imploded to a pinhole of light, just like turning off a television.

I awoke on the floor of my office, on the other side of my chiropractic bench from where I had been sitting at the computer. There were two paramedics attending me. My trousers were damp with warm urine.

There were three women standing quietly against the far wall. One was my wife Joanne, the other my chiropractic assistant Lisa, and the final lady was my local colleague, chiropractic neurologist Helen Sexton.

The paramedics' questions came thick and fast.

"Can you tell me your name?"

"Who is the prime minister of Australia?"

"What day is it?"

"How many children do you have?"

In my awakening state, I correctly answered "four children" to the last question, and there was muffled laughter from the ladies. A few minutes earlier, apparently, I had muttered "Children? What children?"

My left cheek, lip, and tongue felt like I had been chewing on a cheese grater; the taste of blood was salty and raw.

Apparently I'd had a *grand-mal* seizure, where my whole torso had gone into violent extension, and I'd lurched backwards at full power straight over the top of the chiropractic table. My whole left side was thumping super-fast while I fitted on the floor. I bit down ferociously with my left molars on my tongue and cheek.

The paramedics insisted I lie down on a stretcher, even though I felt quite capable of getting up and about, if not a bit dazed. They bundled me into the ambulance for the start of an interesting trip, which was a dizzying rollercoaster of negatives and positives for the next two years, and from which we are only just starting to fully recover from financially, physically, and emotionally now, over eleven years down the track.

I was admitted to the local hospital where a CT scan was made; this showed that there had been a large *sub-arachnoid bleed* over the surface of the right pre-frontal cortex. Reasonably large volumes of liquid, including blood, plasma, or water, can show up as white *shadows* on CT scans. I could clearly see the white shadow of the brain bleed on that first night when I was shown the scan. The *bang* I experienced when I collapsed was likely the rupturing of a sub-arachnoid blood vessel. The bleed formed a white saucer-shaped depression as seen on CT scan, into the surface of the right frontal lobe, between the cranium and the brain. There was also another *sinister* density below it, about 3 centimetres underneath the pre-frontal cortex of the brain. The attending physician told me that it was likely a *glioma*, which is a tumour of the glial cells that form the matrix in which the brain is supported and nourished.

The whole experience was surreal, and very, very confronting. Late at night, here I was in the gloom of a hospital ward, having just had a bleed of the brain. It wasn't a stroke as such; I had all my faculties.

I am not generally a person who panics, however I was in a maelstrom of confusion, and extremely worried, not so much for myself, but for my wife and children. I calmed myself by resorting to praying in gratitude for the experience, and thanking my Maker for my having had a very healthy and fortunate life thus far. I knew enough from all my reading and experiences over the years that *miracles* cannot occur without plugging oneself into the *source*. I asked Joanne to bring my favourite study Bible in, and drifted to sleep after reading the Twenty-third psalm over, several times. You'll know the one; "The Lord Is My Shepherd; I shall not want..."

Over the years, I had often presented at chiropractic seminars on the power of purpose in life, often citing from the book of Proverbs, as well as from my favourite expert on the psychology of survival, Professor Victor Frankel (more on the professor later...). I have studied the ancient origins of the Book of Proverbs in some depth, too. I also presented at the lay services early on Sunday mornings before the seminars started. So, in a way, I was fore-armed and fore-warned by experience, as well as research, in the *how- to's* of surviving nearly anything.

CHAPTER 2

The Lord Of Life Itself

Many people these days cite the *universe* as the source and provider of our needs. Some people openly acknowledge *source*. I am *far* more black and white than that; there is a *universe*, obviously, with its inherent laws, but I feel it's all held in place by the unbounded creative intelligence of God Himself. I *talk* every hour or so with this *bloke*, so wonderfully described by the former Lord High Chancellor of Britain, Lord Hailsham, who once wrote,

> The tragedy of the Cross was not that they crucified a melancholy figure, full of moral precepts, ascetic and gloomy … What they crucified was a young man, vital, full of life and the joy of it, the *Lord of life itself* … someone so utterly attractive that people followed him for the sheer fun of it.

So that's who I've been plugged into for many years now; the *Lord of Life Itself*. He's like my very cool big brother, and he's always looking out for me.

To add to the surreal nature of the experience, the night before my first collapse, I had attended a video *refresher* education night with local chiropractors on the neurology of stroke and other cerebrovascular conditions. One of the subjects we were informed about was a differential diagnosis for stroke from other neurological events. If someone still retained the ability to poke one's tongue into one's cheek on both sides, this indicated there had likely not been a stroke. There are other tests that anyone can use, such as observing for an even smile, the ability to raise one's arms evenly, and the ability to speak clearly.

I told my wife about those tests when I returned home late, about 10 pm.

After I got over the initial collapse, I could perform all of those tests very well, and I was able to get up and about normally, and think and speak reasonably clearly, so I knew I hadn't suffered a true stroke. The physician said that the *bleed* was probably caused by a build-up of intra-cranial pressure within the brain, coming from a *space-occupying lesion*.

Even more surreally, on the Tuesday before my Thursday collapse, I received a copy of *The Four Hour Workweek* by Timothy Ferris. On the back cover came the all-too-prophetic statement:

WARNING! DO NOT READ THIS BOOK UNLESS YOU WANT TO QUIT YOUR JOB!

I had read most of the book on the Tuesday night, however I found Ferris's style to be a bit brash for my taste. To each their own, I guess. Some of Ferris's accounts were hilarious though.

After a night in the local hospital, I was transferred by ambulance to St Vincent's Public Hospital in Melbourne, for exploratory surgery by the highly-regarded neurosurgeon Professor Michael Murphy.

The trip by ambulance to Melbourne was notable for its relative silence. There's not much to talk about cheerfully when the patient is facing a possible terminal situation. It had been raining, and my memory of the trip was of the muted sounds of the wet road under the tyres, broken only by an occasional *ker-thump* as the ambulance struck yet another errant endangered marsupial or rabbit. The gold-green glow of the ambulance's low-level interior lighting added to the sombre feel.

Once at St Vincent's Public, I was given a bed in a shared room on the tenth floor. Like the ambulance, it appeared minimally lit. I was advised strongly to get to sleep, however I couldn't, so I got up and wandered around the half-lit ward, and looked down at the midwinter midnight of the Exhibition Gardens across the road. There were no people or cars to be seen. Only a slowly-moving tram belied the fact that this was not a giant scale model.

"Come on, Keith! You *must* get to sleep" said the nurse in charge of the ward. I was so upset, all I could do was hug her into me as I sobbed for my family, and for myself.

Then I went and slept soundly through the night, with the help of a little pill.

The next morning, I was taken for an MRI study, where MRI-opaque tabs that resembled corn pads were placed on key parts of my head, in order to obtain millimetre-precise accuracy for the neurosurgery later in the morning, of which I have no memory except the preparation, and being wheeled out of the theatre.

Later that day I was told that a group of Bendigo chiropractors, as well as our former associate chiropractors from Swan Hill, Josh and Kim, had banded together to run our clinics for us until we could get a reliable locum. They donated their time to us. Being a chiropractor is like being part of a large family; chiropractors tend to be very gregarious and supportive within the *tribe*. My immediate feeling was that I was loved by many people, regardless of the condition which I now had to contend with, and that everyone was trying their best to help us out in whatever way they could. It was very reassuring to know that there were so many kind people wishing me and the family well; many were former patients who I'd helped in earlier years.

CHAPTER 3

We're All Terminal, Aren't We?

The neurosurgery registrar at St Vincent's Public Hospital in Melbourne was a tall, pleasant younger man named Paul. In the post-surgical rounds, he assessed me and said "Well, Keith- we weren't able to remove the tumour but we did get a biopsy. There's some good news, and some bad news. Which do you want to hear first?"

I immediately said "Shoot with the bad news first". He then replied "It's terminal and inoperable, *but* it's treatable."

He was studying my reaction to this news closely, however I decided to make light of it by saying "That's OK; We're all terminal, aren't we?"

He considered my statement seriously, then agreed with me that in fact, we were all *terminal*.

Initially I was diagnosed with a fairly lethal type of brain tumour with a grim prognosis; this was called mixed anaplastic oligo-astrocytoma, Grade 3; a tumour that sent out a *root system* like a weed would, all through my brain. This condition had a median survival time of 18 months.

After chemotherapy and radiation therapy, the tumour shrank significantly, and remained stable for quite some time.

A year later the tumour *took off* again, changing rapidly to the most lethal of all brain tumours; a grade 4 glioblastoma multiforme. This is unhappily coined the *Brain Cancer Death Sentence*. Apparently in North America each year there are 12,000 diagnoses and 12,000 deaths from this malicious entity annually.

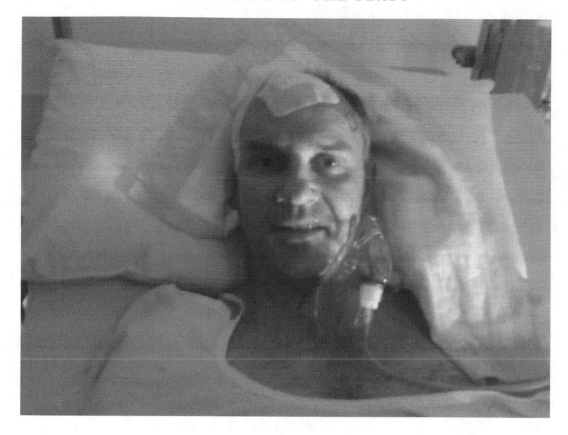

Waking up cheerfully from first surgery

All a man needs is *someone to love, something to live for, and something to do*

The philosopher Immanuel Kant is rumoured to have stated this, as are several other scholarly types over the years. Whoever really said it, it's a pretty good summation of Victor Frankel's observations about Auschwitz survivors, too.

Prisoners who had given up on life were dead within a few weeks from whatever infection was doing the rounds of the camp.

In my case, quite apart from completing my athletics training book, Healthy Intelligent Training, I had something far more important to look forward to. The impending birth of our fifth child.

When I first collapsed in late July of 2007, Joanne was a few months pregnant. Only Joanne and I knew, really. However, as the pregnancy became more and more obvious, and the financial stresses of having had no income for many months grew and grew, and with some specialists trying to convince me that I was in very dire straits with my illness, one thing in particular convinced me absolutely, on top of my mother's exhortations, that I was going to survive; we had been blessed with another child on the way.

If the Good Lord had seen fit that we have another child, perhaps he'd planned that I survive long enough to see the baby born, and choose its name, and perhaps…see him or her reach adulthood. That became my short term, must do, achievable goal: see my fifth child's birth.

When I rang my great childhood friend Gavin on the eve of my first surgery, I apparently rang him to say "Goodbye," as there was no iron-clad guarantee I'd come out of surgery neurologically intact, or even alive. The poor guy said it was like being "hit with a mallet." The subtleties of beating around the bush are not my strong suit.

When I recovered extremely well following biopsy surgery, I apparently rang Gavin to announce I now had two goals that I was going to live for:

> To see my fifth child born, and, God-willing
> To see my child start school.

I decided that this next child was given to Joanne and me to bring up, however the notion of long-term survival was never encouraged, so I was content to be thankful if I could hang about long enough to "wet my baby's head". It certainly spurred me on. Now, I'm aiming to see her children one day, *God willing*.

Joanne and I had some concern that our little baby might suffer developmentally from all the stresses we were under during the pregnancy, but she was cared for by the *Lord of Life Itself*, with prayers being said from all directions, and she thrived against all normal expectations, announcing her arrival on January 3rd, 2008, with a loud cry that her grandmother could hear from outside in the hallway, before being fully delivered. She was three weeks early but still a healthy 8lbs 1oz.

We named our gorgeous little girl *Mietta*, which is a European name meaning *sweet little thing*.

Mietta became the whole family's baby, and gave us all a loving focus with which to forget all the hard times. She's a remarkably happy, cheeky child with emotional intelligence and a sense of humour way beyond her years. I often tell her that she was sent to save my life, and thank her for coming to do that. Every night I say prayers for her and my son Henry, and we usually thank *The Lord of Life Itself* for sending them both to us to be nurtured into *their* life purposes. I am convinced that Mietta and Joanne were protected by all the circles of prayer around them at that time, as well as by God's sovereign will for our lives. It is amazing to look back and marvel at what we all came through.

A few days after that initial neurosurgery, I was earnestly advised yet again that despite my excellent recovery from the biopsy, my prognosis was still very bleak.

I realized I had to extinguish that expectation with my own expectations, very quickly.

> *The moment we want to believe something, we suddenly see all the arguments*
> *for it, and become blind to the arguments against it.*
>
> (George Bernard Shaw)

Following this are the arguments I made for and against my survival after the discouraging prognosis.

CHAPTER 4

Arguments For My Survival

1. If the Good Lord had seen fit that we have another child, perhaps he'd planned that I survive long enough to see the baby born, and my job in this was simply to believe it and get on with things.

That became my short-term, must-do, *achievable goal*: see my fifth child's birth.

I rang Gavin a few days later and told him I was going fine, but the specialists said I had a very bleak prognosis in the longer term. Apparently, I then said I now had set three main goals to achieve:

1. See our baby's birth;
2. See our child start school;
3. Attend this child's marriage one day

As I'm cruising along quite well presently, I think I'll add the next logical goal which is to see her children one day. Time will tell. As Mietta is a delightful ten years old at time of writing, she's a constant reminder of how much time has gone by since my *little issue* first announced itself.

Every night before bed, I pray with my youngest two children and thank the Lord for sending them to us, and ask for a blessing over them as they sleep. Quite often, I'll tell Mietta that she's one of the main reasons I'm still here, and that she saved my life by giving me something exciting to look forward to. She must be kissed or cuddled by every family member many times a day.

Considering all the possible stress factors swirling around us while she was in the womb, there was a conceivable possibility she could have become a stressed child herself, however she is so *normal* on so many counts that she is *outstanding*.

2. My mother said I'd be fine

"Oh... You'll be just fine, son."

These were the very first words my mum said on seeing me on my hospital bed after my initial surgery. She said them with a beaming smile on her face. A mother's instinct has *much* more to it than any data-base. You can't argue with an eighty-one-year-old mother, as she was at the time. She'd seen me pull through from some terrible stuff when I was an infant. One thing she said to me that has stuck with me was "This too, shall pass", an ancient pearl of wisdom that has survived millennia, and ably puts the transcendence of our lives and troubles into perspective.

3. I have a wife to love, and a family to bring up

There was no benefit to anyone for me to leave the planet earlier than desired, and I had a duty of care to my family to stay as strong and well as I could, for as long as I could. In fact, I intend to be around for as long as possible, and, *God willing*, see my grandchildren grow to adulthood someday.

4. I felt in my heart that GOD still had a BIG purpose for my life, and that this was just a *test*.

I KNEW that I could survive and eventually thrive, if I remained calm and thought strategically, using the good brain I'd been given and my higher education in natural health principles, nutrition, and physiology. In my heart of hearts, I've always felt that I had a healing message to share with the world, and part of my purpose is to see the ascension of natural health principles to their traditional status, working together with the modern medical profession in an attitude of mutual respect.

5. I have never, at any stage, suffered true pain or discomfort with this *little issue*

Therefore, I realised that I was being *personally looked after* by my Creator for the duration of this *test*, and only had to *stay the course* by keeping on showing up in good humour. Showing up each day is really not that hard; everyone else does it.

6. I'm in the middle stages of the *race set before me*, and it's just a matter of concentrating on each successive lap

The most apt scripture to describe my overview of the situation can be sourced from the writings of St Paul in his letter to the Hebrews;

"Since we are surrounded by such a great cloud of witnesses, let us throw off everything that hinders and the sin that so easily entangles. And let us run with perseverance the race marked out for us." (Hebrews 12:1).

My understanding of the word *sin* is that it is derived from an Arabic term used in archery for *missing the target*. So, my broader understanding of this term is a bit different to most, in that *sin* can be as simple a concept as missing the *target* or *life purpose* set before us. There are, of course, many specific ways that one can be pulled *off-target* or *off-purpose*; some can be inspired by evil, but many more by laziness or lack of purpose.

What I've been encouraged by greatly is the idea that I'm surrounded by *a great cloud of witnesses*. So, perhaps, Reader, are you.

As an athlete, I nearly always raised my performance level in direct proportion to the number of people watching from the stands. Good athletes tend to be *show-off* types, or good entertainers, and the more people watching, the more energy to feed off, especially if they're our kinfolk, real or imagined.

In effect, this *little issue* and its *fallout* are just a *few tough laps* in the race marked out for me, and just like when I was racing long distances, I'm absolutely sure I'll finish well.

I visualize my father and mother, grandparents, and all sorts of ancestors and family friends in a heavenly stadium yelling at me to "hang in there and *go for broke*". We are encouraged by this great cloud of witnesses to *throw off everything that hinders*, and are given encouragement to *go for it*.

7. I'm descended from a long line of *tough cookies*

My paternal Y-DNA is pure Argyll Highlander, going back thousands of years without any sign of Viking or Saxon interloper. It is extremely likely to be exactly the same Y-DNA the famous Dr David Livingstone possessed, and he was certainly a hardy character himself. My great, great, great grandfather John Livingstone was a first cousin of Dr David, with both being *woolen weavers* in Blantyre, Scotland when young, so we're from the same stock. (My direct ancestor going back seven generations, Neil Livingstone, was Dr David's grandfather as well.)

My great grandfather Neil MacLean Livingstone was a piano importer as well as a professional strongman. He once broke a picket line on the wharves in Edinburgh by knocking stevedores' heads together until they let him through. No-one helped him load his crated grand piano onto his dray, and no-one stopped him leaving, either.

My grandfather James Cooper Livingstone, or *Jock*, was orphaned at 11 when his strongman father died of a heart attack. *Jock* survived the loss of his right leg below the knee on the Western Front, in 1915, when he was blown up by a Saxon mortar shell. Jock took it all on the chin, and as soon as he could he got himself re-trained as a one-legged *aeronautical inspector*, meaning that he had to test those early RAF biplanes for airworthiness and reliability.

On my maternal side, my grandfather Walter Garth Stanley was a pioneering geologist, surveyor and explorer, who opened up vast areas of land in coastal and highland Kenya, often on foot, with many African assistants, often hunting for their food as they went. His father, Dr Walter Garth Stanley, was awarded a military medal for medical service in the First Boer War.

8. This Is a golden opportunity to *achieve something* worth writing about and sharing for the *greater good*

For years I envisaged a future as a writer and a speaker, meeting fascinating people and researching interesting topics around the world. I regard this *little issue* as a blessing in that regard. I keep getting told by knowledgeable people that my survival is *amazing* or that *I* am *amazing*. However, as I am certainly being *looked after,* I don't personally think it's me who is so *amazing*. I have very little to do with it. It's a bit like being carried on an elevator to an exciting destination. All I've got to do is *Believe the Dream* and keep on doing what I'm doing.

When I finally realized that I was not going anywhere downhill in a hurry, I thought that after a significant period of healthy survival, I could write about it and hopefully make some long-term passive income from the nasty tumour that was supposed to finish me off physically and financially.

9. This is really a *Blessing in Disguise*!

After having worked very hard on several fronts for years on end with little to show for it, my *terminal* diagnosis enabled me to have a massive insurance payout which enabled me to take my whole family, including Joanne's parents, around the world, after having paid out all debts from a collapsed real estate portfolio during the *Global Financial Crisis*. We had the *Holiday of a Lifetime,* travelling very cheaply around the world for 14 weeks, because of the oppressive economic times.

There was no way known that I could have given my family this wonderful brain-shaping experience if I had continued to grind away. The northern summer warmth and sunshine, combined with the stimulus of all the new experiences, no doubt helped my immune system kick along nicely, and by the end of the trip I was a lot healthier than at the start! Another *benefi*t is that I have been able to really get to know my kids and spend *time* with them, and there'll never be another opportunity to regain those special formative years with them.

10. None of my family or friends thought it was *time for me to go.*

Despite the alleged severity of my condition, *all* of the many friends and relatives who sent me cards and letters indicated that they were *sure* I'd beat the issue at hand. Not one person who wrote gave me permission to depart. One guy who I hardly knew wrote me an impassioned note saying that from what he'd heard from his colleagues, I was sure to get better, and he was almost congratulating me on this achievement, as if it was an established fact!

One Argument *Against* My Survival

1. There's an epidemiological database somewhere

I choose to believe I'm off that database anyhow, and after ten years have hopped onto the *population survival rate* database now, meaning I've gone so long that my chances of reaching a healthy old age are the same as for other men my age; *except* I'd also say I have learnt to live so healthily that my chances of making a nuisance of myself till a very old age are better than most, *God willing.*

CHAPTER 5

Trouble Comes Calling Again

Twelve months later, the gtumour re-escalated. Emergency neurosurgery by Mr Murphy while I was fully conscious managed to skilfully remove the central core of the tumour, but I was still expected to last only a few months.

In fact, Zurich Insurance paid me out on my life insurance within 6 weeks of receiving the claim form signed by the oncologist and the neurosurgeon. Apparently in the small print of my insurance contract there was a clause covering terminal disease conditions. I wrote a letter to the Zurich insurance assessor for processing my claim, with a photo of our family and letting him know how much it meant to all of us. I received a reply a week or so later to say they were delighted to help out, and that they very rarely received letters from claimants or their families. Apparently my letter and our family photo were placed in their board room as a *reason why we do what we do.*

The seven-figure sum took massive stress of us financially, but after the collapse of my modest real-estate portfolio and paying out all the costs that had accrued after my collapse, including capitalized interest from one niche financier, who knew damned well what we'd gone through, there was not enough left to do any serious investing again. It was time to re-claim my life. I didn't want to let my kids remember me as some ailing guy with a drip in his arm, so I refused an offer of a super-powerful new chemotherapy agent named *Carboplatin* that was thought necessary *to make absolutely sure.* A quick look inside the chemotherapy room to observe several miserable grey– faced people with drips in their arms, convinced me that it wasn't the thing for me just yet.

Not knowing at that stage quite what turn to take, we took the whole family to New Zealand for Christmas, and toured both islands in a motorhome after having parked ourselves in a rental house on the beautiful Coromandel Peninsula at Pauanui, one of my favourite places from childhood days.

We decided to celebrate Christmas of 2008 a week early so that a large group of our New Zealand friends could drive down to Pauanui for the day and catch up for a very sociable *get-together and barbecue.*

Jo drove our motorhome nearly the length and breadth of the country, on both islands. After crossing Cook Strait on the inter-island ferry, Jo manoeuvred the motorhome around the twists and turns of the Marlborough Sounds till we reached a lovely waterfront hotel at Portage, on the beautiful Kenepuru Sound. After a meal with former New Zealand cross-country champion John Dixon and his wife, Dianne, we stayed the night in the hotel before embarking for Christchurch the next day, via Hanmer Springs in the foothills of the Southern Alps north-west of Christchurch. We then parked ourselves with Gary and Helen Shatford, parents of my friend Ivan Shatford, in the small township of Oxford where they'd built their own very comfortable retirement home. Louise Shatford, the youngest of the Shatford children, also came down with glioblastoma multiforme, but is doing well now after quite a few years, and finishing her rehabilitation so that she can return to the family home for her 50th birthday.

In Christchurch, I caught up with Ivan's sister Jacqui and her family, as well as with Brian Taylor, a local running coach who ran a good squad of athletes on the famous Lydiard system that I wrote my book about. Very sadly, within 9 months of our visit, Brian passed away in the second major earthquake that tore Christchurch to the ground. The first major earthquake toppled Brian's chimney, but the second about a month later destroyed the multi-storey building he was visiting, for just a few minutes, at just the wrong time. It was very sobering to think that someone can go from being such a vital force of nature one month to a natural disaster statistic a few months later. Nature is brutal.

In Christchurch, we got to experience the city at its beautiful best, and it didn't seem to have changed much since when I worked there during 1978. Some of the radio announcers I worked with in 1978 were still on the airwaves over 30 years down the track, on the same radio station!

A funny sign in Cathedral Square, which was decimated by the earthquakes later on in 2009.

After Christchurch, we drove down to Tekapo, an old hydro-electricity township near Lake Tekapo, at the foot of New Zealand's highest peak, Aoraki (Mount Cook). We visited a friend of Dad's from his days at the British High Commission in Auckland; Garth Harroway. Garth was the resident schoolteacher on Pitcairn Island in the 1970's, and he and his wife Leslie had retired to Tekapo where Leslie had her own art gallery and studio. Garth regaled us about his time as an *extra* on the set of the *Lord of the Rings* trilogy of films, which was filmed nearby and employed many hundreds of *locals*. Garth played one of the fearsome *Orcs*, and said that each *extra* in the film had to be fully made up over a period of hours with latex masking and heavy-duty clothing and realistic weaponry, and that it was hard work for hours on end.

We took the family on a helicopter trip to about 10,000 feet up Mount Sefton, the next major peak to Aoraki. As the helicopter descended onto the snow ridge that sat perched on the edge of a sheer drop of several thousand feet, it looked as if we were landing on an area the size of a postage stamp! However, as we got nearer the snow, the *postage stamp* grew in size to an area equivalent to several football fields. Despite all the snow, conditions were warm and still.

10,000 feet up Mount Sefton, Southern Alps, January 2009.

When we returned from the flight, we drove up to *The Hermitage*, a site at the foot of Aoraki, made famous as the staging-post from where Sir Edmund Hillary did his training for the ascent of Mount Everest. *The Hermitage* of today bears little resemblance to the weatherboard hostel of Hillary's day. It's a modern 5-star experience. The bronze statue of Edmund Hillary outside the modern *Hermitage* Hotel had a number of Nepalese Buddhist scarves wrapped around its neck, in memory of the great man, who had died early the year before.

CHAPTER 6

After New Zealand; the World!

That New Zealand trip was a lot of fun, and because I was going so well, we then decided to take the whole family on a round-world trip for fourteen weeks, where we hit all the major museums, galleries, castles, and landmarks we could in Europe, went on a very cheap Greek Islands cruise due to the Global Financial crisis, visited Boston, New York, Disneyland (Los Angeles) and Colorado, then finished off with a spell in Fiji. Everything was incredibly cheap due to the *Global Financial Crisis*.

If there is a blessing to be found in this situation, it was being able to take my whole family, including Jo's parents, around the world for a few months during the middle stages of my career. That world trip was something only one of our kids can't remember, but anyone who takes her first steps on the edge of Venice's Giudeca Canal is sure to have benefitted from such a journey in terms of her brain stimulation and social development.

I celebrated the first anniversary of my *likely* demise by taking a jet ski out past the reef into the big surf in Fiji, and showing the bigger kids what their Dad used to do a lot of, before their time. This didn't go down well at first with the local villagers who hired the jet skis out, however I've learnt it's better to apologise afterwards than ask permission beforehand if things are to get done.

Little did they know that I was a past master of the beasts, having hired the older-style stand-up jet-skis from a local jet-ski hire business at Lake Boga, near Swan Hill, every weekend, to the point that I got discounts upon discounts, till I was basically paying mainly for petrol. The second-generation *jet-skis* are not nearly as challenging as the earlier ones I acquired my skills on; they are so tub-like and safe I call them *tug-boats*. It's virtually impossible to get thrown off, even in tight circles, as long as you keep the throttle on near-maximum. I gave chiropractic care to the villagers as a way of atoning, and we were all on first-name terms after that.

Over ten years down the track from the second neurosurgery, not only am I alive and well, but also exercising vigorously most days, and living as if the condition never occurred. How am I so well when statistically I have only *zero* chance of even being alive at this stage? I think it's because I've never allowed myself to worry about it, or admit it has any power in my life.

CHAPTER 7

What You Worry About Controls You

This paraphrases the ancient statement from the Book of Job, in verse 3:25, where the New International Version states "What I feared has come upon me; what I dreaded has happened to me". The New Living Translation of this last phrase is "What I always feared has happened to me. What I dreaded has come true."

I probably did subconsciously *dread* being unable to provide for my family, or being *terminally ill*, so therefore I got *whacked* with both to get my thinking straightened out. This forced me to depend on my Creator, or my Source, as my sustainer; not money or guaranteed cash-flows. I had moved too far from the *path laid out for me*, into a worldly way of thinking and defining my values.

From the spiritual perspective, as a *disciple*, or *pupil*, I re-interpreted the whole situation of being made *nearly* bankrupt and *nearly* dying as a sign of *discipline*, or a very firm *tough-love* correction of my life path to one I was intended for. Clearly, although I was being *allowed* to descend to the very brink of financial and physical disaster, my faith allowed me to feel totally secure and calm throughout, and, as in the final outcome for Job, I am sure that I will regain my total health, and all of my material wealth, and perhaps far more again. If I don't, then that's fine too.

This theme is also what I vocalize, or positively feed my psychology with, on my nightly walks through bushland near home, where I cite the calming scripture of the Twenty-third psalm; "Yeah, though I walk through the valley of the shadow of death, I will fear no evil. You are with me; your rod and your staff; they comfort me..."

I won't deny that I went through some very tough and upsetting times in all of this, but as far as I could I have always concentrated on my best possible outcome. So if you want to get better from a brain issue, keep acting the way you want to end up; in other words- keep *faking* till you get there. It worked for me. You won't get better if you don't take the plunge and do all your favourite things again, and *act well* again!

After continually awaking every day to find I was fine and still going OK, I became more and more used to the idea that I was *supposed* to be here for some time, despite all the doubters. I had my *little issues* with fatigue and financial stresses, but bit by bit I got back to more normal life.

CHAPTER 8

How Stanley Met Livingstone

My mother, Valerie Stanley, a Kenyan-born school-teacher, married former British Army staff-sergeant Chester Roy Livingstone on December 9th, 1957. The Kenyan national newspaper, The East African Standard, at first refused to print their engagement notice, thinking it was a prank with its *Stanley marries Livingstone in Darkest Africa* headline.

After service in anti-aircraft gun emplacements in London during the Blitz, my multi-lingual father was posted to Madagascar, where he served as a translator in a POW camp for Vichy French prisoners of war in the commandeered former Royal Palace in Tananarive. Dad made firm friends with a young French prisoner named Jean Juvené, who he corresponded with for many years after the war.

Jean Juvené later became French ambassador to Moscow, and when he retired, Jean visited Mum and Dad in New Zealand.

Dad later wrote a prize-winning novel based on his Madagascar wartime experiences, published by MacMillan Publishers in 1946. The competition was for the best novel based on wartime experiences by British Empire soldiers, and the book was entitled *The Earth is Red*.

One critic wrote "Sergeant Livingstone has a rare gift for writing", suggesting that he had far greater things in store. However, my father was not interested in fame or fortune as far as I could see. He once told me that he knew he could have gone that way, but he didn't need to prove anything to anyone. He was extremely happy in his own skin, and worldly recognition didn't seem to interest him in the slightest. I admire and envy him for that.

My Aunty Mavis in later years told me that he was known in the neighbourhood as *the boy who'd read every book in the Hendon library* growing up, and it could well be true. Off his own bootstraps, he managed to earn a scholarship to *Kingsbury Grammar School*, where he acquired his Oxbridge accent, and he did exceptionally well in his studies there. School-days were long and disciplined, often starting before 8am and finishing after 5pm. He once showed me his *Greater London School Certificate*, which consisted of 10 subjects, and his lowest mark was still in the low 90's from memory, for a trade subject like woodwork. He never got to attend university, despite his academic prowess, and got a job in an accountancy firm in the years before the outbreak of World War Two in 1939.

Itching for some adventure, Dad had ideas of travelling to Spain to fight as a mercenary in the Spanish Civil War with the *International Brigade* aligned with the Communist-backed partisans seeking to depose the Fascist leader General Franco. His father said "Don't bother with Spain, laddie, we'll have *Adolf* on our doorstep soon enough."

Dad was one of the first to sign up in September 1939. At first he served in England, where I think he manned an anti-aircraft gun during the Blitz. By 1941, when his linguistic ability was noted, he was sent to Madagascar as a translator in a prisoner of war camp for mostly Vichy-French prisoners in that former French colony. He once described his war as being "continually moved by rail, road or ship from one destination to another, then back again." I asked him if he was ever scared of dying, to which he said, "No. When your number's up, your number's up." Dad could speak fluent French, German, Italian, and Spanish, which made him rather useful, and he easily added Swahili to his formidable archive later on.

Later, when the war in Africa started to heat up north of the Kenyan border, he was transferred to the King's African Rifles to be a translator for Italian prisoners. After an epic 1000-mile sea journey north from Madagascar to the Kenyan port of Mombasa by commandeered Norwegian Fishing vessel, with prisoners on board, Dad was posted with the King's African Rifles in Kenya, in 1942. The hazardous boat journey to the mainland was made all the more memorable by a hopelessly slow *escort boat* that was a commandeered steam-tug that continually lagged far behind the fishing boat on the ocean swells. They often waited long periods before seeing its smoke stack poke up above the swells.

Despite the Indian Ocean off the East African coast crawling with German U-boats, the little boats eventually made it safely to the Kenyan coast, with an RAF fly-over near land almost being shot out of the sky by a trigger-happy Cockney anti-aircraft gunner desperate for action.

There had been significant military action in East Africa, with many thousands of Italian troops assembled along the southern borders of Abyssinia.

Dad was posted to British POW Camp 353, in Gilgil, Nakuru County, about 70 miles equidistant from the towering Mount Kenya (17,057 feet) and the Kenyan capital, Nairobi. There were 12 POW camps in rural centres around Kenya, built mostly to house over 14,000 Italian prisoners of war.

As far as one can enjoy a war, Dad did. I'd go as far as to say he loved the army life. We have an album of photos he made when he *diverted* his army convoy driving overland to the coast to the mysterious thirteenth century *lost city* of Gedi on the way. The city had first been reported in *The Archaeological Gazette* in 1934, and presumably it was too good a chance to miss when in charge of a convoy of trucks run at His Majesty's expense.

Dad did suffer a *war injury*, but even then the *Guiding Hand* was at work. He was a dispatch rider, able to fully indulge his love of speed, when he felt his motorbike's front wheel slide away beneath him on loose gravel coming out of a turn. He slid sideways with the bike for several metres, badly grazing his left knee, wondering why he had come to grief with such a simple manoeuvre, when he looked up behind him and saw a tight strand of copper wire strung across the road at dispatch-rider neck height. He was able to re-start his motorbike and complete his task. In 1943, he caught malaria, which came back to haunt him forty-three years later when hospitalized in Auckland Hospital, greatly confusing his medical staff who were not used to treating tropical diseases.

It was in Gilgil that he became friends with Anne Potgieter, a young Bavarian emigrée who worked in the records office. Her husband was staff-sergeant Smartie Potgieter, a tough-as-teak Afrikaaner who was in the Transport Division. Smartie was reputed to be the man who *dropped* the hulking young African regimental heavyweight boxing champion and confirmed bully, the Ugandan Corporal Idi Amin, for refusing to follow his orders in loading a truck.

(Certainly, Smartie could still handle himself extremely well when he was nearly 70. He *laid out* a very angry younger man with a reverse punch in the Trentham pub in Central Victoria, two weeks before I visited the same pub with him in 1981. I once joined Smartie for a pleasant afternoon of serving court summonses, which was his retirement job. Apparently the angry young man refused to accept his summons, and made the *huge mistake* of trying to *coward punch* Smartie from behind as he laid the summons out on the bar for the whole pub to read. The very impressed barman voluntarily told me that story.)

Anne's brother, Horst von Kaufmann, was a friend of Dad's too. Horst soon became renowned in the area for the 1926 Rolls Royce he converted to a flat-deck utility to transport sheep, to the horror of Rolls Royce's East African agents. Anne's earliest memories of my father were of a very polite, self-contained man who was given to whistling happy tunes, even while he typed out court-martial documents. She found that absolutely hilarious.

For Italian prisoners of war, there was no better place than Kenya to be *imprisoned* during World War Two. The Potgieters' three tiny girls grew up with Italian prisoners of war tending vegetable gardens, playing guitars, cooking pasta, and teaching them Italian nursery rhymes. *Escape* back to Italian-occupied Abyssinia was made nearly impossible by wild carnivores, and the rugged, arid desert lands to the north, where only native Turkhana and related tribes were able to survive.

It didn't help escaping POW's chances that earlier in the war, when thousands of Italian forces were assembling to the north, tribesmen were allegedly promised large bags of sugar and flour for each enemy head delivered to District Commissioners' offices.

However, on January 24, 1943, several Italians did manage to escape from POW Camp 354, at the base of the forests below Mount Kenya, without coming to much harm. In a hilarious departure from a normal POW escape story, the Italians, two of whom were seasoned mountaineers, *escaped*, just to have the thrill of climbing the formidable peak that gazed down at them from outside the wires of the camp. The third member of the party was a non-mountaineer, chosen specifically because he was a known *mad bastard*. Using camp-made climbing gear and hoarded rations, the three escapees managed to traverse miles of thick rainforest teeming with wild rhinoceroses and large carnivores, before ascending one of the mountain's three peaks.

They used an image of the southern side of Mount Kenya that was on the lid of a can of *Kenylon* meat and vegetable rations to work out what lay on the opposite side of the mountain. The sole motivation was to escape the ennui and boredom of the camp, and to have something constructive to do rather than walking around talking to equally bored and disheartened prisoners.

Having reached the one peak, and with one of the party suffering distress, they returned to the prison camp and *broke back in*! No-one came after the trio when they walked out, and their escape was only noticed when they returned.

The Welsh-born camp commander congratulated the returning climbers, then chose to punish them with four weeks in 'solitary'; representing the 28 days they had been *Absent Without Leave*. The sentence was then commuted to just 7 days, in recognition of their *magnificent sporting effort*.

The instigator of the adventure, Felice Benuzzi, wrote a best-seller named *No Picnic on Mount Kenya* that was first published soon after the war. Benuzzi died in 1988. The book was republished in 2016 and is still available. A movie based on the book, named *The Ascent*, was filmed in 1994. According to a son-in-law of the actual camp commander, the original story had been "sidelined with a ridiculous story involving climbing and love rivals."

We have photos of my uncle, Tony Stanley, who was a captain in the King's African Rifles, high up on Mount Kenya with some Italian prisoners of war, all obviously enjoying an *outing* up Mount Kenya.

Anne and Smartie still lived in the forestry home where Smartie had been a manager before the war, and Dad was often a house-guest. Smartie once told me that my Dad wasn't overtly brave or brash, but that he would happily venture into life-or-death situations because "He didn't have nerves of steel. He didn't seem to have any bloody nerves at all, the mad bastaard!"

Smartie was referring to a full-moon romp across grasslands on his motorbike during a Mau-Mau War blackout in the early 1950s, where Dad arrived at their home in the small hours of the morning, covered in insects, dirt, and grasses.

Apart from his motorbikes, Dad had acquired a small fleet of classic sports cars after the war; one was a Riley 1500 MPH, which even then was a very rare sports car.

However, it was to be another 14 years after his arrival in Kenya before the *fates* conspired to introduce Chester Roy to his future wife.

At some stage in1956, Kenya-born school-teacher Valerie Stanley was still reeling from the death of her mother, Una, who she had been caring for. She was invited to the up-country farm where Smartie and Anne and their brood of three girls and one little boy were residing, to relax for a few days. When she arrived, she complained that her car, a 1952 Ford Prefect, hadn't been running particularly well on the trip up from Nairobi.

She was introduced to a genial, well-spoken *younger man* who was also a friend of the Potgieters. After dinner and some convivial conversation, the *younger man* excused himself about 9pm, and Mum thought he'd retired early to get some sleep.

When she got up after midnight to use the outside toilet, she spied a pair of long legs sticking out from under her car. They belonged to the *younger man*, who was busy tinkering with her car by the light of a kerosene lantern. She thanked the person attached to the long legs, and offered to make him a cup of hot coffee, which she duly left beside the legs when she returned.

In the morning, the long legs were still under the car, and the coffee was stone-cold. Later on that morning, the *nice young man* had the car purring like it was brand new, and she was intrigued when he turned out to be a very well-preserved bachelor some eight years her senior, who shared her love of literature and animals, but knew far more about machinery.

I am not sure how my mother's family came to know the Potgieters, but Mum's older brother Tony, eleven years her senior, served as a captain in the King's African Rifles with Smartie and possibly my father, and her mother Una worked with the Army during the war years as well, as a stenographer. The European population of Kenya was very small, and *everybody knew everybody* in the early days.

Valerie had a fascinating upbringing, being the daughter of one of Kenya's earliest surveyors and geologists, Walter Garth Stanley. Her mother, Una, was one of the seven daughters and one son of Charles Coldrey, who was principal of one of Johannesburg's first schools.

Mum spent part of her childhood living in the high-country community of Kakamega, where the family lived in a thatch-roofed home constructed by the local Luhya people with traditional methods, under the firm instruction of Chief Mulima, who became a good friend of my grandfather. Mum said their home had mica windows, and a hard-packed dirt floor. She often went to sleep at night to the sound of distant drum-beats.

This upbringing was totally at odds with that of her first cousins in Johannesburg. Walter Garth's sister May married Bill Gallagher senior, an American engineer from a wealthy diamond-mining family who later over-saw the operations of the world's largest alluvial diamond mine, the De Beers mine, with its famous *Kimberley Hole*, said to be the largest hole ever dug by pick and shovel, with 50,000 miners working it between 1871 and 1914.

Her first cousin, Bill Gallagher junior, who we referred to as *Uncle Bill*, was quite a bit older than her, and was only known to us by his legacy of *Uncle Bill's egg*, which was a novel way to eat a soft-boiled egg that involved mashing the egg into a cup of diced buttered toast, with salt to taste. When we were first in New Zealand, *Uncle Bill* sent us some beautiful model plane kit sets, and also generously offered to buy a house for us, which Mum refused on a moral platform of her own making.

Mum later said that while she was extremely appreciative of the care extended to her by her uncle while she was at university during the war, as an independent adult with children she now had a moral duty to make sure we grew up knowing that any home we lived in wasn't purchased with money earnt off the sweat of the black man, but with money we had earned ourselves. So while we had second cousins living on a grand estate near Johannesburg, we were living in a tiny two-bedroom rented flat in Auckland.

The *disconnect* between this fabulous wealth and my mother's upbringing was so big that I only knew the bigger story when I visited South Africa in 2002. My cousin Tim Stanley informed me that our *Uncle Bill* (Mum's first cousin) Gallagher had left a sizeable property to the City of Johannesburg, and if I had the time, I should visit his widow who was living in Johannesburg. The *Gallagher Convention Centre* is touted as one of the largest and most sophisticated conference venues in South Africa and offers professional conference facilities for up to 12 000 delegates.

As he was by then a board member of Anglo-American, the world's pre-eminent diamond-mining conglomerate, buying a small house in New Zealand for his youngest cousin would have barely dinted the coffers.

Mum's father was away on safari so much that her first recollection of him, when she was about three, was of a "smiling man with glasses who walked through our gate, said 'Hello Valerie', and then hugged and kissed Mummy. I liked him, because Mummy did, but I wondered who he was!".

Her father died of *black water* fever, the third time he had contracted that terrible form of malaria, in May 1935, and his death was noted on the front page of the East African Standard, which is still Kenya's main newspaper. The article described him as a popular man with a wide circle of friends throughout many districts of Kenya, and how he would attend *sporting events** whenever his safaris would permit. (* horse racing)

The Catholic funeral had a European service at the local church in Kakamega, and Walter Garth was laid to rest under a large *mikumu* tree (fig tree) in the cemetery. The day after the funeral, Mum remembered local Africans visiting his grave and leaving flowers. Mum said her father and mother had a very respectful relationship with the local Africans, with her mother providing first aid when required, and her father employing quite a few men on his wide-ranging safaris.

In 2002, I visited Kakamega to find my grandfather's grave. Eventually, with the help of an amazingly fit 87 year old Dutch Catholic priest, *Father Gerardo* (Gerard van de Laar), Walter Garth's terrazzo marble gravestone was found in thick foliage, with the old fig tree having long since rotted away. Kakamega, far from being the small high-country settlement it was when my grandfather died, had now become a sizeable town of about 100,000 people, and on the day I visited, there was a religious revival going on, with groups of people gathered around preachers with boom-boxes all around the green lawns of the main *cathedral*, under large shady fig trees. The *cathedral*, an open-sided concrete structure, was full to overflowing with about 3000 people. Ironically, a few years later, that very part of the highlands was swept with inter-tribal warfare and vicious killings, after a disputed election result.

CHAPTER 9

You Can Take the Boy Out of the Country, But You Can't Take the Country Out of the Man

If there's a theme that looms over my early-life recollections, and has been a backdrop to my whole life, it's total immersion in the eccentric, odd-ball life of colonial Kenya. One would have expected that immersion to gradually fade away once we had emigrated to Auckland, New Zealand; however *Kenya* emigrated with us.

During the first couple of years in Auckland, we attended the *Jambo Club*, where we met and played with other *Kenya kids* and their families, in an upstairs dance-hall in a long-since-demolished building opposite the Victorian-era Symond's Street cemetery, on Karangahape Road.

Right from the start in Auckland, we were surrounded by fellow Kenya immigrants, many of whom knew Mum and Dad in Nairobi. Auckland was a very staid, homogenous city in 1965 when we arrived. Not many people were well-travelled, apart from the war veterans, of whom there were still quite a few. As an English and Geography teacher, Mum was amused that the man who was in charge of the geography syllabus for New Zealand's school certificate had never left the country. She certainly sorted him and his syllabus out. There was a popular book titled *The Quarter Acre, Half-Gallon Pavlova Paradise* by Austin Mitchell that described suburban life in Auckland in the 1960's. On weekends, the air would come alive with the drone of lawn-mowers. It seemed as if most men were *do-it-yourself* types who could fix or make anything in their workshops.

I'll take the opportunity here to talk about the close network of *Kenya friends* my mother and father had in Auckland, who, in the absence of grandparents or uncles and aunties in a new country, became our New Zealand *family*.

The Brochners

I can't imagine the adrenal jolt the residents of Torrance Street in pleasant middle-class Epsom got when *Aunty Marietta* Brochner revved out of her driveway in her MG sports convertible, talking loudly in her thick Bavarian accent and gesticulating wildly while her scarf fluttered in the breeze. The former Contessa Marietta Johanna Paula Albertina Grafin von Pocci was married to Per Brochner, the son of a Danish cavalry-man. *Aunty Marietta* was appalled by Adolf Hitler when she was a young girl, patting children on the head during public parades; "We were all told he was wonderful then, dahling. We didn't know anything then, you see! No-one knew!"

Marietta nursed me and my brother in Gertrude's Gardens, the children's hospital in Nairobi, and reminded me whenever I saw her. I have no idea why a legitimate Bavarian contessa would take up nursing and move to Kenya.

Many Christmas Days were spent in their ample Auckland weatherboard home, with a huge Bavarian-styled traditional Christmas roast followed by an amazingly rich traditional Christmas pudding with brandied cream; all prepared by Marietta. The antique dining table and chairs belonged to Baroness Karen von Blixen, the Danish woman who wrote *Out of Africa*, which was later made into a film with Meryl Streep. I have a copy of the original book, and her name is simply *Karen Blixen* on that.

Marietta and Per were very generous, but both were complete opposites. Per was very blunt and to the point, or *practical* as my Mum would say, and Marietta was very empathic, highly observant, and caring. They had three children: Olga and Hugh, and Richard, who was much younger. We still keep up regularly with the oldest, Olga, who is now a specialist ophthalmic nurse in Auckland after years at Moorfield's Eye Hospital in London.

When we were little, we'd clamber in and out of the windows of a long enclosed verandah that was the kids' playroom. Pride of place was occupied by a large, beautifully detailed dolls' house that was two stories high, and possibly already over a century old.

Christmas Lunch with the Brochners, 1980.
L-R: Connie Binnie, Colin, Olga Brochner, Marietta Brochner, Dad, Richard Brochner, Mum.

The rest of the house was filled to the brim with an eclectic mix of valuable European family antiques and mounted hunting trophies. The umbrella stand was fashioned from the hard-bristled lower leg and foot of an elephant, and had a polished hardwood lid. There were two massive elephant tusks on either side of the fireplace. There was a small hand-sculped stone bust of Per's sister Karen, done when she was about twelve.

There was a massive ancient wooden chest that held crystal-ware and ivory-handled silverware and crockery that were very old, engraved with the Von Pocci family crest. We were encouraged to drink from the ancient hand-cut crystal wine glasses. There were coffee tables with silver trays resting on upside-down antler horns as legs. Despite the age and value of this antique-ware, it was used with impunity at Christmas time. "Eat up, Dahling!" was Marietta's signature phrase; "It's there to be enjoyed!"

There was a buffalo head with seriously big horns, mounted high above the dining area. I always assumed that Per or his father had shot it. A few years ago, I finally asked him who had shot it. "That was the first buffalo my *mother* ever shot!" he replied. *Hilarious!*

Looking back, there always seemed to be Kenyan friends visiting our house or the Brochners' at weekends, and we were privileged to know some older people who had led truly fascinating lives.

There was *Rhys Jenkins*, a quietly-spoken man who had been employed to open up aerial routes from the Mediterranean to South Africa in the 1920's for an emerging firm named Imperial Airways, which was later subsumed under British Empire Airlines, then became BOAC, which is now British Airways. We still have hundreds of his original black and white photographs of an Egypt that could have been straight from the time of Jesus. There are beautiful aerial shots of the pyramids and the Sphinx, with their bases half-covered by vast sand dunes, and not a tourist in sight. A bit of Rhys stayed with us for many years in the form of his 1939 Morris 10, which Dad kept purring for many years as our family transport.

His chatty wife, Kath Jenkins, survived him by many years, and was often at our home, which on weekends was always "open house" for any visitors. Kathleen was a former dancer with a London dance company, and she was often brought around to the house by another member of our 'extended family, our most outrageous favourite, *Aunty Connie* Binnie.

Connie Binnie was at my parents' wedding. She is the dark-haired lady in my parents' wedding car photo, standing in front of a large window. Connie was a very high-energy, intelligent lady who hailed from Glasgow, and she was quick-witted like a female Billy Connolly, with the same Glaswegian accent. As a young journalist, she had been based in the Caribbean for a few years, living in Haiti. She was with the Kenya Police during the Mau Mau campaign, where she went undercover as a Bebe (*bee-bee*, or matronly Kikuyu woman), with theatre make up and wiry wig under a head scarf. She reckoned her fluent Swahili, *thick lips and large bum* made her an *honorary Kikuyu*. She was a rare character who livened up any gathering.

When we first moved to Auckland, New Zealand in early 1965, we had a tiny flat in Owairaka Avenue, Mt Albert. Connie shared it with us until Dad arrived in NZ some 18 months later. We were only 6 years old and took to Connie's amazing sense of fun straight away.

Here are a few of my favourite Connie memories.

The mouthwash

I came home from Owairaka Primary School one day very impressed with what I'd seen a Maori kid at school do to my Primer 4 teacher, Miss Powell. His name was Jerry Mahouri, and he was always in some sort of altercation with Miss Powell, usually getting the better of her before he was evicted from the class. On this occasion, a particular phrase he used got a powerful response from Miss Powell, and struck a literary chord within me:

"That's for me to know and you to find out".

At about 7 years of age, and largely innocent of the machinations of the world at large, I had no idea of the possible impact a statement like this could have if I tried it out randomly. I was soon to find out.

With her newspaper journalist hours, Connie was often home when we got back from school. On this occasion, she enquired what I'd got up to that day at school. I decided to use the Jerry Mahouri line because it had been pretty effective with Miss Powell.

"That's for me to know and you to find out".

"What did you just say, Keith?" said a bemused Connie.

"That's for me to know and you to find out", I replied.

"Don't you be cheeky to me, young man! If you say it again, I'll wash your mouth out with soap!"

"That's for me to know and you to find out", I replied again.

No sooner had those words left my mouth than I was lifted bodily into the tiny bathroom, and a block of yellow *Sunlight* laundry soap was procured. Connie wet it under the tap, and made me get my toothbrush and scrape it over the block.

"Now brush your teeth with it until I see the soap bubbles, you cheeky little monkey!" she said.

I clearly remember the taste of Unilever Sunlight soap to this day, but more to the point, I realized then and there that Aunty Connie was a force of nature not to be mocked, and that words certainly had power.

These days she'd be accused of *child abuse*, but we just loved her to bits.

The Al Capone Incident

In about 1967 Connie, Mum, Colin and I ventured on the old steam ferry to Waiheke Island in the Hauraki Gulf, to visit Olive *Teddy* Bear, a former school matron who'd worked with mum in Kenya, and who was then the island's district nurse, based in Onetangi.

We all had a lovely time there, and Colin and I were allowed to bring our recently acquired *Lincoln International* black plastic machine guns with us. Those infernally loud toys looked and sounded quite authentic when *fired*.

Teddy was driving us all back down the little gravel road to the wharf at Matiatia for the return trip, in her standard-issue district nurse Morris 1100, when she slowed down as she passed two little old ladies walking down the road in the same direction, on the right-hand side of the road. Evidently they were clients of Teddy's.

Connie was seated between Colin and me in the back seat, supposedly to stop us fighting. However, with lightning speed, Connie grabbed a machine gun, and gave the old girls a healthy dose of machine gun fire from behind. She was halfway out the rear window.

The old girls shot vertically a good two feet while shrieking, and this had Colin, Connie, and me in fits of laughter till *Teddy* and Mum both railed on us and let Connie know how *irresponsible* this act had been.

Irresponsible as it may have been, I still find it very funny. You wouldn't know what could happen with Connie around.

She had a particular *thing* for stirring up old ladies, and got away with it with impunity because it was all done with mischievous fun. Poor old Kath Jenkins was the butt of her humour on many occasions, but obviously enjoyed the fun of it all.

There are many other very happy memories of shared trips to Rotorua and the Bay of Islands with Connie, as well as to her beach-house at Whangaparoa, north of Auckland, which had a lovely view over the beach.

Connie was very fond of animals, and I recall she had one particular little dog which was her constant companion, when she lived in Freeman's Bay in Auckland,

When I first started to do well with my running, Connie was very encouraging and surprisingly knowledgeable about athletics. A real enthusiast. A former top-class hockey player, she even took up jogging at one stage in her 50's, while still a heavy smoker, but enjoyed running so much she gave away smoking by default.

She suffered the first of several cardiac events while holidaying in Durban, South Africa, when in her late 60's. She loved the fact that she was given the *kiss of life* by a *gorgeous young life-saver who had muscles on his muscles.* She was flown back to New Zealand with a personal nurse courtesy of her travel insurance.

It's sad to realize Connie has left us now, but I like to think she is in a better place now, creating a ruckus with all the other family friends who've left us.

Colin, Connie, and Mum at Whangaparoa

Dr Ken & Meg Morris

Several Christmas holidays in the late 1960s were spent on the shores of the delightful Lake Rotorua, where we rented a holiday house in the same street as Dr Kenneth Morris and his wife Meg. Dr Morris was a crusty older man with a wiry build who delighted in fly-fishing for trout from his own lawn frontage to the Ngongotaha stream. He had a hearing aid, and he'd deliberately turn it off while he fished, so that he couldn't hear his wife calling to him from the house. He was world-famous for his research on the scourge of *sleeping sickness*, or *Human African Tryptomaniasis* in East Africa, spread by the tsetse fly, however he wore that title very lightly. He made plenty of time for me and Colin, kindly showing us how to cast a line for rainbow trout.

Ken Morris's wife Meg had a fascinating ancestry, being a direct descendant of Oliver Cromwell. She happily shared a unique feature of the Lord Protector's physiognomy: namely a prominent bump on her nose.

If anyone in the sleepy little hollow of Ngongotaha at that time had any criminal tendencies, the Morris's rambling weatherboard home was stacked with *priceless* art treasures, including an exquisitely detailed painting by the renowned Venetian-born artist Giovanni Canaletto. The large gilt-framed painting was of Venice's Giudecca Canal, complete down to the rigging details of small boats moored in front of the Doge's palace. In 2011, a Canaletto painting achieved the highest-ever price for a landscape at auction, fetching £11,432,000 at Christies in London.

Around the corner from the Morris's home was the local Maori *pa*, or traditional village. A few of the local Maori boys made friends with us on our first summer there, and after having introduced us to playing *marbles*, they promptly relieved us of our freshly purchased marbles on further visits, turning up on the doorstep within minutes of our arrival. The boys showed us how they found *kouras* (freshwater crayfish) in the cold clear water of the Ngongotaha stream. This was a right reserved solely for local Maori at that time. We were shown how to feel around inside the hollowed out stumps of old tree ferns that had fallen into the creek.

Irene Horley

Not all of Mum's older acquaintances were from Kenya. One, Irene Horley, was a genteel lady with an English accent, who had an immaculate flat with pristine cream carpet and Queen Anne styled furniture. We suffered her wrath when we were about ten years old and were about to trail outside detritus into the house. The reasons for her sense of household cleanliness and decorum were easily explained in later years when we were informed that Irene was one of the few survivors of the brutal enforced march from Singapore to Sumatra after Singapore fell to the Japanese. You would never have known it; we just thought she was a nice but fussy older lady. The tale of that long march was told in the 1997 film *Paradise Road*.

CHAPTER 10

Little Adventures Along the Way

The first few weeks of oncology treatment included 6 weeks of intense radiation therapy on 5 mornings each week, followed by 3 months of chemotherapy with an alkylating agent, temozolomide (*Temodal*).

Stereotactic radiotherapy (SRT) is a special type of radiation therapy, not a type of surgery, so no cuts are made in the skull. It is used to treat some brain tumours. A high dose of radiation is targeted precisely at the tumour, in very thin beams, with very little reaching surrounding areas of healthy brain tissue. Several beams are aimed sequentially from differing angles, with the central focus being the specific location of the targeted tumour.

In order to make the therapy as accurate as possible, the head has to be held completely still, in as accurate a replication of the position in which the diagnostic MRI images were first made. For this, a flexible plastic mesh cast of the patient's face has to be made. This is cast from a surgical plaster-cast mould of the face, which can be quite a fun process for kids to get involved with.

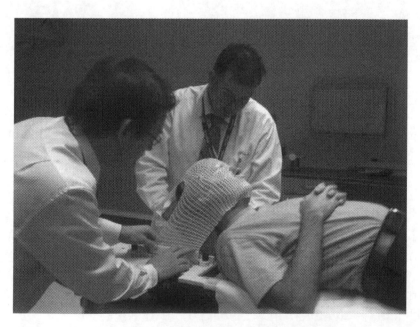

The plastic mesh face-mould being fastened down prior to stereotactic radiotherapy.

When I told my children about the plaster-cast of my face, my daughter Miranda's face lit up. She suggested we *do another one*, and paint it to look just like my own face. At 9 years of age, it was the perfect time for her to *cast* me in the shed. I had to shave closely and cover my face with Vaseline Petroleum Jelly so that the plaster mould could be peeled back easily.

The resulting mould was passable, and with a good coat of skin-toned acrylic paints, with the addition of a pair of genuine glass eyes sourced from North Wales, there was my own *dial* staring out at me. Making the ears was a bit of a problem, so we settled on making large flappy ears like a buffalo's, to accompany the set of buffalo horns I'd acquired on a family holiday in Queensland.

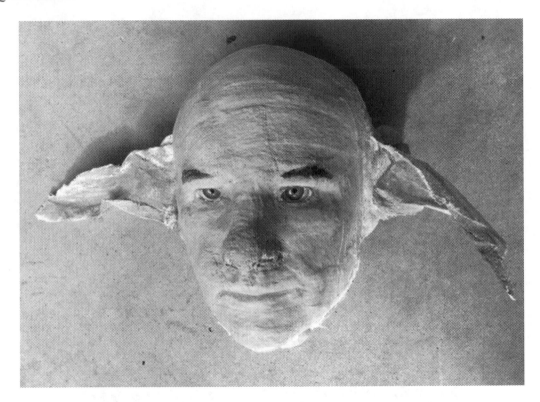

The initial idea was to whack this buffalo-horned head up on a wall in my office in the shed, staring down from behind an old pair of my glasses. By the time we'd finished the project, little Mietta was with us, and even though she was a very new and tiny baby, she made it very clear that she didn't like the face, with or without horns.

She also couldn't stand the *portrait* that I'd given to Joanne at our wedding, originally meant to show us still together in advanced old age. So the portrait which had overlooked our bed since 1991 had to be hidden away from *Her Majesty's* sight pretty much from when she was a few months old in 2008.

Now that Mietta is older, full completion of the mask on the horns for my current shed space is looking good, and re-hanging of the original portrait may be viable.

We were fortunate at Bendigo Hospital to have Joanne Maree Turner, an extraordinary orderly, working in the Peter MacCullum Radiation Oncology department.

The first time I met Jo, I wondered exactly what role she played. She seemed *too free and easy* to be working in a serious hospital setting, stirring up staff and patients alike with her zany sense of humour.

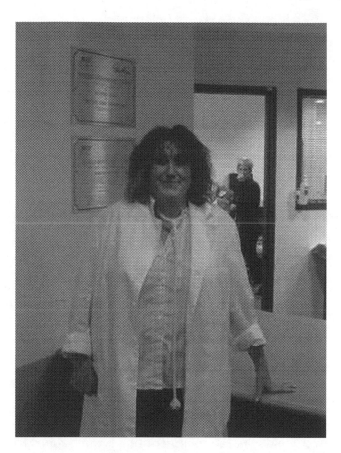

Doctor Jo Turner

Jo introduced herself to patients as *Doctor Turner*, complete with a toy stethoscope. She maintained that she *ran the Department* in Bendigo, and she even applied through official channels to run the Department when the job came up. She actually received a personal reply from the professor who headed up Oncology Radiation for the Peter MacCallum Hospital in Melbourne. His main caveat was that although she had years of experience in the Department, the lack of a bona fide medical degree was a bit of a problem. He suggested that if she obtained her medical degree, that she should re-apply in a few years.

This letter was kept in a folder that she asked every new client to peruse. At the cessation of the six-week radiation oncology treatment programmes, patients were asked to submit a formal resignation letter to *Dr Turner*, and these were proudly displayed too.

It was amazing how responsive *most** clients were to her humorous and caring approach.

*(There are always some grumpy people in any crowd, but my involvement with this group of patients, undergoing whatever personal hells their radiation therapies were for, was pretty good. Most were *up for a laugh* as far as I could see, and I got to meet some pretty interesting people in the reception area.)

The *Temodal* was so toxic that it was only given for about five days every four weeks, with twenty three days' recovery in between doses. The first week, I felt very grey around the gills, because I had neglected to take *Maxolon*; an anti-nausea medication. Having never had anything more medicinal than vitamin supplements in thirty-seven years, getting used to prescription medication routines was a bit of an issue for me.

The next two five–day doses were easier on me because of the *Maxolon*; however, about a month after I'd finished the chemotherapy I was plagued with thick mucus plugs that blocked my bronchial airways, making me cough loudly. I believe the coughing was my body's attempt to get rid of the last of the toxins.

I was staying with my mother and stepfather in their little cottage in Titirangi, Auckland; sharing a bedroom with my brother for the first time in over thirty years. Because the mucus was so thick and congested, I had to sleep semi-upright on my bed in order to not choke, and Colin was kept awake in the same room, not able to sleep his jet-lag off. It made him pretty grumpy. At one stage I had a paroxysmal spasm in my airways which was pretty scary.

Colin went away for a few days to visit friends, while I continued staying at the cottage, where I continued to struggle each night and into the day with getting enough air to breathe. I probably should have seen a doctor for some bronchodilation treatment, but at that stage I'd had enough of the medical approach, so I soldiered on, perhaps needlessly.

A couple of days after Colin had gone, about lunchtime, I experienced true panic as my airway was totally blocked with a thick mucus plug. My mother was in the kitchen, and I thought she'd have realised after a week or so of my coughing that I had an issue of some concern. Nope. No such luck.

As I was struggling desperately to suck in a breath, I made frantic signals to Mum to hit my back as hard as she could. I couldn't speak, because I needed to breathe to be able to speak. She just looked at me quizzically. At 82, although very lucid, she wasn't as quick on the uptake physically as in earlier years, so I did a running reverse thump into the door jamb of the kitchen, and thumped my chest like Tarzan, with a closed fist, dislodging the offending blockage enough to go outside and spit it into a bush. It had a bit of blood in it, but at least I could breathe again. My throat was sore for a week or so afterwards. There are kinder nutritional ways to alkalise the system than with chemotherapy.

There were a few quirky happenings while I was undergoing my therapies. Each radiotherapy morning I'd get picked up by a Red Cross volunteer driver, then after my treatment, I'd walk the three kilometres home just to get some nominal exercise in. I didn't necessarily look my best, with the remains of an angry scar, and at times I was unshaven. Because it was winter, and cold, I often used to wear a big Bomber jacket, and with my scar and shaved head I may have looked a bit dodgy.

Two people thought so, anyhow.

The first was a friendly chap who poked his head out of the passenger door of a white van, asking if I wanted to purchase a *cheap stereo system* that he happened to have with him in the back.

The second was a poor woman who was delivering newspapers from a hand cart. That looked like a good part-time job for Miranda to do with me, so I ranged up to her from behind and just said "Excuse me, madam. Where do you go to get a job like yours?"

She took one look at me, then turned on her heels and started dialing on her mobile phone, while scuttling away from me as fast as she could. I imagined that she'd called the police, so I walked along the creek banks, off-street, all the way home.

CHAPTER 11

Give Me a Child Until He is Seven, and I Will Show You the Man - Aristotle

It's not really possible to give a context to my attitudes and relaxed approach to new adventures without an account of my first seven years on the planet, which were as varied as anyone's I've met, spanning colourful experiences at the end of the British Colonial era in Kenya, Bombay (Mumbai), Sri Lanka (we called it Ceylon), and Australia enroute to Auckland, New Zealand.

This is a rushed account of the first seven years of my life, but it may contain clues in it as to why I have been able to *roll with the punches* later in life.

My birth was probably pretty normal as far as I know; but it was far from uneventful.

Somehow, the presence of me or my twin brother in the womb was completely missed by attending physicians during the course of the pregnancy. In later years, my mother, for whom this was the first pregnancy, said she thought she was *giving birth to an octopus*, such was the lively physicality of two boys in her womb, who she thought might be just one budding Hercules. She went into labour two weeks earlier than expected with *Young Hercules*.

STARING DOWN THE BEAST

Five minutes after my arrival at 10 am on October 18th, 1958, in Nairobi, Kenya, my brother Colin also arrived, completely unexpected, in a separate sleeping bag of his own. (Of course, who is to say whether the doctors weren't listening to Colin's heartbeat instead of mine?)

My father was stunned, not to say my mother, and apparently he spent quite a bit of time down at the RAF Mess at the Nairobi Aerodrome, celebrating twice the number of babies he was expecting earlier that day, as a first-time father at the age of 40.

As Mum was a popular teacher at the Kenya Girls High School, she was inundated with cards and gifts and a huge number of Teddy Bears from pupils and staff.

Mum made the observation that we always seemed to be happiest before we could crawl by being placed close to each other in a cot, kicking at each other and giggling. (That vigorous relationship has continued to this day, and often when we were growing up people thought that what we thought was merely *vigorous discussion* was about to blow up into a full-on fight!)

Colin and I are both very fortunate that we have extremely good memories of our early childhood, and are able to remind each other of significant events that keep those memories alive. However, the most significant event in my early childhood is one I can't recall at all.

A couple of years after our unforeseen dual arrival, I suffered from a nasty abdominal condition called intussusception, which announced itself with projectile vomiting across a room when I was two years old. This was a type of self-strangulation of the small intestine, where the small intestine doubled up on itself, and it demanded emergency surgery from an off-duty resident Kiwi surgeon who had to scrub up, gown, and operate while still in his tennis gear!

He had to remove a decent length of dying, obstructed small intestine. I was suitably stitched up, and sent home when the stitches were removed after several days. Once it seemed I was well and truly on the mend, my mother returned to teaching at the Kenya Girls High School, where our family had a small flat, and where she left our trusted servants in charge of Colin and me while she taught.

Our high-country *Kipsigis* house-boy, Arap Chuma, who was from the same tribal group as many of Kenya's greatest runners, appeared, looking distressed, in the doorway of her class soon after, and Mum realised straight away that something was badly amiss.

Apparently, the incision of my scar-line, now minus its stitches, decided to peel itself wide open, exposing my intestinal contents. Arap Chuma covered the gaping wound with a clean kitchen-towel, and left Clara, our *ayah* (nurse-maid) in charge. After being firmly re-stitched, it was decided to leave the stitches in for another nine days just to make sure that nature didn't repeat itself. To this day, I have a vertical *tree* on my abdomen to remind me of that early adventure.

I must've been getting *looked after* quite a bit, even back then! According to some old letters my mother wrote to Jock, her father-in-law, that have resurfaced in our family archive, I'd had three haemmorhages where I'd passed blood, over several months. The local paediatrician was confused about my case because I'd be listless for a while, without a temperature; then be in a lot of pain with my body racked into a foetal position; then I'd pass the haemmorhaged material; and then get better again. My most recent reading about intussusception on *Medscape* states *If left untreated, however, this condition is uniformly fatal in 2-5 days.* Just as well that I was too young to understand that in 1961.

We enjoyed an idyllic early childhood in Nairobi, especially when we moved to the emerging area of *Kitisuru*, where Mum and Dad built a small home on about eight acres of old coffee plantation across the road from natural forest leading down to a small stream. *Kitisuru* provided room for Dad's expansive collection of veteran cars scrounged when the *top brass* of the British military left Kenya at the end of the war, minus a 1920's Hispano Suiza that my mother never ever knew about, *stashed* on a family friend's farm up-country.

At Kitisuru, I remember literally walking into a *hornet's nest*, aged about four, when Colin and I decided to hop onto the newly-horizontal trunk of a large tree that Dad had just cut down for the express purpose of–: *getting rid of the hornet's nest!*

Colin still remembers me being festooned in hornets, and I remember being stung all over my arms, neck, legs, and head. What I particularly remember is being dotted in gentian violet antiseptic, a purple substance which lasted longer on my skin than the sting scars did.

I am likely to be *immune* to all kinds of insect-derived toxins after that massive exposure at that young age.

Around about that same time, Colin came down with two successive illnesses that both required hospitalization. One illness progressed from a nasty *strep throat* to full-blown *rheumatic fever,* and the other I remember as *tick fever* (probably *tick typhus* or one of the *rickettsia* infections transmitted by tick bites in East Africa).

As he was presumably quite infectious, he was isolated in his own room at *Gertrude's Gardens,* the children's hospital in Nairobi that featured far too many times in our early childhood. After a week or so, we were missing each other desperately, so Dad hatched a plan that incorporated our favourite movie of the time, a silent black and white *Noddy and Big Ears* cartoon he ran on his Standard-Eight projector. He got permission from the matron to bring the projector into Colin's room, so that she knew everything was *above-board.*

Before Dad went into the building, he'd instructed me to stay below Colin's window, and then when the *coast was clear* he hoisted me up and deposited me under Col's bed, to watch *Noddy and Big Ears* while not making too much noise. When the movie was over, he opened the curtains and dropped me out of the window, at which point I walked back to the car to wait for him.

The first part of the plan went very well, with me happily looking up from under the bed, while lying on my belly. The room was dark when *Matron* made a surprise visit, presumably to see what Colin was laughing so much at in the movie. The loud laughter was likely me and Colin laughing together. I could easily have touched matron's bristly lower legs and sensible shoes as she stood at the foot of the bed, but she left after a short while.

Dad then lowered me out of the window, as planned, into the garden bed, before packing up the projector and meeting up with me at the car.

Even though the very serious part of the Mau-Mau Emergency was long since over, we did have one spot of bother I can clearly recall. I remember awakening to unusual sounds outside our bedroom window at Kitisuru, and getting out of my bed to watch as two Africans were slowly rolling Dad's favourite veteran car backwards down the scoria-graveled drive, while an accomplice scampered up a telephone pole. I wasn't seen by the interlopers, and went into Mum and Dad's bedroom to rouse Dad. He was a very heavy sleeper, so I had to shake his foot quite a bit before he woke up. It must have been a bright moonlit night, as although no outside lights were on, I could clearly see what was going on.

Dad put on his robe, and then retrieved his old Army service rifle, a *Lee Enfield* 303 stashed in the top of the in-built wardrobe, and after quietly prising open a window just enough to put the barrel through, he proceeded to let a round go into the wooden pole just inches from where the erstwhile thief was still busy trying to cut through our telephone wire. The thief flew backwards off the pole from several metres up, and couldn't have been hurt too badly as he jumped straight up and took off howling down the drive into the darkness of the forest. His friends took off after him, with Dad soon after them, in his dressing gown and slippers, armed with a torch as well as his *Lee Enfield*. Mum then proceeded to ring the police.

We were allowed to watch the policemen- mostly African-dust the car for finger-prints. It was pretty obvious that the thieves were not locals, as all the local Africans knew that Dad was a former British Army man with a rifle, and therefore a *memsahib* to respect. It was also pretty obvious that the *thieves* were clueless about what they were *stealing*: the car was extremely rare, and was the only super-charged 1926 Vauxhall 3098 in Kenya.

When it was parked at the top of our driveway, Colin and I used to love clambering up and down the wide running-boards of *Barcus*, and we often hopped behind the wheel, pretending to drive. We were doing this one day when Mum and Dad were entertaining friends on the front verandah, when Colin somehow managed to disengage the large externally-mounted hand-brake, and *Barcus* started to slowly roll backwards down the drive. I promptly hopped off, watching the very large vehicle roll away without thinking to alert anyone.

My Dad was soon aware that his *pride and joy* was disappearing down the drive, with another *pride and joy* somewhere in the cab, and sprinted hard to jump on the running-board to haul up the hand-brake. He succeeded, just as the rear-end of the car crashed into a fragile frangipani tree, on the edge of a teetering drop. Colin's memory of the incident was of falling into the foot well in front of the driver's seat, looking up at the surrounds starting to move, but not feeling any particular panic, then feeling the jolt as the car stopped, only to see Dad's head appear above him. Neither the car, nor Colin, suffered any permanent damage.

That particular car was in our parents' wedding photo, and in later years, repainted white, it appeared in the 1987 film *White Mischief*, starring Greta Scacci, (Our childhood friend Olga Brochner, who was in Kenya at the time, was an extra in that film.)

On another occasion when I was about four, we were visiting family friends on a small farm not far out of Nairobi. They had a small bay pony with a thick, long, dark tail. It was near the back door, and I decided to pat it while eating a thick *Golden Syrup* sandwich.

I decided to stroke the horse's tail, but because my tiny fingers were covered in the sticky syrup, I had to tug my hand down quite hard through the horse's tail to get it out. The pony's immediate response was to flick me several metres across the yard with a swift, very hard kick from its rear legs. He got me in my lower legs. I was in a lot of pain, so on that visit to hospital I was very pleased to have X-Rays taken of my legs, hoping that I had suffered a broken leg so that I could walk around in a plaster cast with crutches and be a *wounded soldier*. (This was only about 17 years after the end of World War Two, which still hung like a large psychological backdrop for many kids born in the 1950s. Adults very often referred to *the war* as if it had only just occurred very recently).

I remember being very disappointed when we were informed that my leg hadn't been broken, but that disappointment was addressed when the nursing staff wrapped my leg from foot to thigh in crepe bandage, so that I had something to show for my heroic exploit, at *Mrs Drummond's Nursery School* the next day. I loved it when, after so many of my childhood rough-and-tumbles, my Dad would say something like "You're a brave soldier, aren't you, laddie? You always get up to fight again!" He was kindness and compassion itself, and he was the absolute hero of my early childhood.

With Kenyan Independence Day occurring on 12th December, 1963, although I had only just turned five, I can remember the perceived need for all Asian or European residents to leave the country. Jomo Kenyatta, the first black president of the Republic of Kenya, ushered in moves to have all non-indigenous residents apply for work permits which they wouldn't necessarily receive by birth-right. The xenophobia particularly extended to the Chinese and Indian populations, who were the mainstay of commerce, as well as the colonial public service. Thousands left Kenya, leaving administration of infrastructure for things like the East African Railways to go to seed.

This was the *beginning of the end* for many people like my mother, who had been born and bred in Kenya. There was a mass-migration of Kenya-born residents to the U.K., Australia,

Canada and New Zealand from 1963 to 1965, and our little family eventually joined this exodus.

One occurrence I clearly remember was when my father drove Colin and me home from school at the Loreto Convent. We were at one of the few intersections in Nairobi with traffic lights, and we had been waiting for some time for the red light to change to green.

However, when the light did change to green, a police car with siren blazing stopped our entire queue of cars, while the presidential cavalcade sauntered across, taking as long as it liked. Even at that age, I felt outraged at this cavalier rudeness, however in retrospect, this was Jomo Kenyatta's time to thumb his nose at the Colonial administration that had him jailed for a number of years, for his long association with indigenous self-determination.

Like most European families in Kenya at that time, we had *servants*. The arrangement wasn't one of *white superiority*; it was really more of a moral duty to provide employment and accommodation to Africans who otherwise would be unemployed and homeless. Once an African had been allowed to join the household, the understanding was that he or she could build a *shamba*, consisting of a traditional hut at the rear of the house, complete with chooks, chicken-wire fencing, and a small home-garden. In return for household duties, they were provided with basic groceries like sugar and flour, and a small income as well.

Any presumption of superiority over our African servants from me or my brother was doomed to failure with Mum's unflagging interest in our staff's wellbeing and their life stories, and Dad's gentle nature.

It was not unusual to walk into our kitchen and find several *watotos* (small children) sitting under our kitchen table while their parents prepared our meals.

I had a major *life lesson* when I was about five, and decided to enter a shamba behind the house with a degree of the memsahib's self-entitlement. The first thing I noticed in that dark little hut with the hard-packed dirt floor and the smell of wood smoke and sweat was a small, old leather clasp-purse lying close to the embers of a small fire. I picked the tiny purse up and undid the clasp, finding only a solitary coffee bean inside. Then I became aware of an old man looking at me from across the hut. I felt desperately ashamed for waltzing into his very private space, and his look of helplessness and loss of natural dignity is with me to this day.

What we were too young to realise at that time was that our own *ayah*, or native nursemaid, was Jomo Kenyatta's first wife, Grace Wambui Kenyatta. She was also known as Grace *Wahu* Kenyatta, or simply *Mama* in her later years, long after Jomo's death. Despite being fluent in Swahili, Mum didn't realise until many years later why all the other servants held Gracie in such high esteem, but Dad, who must've arranged the job for her, obviously did.

Colin playing at driving, with Gracie.

The Colonial administration was looking high and low for Kenyatta's immediate family, and I'd say that Dad felt it wasn't fair-minded at all. He knew Gracie was caught between a rock and a hard place. From what I can piece together years down the track, he decided to give Gracie safe harbour right in the least-expected place; a former British soldier who had fought in the Mau Mau campaign would be the least likely person to give employment to a so-called *Mau-Mau sympathiser*. Dad often used to cryptically say that "the best place to hide is right under someone's nose". A *secret stayed a secret* with Dad. I actually visited *Gracie* in Nairobi in 2002, when she was over 100 years old. I'll write about this now, before resuming my tale.

Finding Gracie Again

In 2002 I managed to visit *Gracie*, at the large home Jomo left her on Ngong Road, opposite the race-course. It took a few days and repeat visits to the compound to convince the *askari* (armed guard) that I wasn't a journalist, but eventually, after some annoyed eyeballing from me at very close quarters, he phoned the house. Gracie's daughter, Margaret, said to "come on in". I hadn't come all that way to be turned away by someone with his own agenda, whether he was black or white.

Margaret was about 74 at that time, and said that Grace's income as our *ayah* helped nine of her extended family and supporters get through a very lean time for several years. Grace was 100 years old, and Margaret and a grand-daughter were caring for her.

Keith and Gracie in 2002: she was over 100.

Gracie lived in an extremely modest way, with a bedroom off a ground-floor lounge, and it was lit by a single bare light-globe, which is why the video-photo had to be taken with night-vision. She had an old *Church of Scotland* hymnbook written in Kikuyu on her bedside table, and she was very glad to meet me, even though I am quite sure she didn't realise why I was there for a good half-hour. She sang me some of her favourite old hymns, and patted my hand as I sat beside her.

When I showed her a photo of me and Colin when we were tiny, she made the association, but it took a good half-hour during which she didn't quite know who this visitor was, but was very happy to entertain him anyway.

I was there for about an hour or so, talking and drinking *chai*, (native tea brewed in heated milk) before I realised that my poor Kikuyu taxi-driver was still outside the front gate. "Bring him in!" said Margaret.

I walked out to the taxi, expecting the driver to be a bit angry, but he was in animated conversation with the *askari*, and had decided to stop the meter while he waited.

I said "Would you like to come inside and meet Mama?", to which he gave a delighted "Yes, sir!"

I winked cheerfully at the surly askari, who had deliberately prevented me from even making contact on several occasions a couple of weeks earlier. My taxi-driver refused to charge me for the return journey of the trip, saying he was thrilled to have met *Mama* and to have had a cup of chai with her, and that he had something amazing to tell his wife and children now.

For the local Africans at the time, meeting someone like that was akin to meeting the Queen. I paid the taxi-driver anyway.

Emigration to New Zealand is First Talked About

I still vividly remember when the decision was made that we would emigrate to New Zealand, where mum had friends already settled in Auckland. Mum had decided unilaterally that New Zealand would be better for us, after her experiences as a teenager dealing with servicemen from several British Commonwealth countries as a girl guide volunteering with the Red Cross during the early years of World War Two. Mum said that the Canadians and New Zealanders were *gentlemen,* but that the Australian soldiers were *uncouth.* So, as Canada was *too cold,* New Zealand was *it!*

The picture-book of New Zealand we kept looking at had a beautiful front cover of a scene overlooking an idyllic harbour from high up a very rugged hill. This looked to be very exciting to us, and we were *ready to go*!. (Years later, when I was running high in the Port Hills overlooking the South Island city of Christchurch and its port of Lyttelton, it struck me where I had seen that scene before.)

We turned six before we left Kenya, and as Colin and I had never seen the sea because we lived too far inland in Nairobi, we went on a wonderful overnight trip by steam engine with East African Railways to the coast; 500 miles or 800 km to Mombasa, Kenya's ancient Arab trading port. We went *first class* and had a family cabin and bunk-beds! The trip was extremely exciting for little guys!

Unfortunately for our parents, every time we so much as sighted a large pond in the moonlight we'd wake them up! As the train passed small villages in the morning, we'd see women pounding maize, and mobs of *watotos* running excitedly while they waved at us. In some areas we'd see wild animals grazing on grassy plains.

The formal *evening meal* in the dining car was something else again! We dined with ivory-handled silver service and proper porcelain crockery with the East African Railways logo; the meal was *kedgeree,* a delightful Indian fish and rice dish with mild curry flavouring.

The train sinuously wound the many long bends on its 5000–foot descent to the coast, and after a scrambled eggs and bacon breakfast we drew into Mombasa, after several excited sightings of a distant sea.

When we were eventually transported to our accommodation for the week–the Grosvenor Hotel on the coast at Kikambala Beach, our excitement was at fever pitch. "It's a far, far place with no country!" was my first reaction to the expanse of Indian Ocean.

The Grosvenor Hotel was true to its Colonial origins, with African porters and concierges resplendent in their crisp white shirts and red fez hats. The smell and feel of crushed coral sands, sponges, seaweeds and light Indian Ocean breeze has stayed with me ever since.

We had to wear sand-shoes when we walked out onto the reef, largely because of the *Reef Stonefish*, the most venomous fish in the world with its brilliantly disguised toxic spines. We did see one on the beach, however it was corralled in a child's paddling pool near the hotel, with beach-sand on the floor of the pool making it almost impossible to see.

For two extremely inquisitive young boys, *mortal danger* was not to be found on the reef, but within the hotel itself! Somehow, we managed to find our way through a window into the adjoining suite to ours, and made a bee-line straight for a free-standing wardrobe with tall mirror door and full-width drawer beneath the closet space. We opened the door wide, and clambered into the empty closet space, then I pulled the bottom drawer open, and hopped into it as one quite naturally would at that age!

Even though I was tiny, my weight in the front of a fully-opened drawer in an empty wardrobe with its heavy mirrored door wide open, as well, was enough to slowly lever the whole wardrobe forwards on its front legs.

Miraculously, Colin got out of the way somehow. I can remember the uncertainty of what was happening, and somehow managed to stay inside the drawer as it slammed shut rapidly with the mirror door above smashing apart.

I was in a dark, muffled space, and was extremely worried that I might not be able to get out of there without getting into trouble. My Dad and a hotel porter got into the room after hearing the crash, and managed to lift the smashed wardrobe off the floor slowly, to a point where I was able to roll aside as the drawer slid out of the wardrobe carcass. I had to crawl around all the shards of smashed mirror. How I didn't sever a limb I don't know, and how I avoided a huge thrashing is even more of a miracle. I think in all the relief that I was OK the need for a thrashing petered away. My over-taxed *guardian angel* must have been whitehaired and red-eyed by this early stage of my life, already.

The high-walled monolith of Fort Jesus that dominates the harbour-line was built by the Portuguese on Mombasa Island in the 1590s. When we were there, clinker-built Arab dhows, just like those seen on the Nile, plied the small harbour, and I believe the same can be said of Mombasa's harbour even today. Mombasa became the major port city of pre-colonial Kenya in the Middle Ages and was used to trade with other African port cities, the Persian Empire, the Arabian Peninsula, the Indian Subcontinent and even China.

Other memories of that wonderful holiday were on the beach in front of our hotel.

We discovered hollowed overhangs with coral-sand floors in low cliffs along from the beach, which became our *pirate caves*.

One morning, we were up as usual at the crack of dawn, and the rising sun made the whole coral-sand beach appear a glowing pink-red. Then the *whole beach got up* with a collective clatter, as many thousands of crabs scuttled into the water at our approach.

On the same beach one evening, we saw a very refined middle-aged English lady, dressed from the knees up as if she was going to a civic reception, but below the knees she was dressed in sandals. She was walking a cheetah on a leash, as one does. She was smoking a cigarette in a holder, like a 1920's film star would. She wafted up to us and said "Would you like to see my pussy-cat run?", and without waiting for a reply she let the cat off its leash, at which it took off at amazing speed till it was hundreds of metres up the beach. Then she called out to it with a high-pitched appeal, and it zoomed back to us at much the same speed. The lady then resumed her walk along the beach with her spectacular cat, and it seemed totally the appropriate thing to happen in that exotic part of the world.

When we returned from that trip to the coast, we moved back into staff accommodation at the Kenya Girls' High School, as Mum and Dad had sold our *dream property* in Kitisuru in anticipation of emigration. With mass-emigration of many potential buyers, it was exactly the wrong time to be selling Kenyan property, however pleasant. The school provided comfortable two bedroom flats for staff on-campus. Colin and I quite enjoyed living at the school, as we were partial to all the attention of numerous *big girls*, who thought we were *cute*.

We were back with our former ayah, Clara, and we'd often play with her son Peter, who was our age. We used to look at Peter's hands, and see that his palms were almost as light-skinned as ours, and wonder how the rest of him was so dark, and his hair so tight and curly. In turn, he used to marvel at our blonde hair, and would want to stroke it.

I built a small hut with rocks, sticks, twine, and old sheets under a tree beside the flat, and one day got into a fight with Peter which resulted in me hitting him hard on his forehead with a small rock. I opened up a big gash on his dark skin, and I was astonished at how lustrous his bright red blood was against his ebony features. I was also surprised at how loud he could scream. For the most part, Kikuyu *watotos* were made of hard stuff, and weren't given to crying and screaming, however for some reason Peter's wailing was loud; too loud.

Clara went apopleptic seeing her son's head covered in blood, and I got a severe thrashing from Mum for that episode. She usually took her flat shoes off and hit me across the back of the legs with one of them, leaving a healthy red patch of stinging skin. Peter was OK once he'd received stitches from the school doctor, and we played quite happily again a few days later, once I'd apologized to him and his mother, with Mum standing behind me with her hands on her hips.

Poor Clara really was put through the mill trying to look after Colin and me. One day we took off and hid behind the organ pipes in the school chapel, while she yelled outside for us, not knowing where we were. We thought it was funny, but obviously it wasn't, as we received a good hiding for that, too.

The Kenya Girls High School provided lots of opportunities for new adventures. Another day we decided to see what would happen when we rang the big red bell in the school quadrangle. Quite a bit happened, as several hundred well-drilled girls spilled out onto the quadrangle, with puzzled teachers in tow. We observed from a great distance, and we were never found out for that stunt.

There was a galvanized iron and wood *canteen* thrown together on grassland a couple of hundred metres away from the school, and sometimes we would wander over to buy a Fanta or a Pepsi. The Africans never seemed to mind.

Another time I can recall us being baby-sat by *Uncle Tom* Chote, an absent-minded bespectacled Scottish bachelor who was good-hearted but not the best choice for the job. Once Tom had his nose in a book, that was the end of his present-time consciousness. He started a bath for us, as instructed, but soon got caught up in one of the many interesting books Mum and Dad had in the lounge area. For some reason, Colin and I had decided it'd be a good idea to see if we could close the bathroom door while the bath was still running.

Unfortunately, the bathroom door stayed locked, and Mum and Dad came home to a stream of warm water spilling down the concrete steps from the first-floor flat, with Uncle Tom still with his face in a book, and Colin and I in our room wondering how to explain everything. *Uncle Tom's* most hilarious act of absent-mindedness was when he constructed a wooden dinghy in the living-room of his rented house, whereby an external wall had to be taken down to get it outside!

Looking back, trouble just seemed to find us. Two little guys with boundless enthusiasm and curiosity can create a lot of strife, without any harm or malice intended. We definitely regarded ourselves as *good boys*.

We started school at the Loreto Convent in Bishop Avenue, Nairobi, when we were five

With Uncle Don, a former RAF Spitfire pilot friend of Dad's, on first day of school.

We had photos taken on that occasion, in the Kenya High School grounds, with *Uncle Don*, Dad's friend, who was stationed with the RAF in Nairobi. Don and Dad had half-shares in a Tiger Moth biplane, and now and again they would *buzz* the school, and Dad would take aerial photos. Don flew Spitfires during the war, and to us was the epitome of dashing bachelorhood. He was quite a raconteur, and his small flat at the RAF base had an esoteric collection of militaria and African weapons that was fascinating to small boys.

The Loreto Sisters were the same order of nuns who had taught Mum when she was at school in Nairobi, after her father had died. I can remember sit-down lunches supervised by the *big girls* (probably no older than twelve) in their gym-frocks. For some reason, rhubarb was served quite often, and the plates were watched like hawks by the *big girls* to make sure the little ones ate everything served up. Disposing of the rhubarb without being caught eventually involved deftly spooning it into an empty glass, then into a communal jug of milk on the table, where it was hard to see unless one looked hard.

The Loreto sisters dressed according to the prevailing fashion for nuns back then; the *Penguin* look epitomized by *The Penguin* in *The Blues Brothers*, the classic 1980 movie.

We were taught the *three R's* on a reward system, right from the start. The *reward* for getting one's spelling or sums correct was being able to play with plasticine, a coloured dough-like modelling material that was very popular with children back then. Because we loved playing with plasticine, we learnt very quickly. One warm afternoon, when old Mother Breed was dozing off at her desk, I chose to throw a well-kneaded ball of the stuff up onto the ceiling, to see if it would stick. It did indeed stick to the ceiling, in a flattened circular blob, and after observing it for a while I forgot about it.

I remembered it again with a jolt when the little girl in front of me screamed when it dropped into her hair. She screamed even more when I rushed to *help* by getting the plasticine out of her blonde strands with my hands. Mother Breed immediately demanded that I go and stand in the corner for the rest of the lesson, in disgrace. I was probably lucky that she didn't hit me; the good sisters were given to a bit of *capital punishment* on occasion. The pretty little girl returned to school the next day with her hair cut off. I wondered why she didn't like me anymore; the start of many years of being *dumb and dumber* with the female species.

Around that time, I also managed to get attacked by a small vervet monkey in Nairobi's wild animal orphanage. It took exception to me putting my tiny hand and wrist through the enclosure's chicken-wire to pat it, while it sat on a small branch. It clamped its ferocious little teeth down hard on the tip of the fourth digit of my right hand; I can still identify the tiny round scar today. I was rescued by a tiny old Indian lady in a sari, who screamed at the monkey while pulling my hand out, and jabbed the monkey in the eyes to get it off my finger. The open wound bled profusely. That episode required a tetanus shot, a couple of tiny stitches, and a large amount of bandage. I haven't fully trusted small primates since.

It was at Loreto Convent that Colin and I did one of our best-ever double-team stunts. The nuns were extremely strict about class-times being adhered to. One lunchtime, when Colin and I had been playing in a sandpit down the stairs, we got up to the class to be prevented from entering by a kid we called *Jerry Hair*, who we disliked because he had very curly hair and an *attitude* to go with it. He had pulled the multiple-paned steel-framed glazed doors shut from the inside, and we pulled one door back as hard as we could in order to get inside before the *penguin* arrived.

We soon realized that it was going to be an impossible task to get inside in time, but in unison we both decided to pull the door back towards us with one big heave, with several boys pulling from the inside. Then we let the door go in complete synchronicity! The door hit its steel framing so hard that all the glass shattered inwards over our opponents. Colin and I both decided the safest place to ride that scenario out was back at the sandpit, where we were soon rounded up by a penguin who decided that we truly were just playing downstairs where we always did, and hadn't heard the bell. The boys who had just blamed us for the shattered glass were severely reprimanded for making up stories; – "clearly Keith and Colin were nowhere near the scene".

When I visited Kenya again, in 2002, over 37 years later, I stayed at The Fairview, a hotel situated across the road from the Loreto Convent. The owner, Mr. Slapack, had gone to school with my step-father, Brian McCabe. To visit the convent, I had to get permission from the Israeli Embassy, which was sited next door. I was warned by hotel staff that the very muscular, highly-armed Israeli security staff hated being photographed, with the 1998 destruction of the US Embassy in Nairobi by the newly-emerged terrorist group Al Qaeda still being fresh in their memories. They had been known to rip cameras from people and destroy their cameras. Each security man was armed like Rambo, minus the head-scarf and bare torso.

After obtaining clearance, I toured the convent grounds with the headmistress, and noticed how it was *exactly* the same as when I last remembered it, except a bit more tired and dusty. That seemed to be the way it was in Nairobi, with a visit to the National Museum of Kenya being a tired, faded, and dusty version of the museum as it was in 1964. None of the exhibits I remembered so well had even been changed, or re-mounted on fresh mounting-board!

We turned six while living at the Kenya Girls' High School, and had a big party in one of the reception rooms in our accommodation building. There were many beautiful presents, including beautiful wooden scale-model yachts and many other toys, given by staff or students or family friends. They covered several tables, and there was a very tall multi-tiered cake. Unfortunately, we couldn't take much with us on our trip to New Zealand, so Mum gave most of the presents to an orphanage, as well as her mother's very valuable antique violin, given to her own mother by a German violin teacher in Johannesburg. No doubt, somewhere in Nairobi, several orphaned *watotos* learnt on that instrument.

Eventually it came time for Mum, Colin and me to depart for New Zealand. Dad had to remain in Kenya to honour the remainder of his contract with Gill & Johnson, an auditing firm. At one stage he was required to monitor the illegal transfer of UN-sourced grains from Kenyan government officials to Ugandan politicians, while working anonymously in the border city of Kisumu, on Lake Victoria, as a mild-mannered accountant. The grain was intended for famine relief in northern Kenya. Dad suffered a nasty dose of food poisoning in Kisumu, and what was supposed to be a short interlude stretched out to about 18 months, before he was able to finally board a plane out of Kenya.

Before we went, Dad gave each of us a wind-up watch and a Fujica camera, and some great cowboy cap pistols. I took my watch apart by the time we reached New Zealand, just to see what *made it tick*, but I still have the Fujica camera in original working order. Some of the photos in this book were taken with that camera.

The Long Journey to New Zealand.

A week or so before Christmas of 1964, Mum embarked for New Zealand with me and Colin. An abiding memory of that trip was her *white vinyl handbag*, that was last sighted residing in one of her cupboards, only a few years ago. I have a photo of me and Colin with our cousin, Tim Stanley, where we were holding the *white vinyl handbag* while Mum took the photo. The photo was taken with Tim at Nairobi Railway Station. Tim was about to embark on his merchant navy training in the UK, at HMS Conway in North Wales.

We departed from Kenya by B.O.A.C. (now British Airways) in a De Havilland *Comet* jet, bound for the British Protectorate of Aden, in what is now called Yemen. The airport walkways were patrolled by armed British troops in their camouflage gear, which impressed us greatly. On the plane, the B.O.A.C. stewardesses made sure we enrolled for the *Junior Jet Club*, which entitled us to enameled winged badges, membership cards, satchel carry-on bags with the J.J.C. logo, and most importantly, flight logbooks which were to record all our international flight details including cumulative flight hours and statute miles, as well as individual trip data, to be signed by the captain after each trip.

The next stop was Karachi, in Pakistan, where heavily armed soldiers in dark uniforms and bullet-proof vests glowered menacingly, while the Comet was refueled, which seemed to take a very long time in a sweltering airport concourse.

From there we flew to Bombay, (now known as *Mumbai*), and the strongest memory I have is of the absolute stench emanating up with a heat-haze from the city below as the plane circled overhead for landing. It was as if a septic tank had been prised open in the passenger cabin. The heat haze was so thick that we could hardly make out any buildings. (In those earlier days of pressurized cabins the stench of the city thousands of feet below couldn't be filtered out! The stench seemed more bearable on the ground.)

We stopped over in Bombay at a hotel in southern Bombay situated close to tourist attractions like the spectacular *Gateway to India*, a triumphal arch of similar proportions to the Arc De Triomphe in Paris.

The *Gateway* overlooked half a kilometre of beach on each side, sited as it was at the top of a small bay opening out onto the Arabian Sea, and there was a large paved public space of several acres in front of it, packed with market stalls and people. Around the perimeter of the square ran a poorly defined *road* which had Bombay's ubiquitous yellow and black Morris Oxford taxis avoiding more ubiquitous street dogs and innumerable Brahman or cross-breed cows. The dogs and cows seemed to do their own thing, with impunity. In the marketplace, we took particular notice of an elderly snake-charmer and his beautiful cobra. We stayed watching them for a long time before walking back to the nearby hotel, reluctantly, with Mum.

The next day we were taken to see Mahatma Gandhi's former residence, *Mani Bhavan*, in Bombay. It was up a steep flight of wooden stairs in an old two-storey building a few kilometres away from the Gateway to India. The room itself was pleasant, of early 1900s ambience, but very sparsely furnished. There were a couple of Gandhi's Indian-style wooden *spinning wheels* on one side of the room, and what looked like a futon mattress on the wooden floor. Apart from that, all I can recall was a white enameled tin hand-basin on the floor as well.

When we left the Gandhi residence, we noticed a wooden cart drawn by a donkey, going in and out of the narrow laneways between buildings. The cart had a red lamp on the back, and a little bell on the front. The two men guiding the cart were picking up the corpses of the recently-deceased poor who lived under large sheets of cardboard or makeshift shelters in the alleys. They placed them on the cart, covered by old grey blankets.

This theme of indifference to death was reinforced when we were driven up *Malabar Hill*, a tree-clad promontory overlooking southern Bombay from the west. This was where the elite of colonial India built their exclusive residences with glorious views over the southern city and out to the Arabian Sea to the south and west. Those views were not what got two little boys' imaginations stirred though; what was far more impressive was a large grey wall surrounded by tall trees, with large vultures sitting on the top of the wall, or circling around overhead in menacing sweeps. They clearly had food in their beaks, and it turned out that this was a Parsi (or Zoroastrian) temple, where the dead were laid out on stone slabs for nature to take them back.

We returned to the hotel, ready for an early departure the next morning on the airport bus, where our journey was to re-commence: this time, to Colombo, in Ceylon (now Sri Lanka).

After breakfast, I can remember getting as far as the bus door with Mum, however the lure of one last look at the old snake-charmer proved irresistible. I don't know how we managed it, but we were off in no time around to watch the snake-charmer. My poor mother must have been absolutely frantic! My memory of being that age is that I was a *good* little boy, but extremely inquisitive, as I still am.

When we arrived at the snake-charmer, minus a supervising mother as we had been a couple of days earlier, the friendly old guy signaled us to stand right beside him and not go anywhere. That was OK with us. The next thing I recall was being hit by several hard whacks from Mum's *white vinyl handbag.*

Mum was purple-faced and furious! After an exceptionally severe and hurried dressing-down, with a few very hard bare-handed slaps to the back of the thighs for good measure, we were marched around to the hotel, where the airport bus was still waiting for us all.

THE PUNISHMENT

We weren't able to sit down comfortably for a couple of days.

Our biggest punishment was that Mum said we couldn't be allowed to be out of her sight for the rest of the trip, and we were to be with her at all times, even with nature calls on the plane, where we were made to stay outside the toilet door while she had her visit, with the stewardesses watching us.

Mum was true to her word, even in airport layovers, the whole way to New Zealand where we arrived about 6 weeks later. At every stopover on the rest of the trip, she even made us accompany her to the women's toilets, where she requested fellow women passengers to keep an eye on us while we guiltily absorbed the ambience and strange communal lipstick rituals of the sisterhood in front of mirrors in women's rest-rooms, and noted the complete absence of stand-up urinals. Very strange.

A MONTH IN *SERENDIP.*

Sri Lanka, or *Ceylon* as I still remember it, was also known as the legendary *Island of Serendip.* This Persian-Arabic name gives origin to the word *serendipidity*, having been coined by the English writer Horace Walpole in the eighteenth century, when he was inspired by the ancient Persian fairy tale *The Three Princes of Serendip*, whose heroes often made discoveries by chance.

The island of Serendip is still very much an island of ancient mysteries, and was well-known to Chinese, Persian, and Arab traders, long before the Portuguese and British colonists of recent centuries. It was well-known to Prince Gautama of Nepal, who according to ancient writings travelled on three occasions to Serendip as the *Buddha.*

If our colourful Kenya memories weren't enough to stimulate our young minds, the Bombay *brain-blast* followed by a fascinating month or so travelling around the full length and breadth of Sri Lanka further seared life-long shared memories of an era that has gone forever, deep into our psyches.

We arrived in Colombo after a long, eventful flight through the night. Still flying by Comet jet, we were buffeted by a tropical lightning storm over southern India. Mum said she would always remember Colin and me excitedly looking out of the window at the bolts of lightning, while the plane lifted and plummeted, oblivious to the sheer panic of many adult passengers, who were groaning or spewing into the paper bags specially provided for that purpose. It was most exciting when lightning sparked off the end of the wing. My memory of most flights on the way to New Zealand was that we were glued to a window, whether flying during the day or night.

We were to stay with *Aunty Elizabeth* Sharp-Paul and her young family in Colombo. Elizabeth had studied at Rhodes University in Grahamstown, South Africa, during the war years, where she and my mother shared a house on the grounds with two other *girls* who also stayed life-long friends for many years. The house was nick-named 'Kenlonsia' in deference to the girls' home countries of Kenya, Ceylon, and Rhodesia.

Elizabeth passed away, in her ninety-first year, just a year ago as I write. Like my mother, she was mentally agile right to the end, having uncovered the previously unknown genealogy of *Gundrada*, the grand-daughter of William the Conqueror, when she was in her 70's, and having written a book on her findings. This possibly ruffled the feathers of professional historians along the way. Elizabeth's funeral at Ballarat Anglican Cathedral was very well-attended; she had lots of friends of all ages and vocations, in the local community.

Elizabeth had three of her four children with her in Colombo while we were there; Graham and Margaret, who were a few years older, and Fergus, who was probably a few months younger. Alastair, the oldest boy, was away at boarding school in the U.K. We stayed with the family in Colombo for a week or so, where the sound of Buddhist rituals with fireworks were noisy nightly events. There was a very large *Golden Buddha* presiding over a small park on a main road a few hundred metres away.

We liked their cook, Sinaia, a beautifully muscled Sinhalese who would flex his biceps for us at every opportunity. We also were fussed over by *Nanny*, a tiny Sinhalese lady who was a sort of governess for the family. She was heart-broken when we left, asking if she could come with us to New Zealand. Ever-diplomatic and caring, my mother explained to the dear old lady why this couldn't happen.

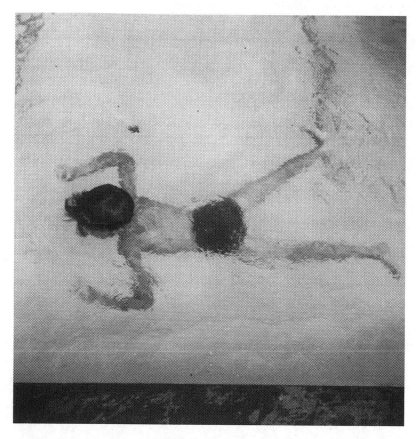

Elizabeth taught me to *swim* at the Colombo Baths, with the simplest swimming lesson possible. She said "Have you seen a frog swim, Keith?" "Then do just that! Go under the water for a few strokes and come up again when you need to breathe!"

I promptly managed to cross the swimming pool on my first attempt, and could *swim* confidently after that.

The family had gone to some trouble to include us in their Christmas celebrations while we were at their home. I remember being given quite a nice leather soccer ball, and a snorkel set, and loudly pronouncing "Is that all?", receiving a sharp kick under the table, with an accompanying glare from Mum, and I was made to say "sorry".

I was used to being thoroughly spoilt with lots of presents from staff and friends of Mum's at Kenya Girls' High School, where we were doted upon. (Colin and I are possibly still *covered all over in dote-marks*, to borrow from Spike Milligan.)

Elizabeth's husband Alan had a position managing tea estates in Ceylon. Alan was a former Royal Navy officer who had been managing tea estates for some years. Elizabeth managed to secure a tea estate car (a black former London taxi-cab) with estate driver, for what I can only describe as a *Grand Tour* of Late-Colonial Ceylon. In the north of the country, we were privileged to visit areas that outsiders in the years since had no access to due to ethnic tensions that eventually built into full-blown civil war, ending only in 2009.

First stop was *Bentota* or *Ben-tot*, a delightful west coast beach about 40 miles south of Colombo, where we stayed in a holiday house surrounded by palm trees, backing onto the local river. We were forbidden from setting foot in the river due to a water-borne parasitic disease, (probably *schistosomiasis*), spread by aquatic snails. This was a great pity, as the gentle river looked an idyllic place to swim or paddle during the sultry tropical heat of the day.

The *refrigerator* was a big steel chest that was filled with a large block of ice every day, and could be drained from the bottom. The beds all had mosquito nets, and the house had very fine screens on the inside of louvred window spaces that allowed cooling cross-breezes.

One day we saw a very annoyed man, screaming out loud while kicking an elephant in the leg, while it ate the thatching off his house roof, with the *mahout* atop the hungry pachyderm laughing his head off. Somewhere I have a photo of the incident, taken with my little *Fujitsu* camera.

One day we were taken to a small nearby island off-shore by outrigger canoe. At six years of age, I could barely see over the top of the hollowed out hull while standing in the canoe. The tiny island was dominated by a white lighthouse, and the people who lived there were very dark-skinned and muscular; they seemed to be a different race to the more Indian-looking Sinhalese living a few hundred metres away on the *mainland*.

There were water buffalo on the beach which were being used to thresh rice by the locals.

The canoe was carved out of a single large tree trunk, and was poled across a shallow strait of water by a man who stood on the prow. This little island was called Barberyn Island, off-shore from a little town called Beruwala a few kilometres north of Bentota.

With my new-found swimming ability, and the snorkeling set I'd been given for Christmas, I was encouraged to *dive* in the reef near where the outriggers were pulled up. I ran straight out of the water after only a minute or so, having dived close to a sting-ray. A couple of the local men dragged the poor creature up on the sand after spearing it, and flipping it on its back. I felt sorry seeing the strange creature die upside-down on the white sand, with its *eyes* rolling backwards. It was only a couple of feet across, and hadn't attacked me.

When Mum and Elizabeth took Colin into the water, he fought them furiously, absolutely refusing to put his head under the water. There was no way that the two grown women could over-power tiny Colin. The reason for this bizarre behavior became apparent after a visit with a local doctor who said Colin had one of the worst cases of *otitis media* he'd ever seen in a child, with the ear-drum completely ruptured with pus and blood. Colin informed us in later years that at that age, he thought "everyone felt sore like that in their ears," and assumed that the high-pitched whistle he constantly heard was *normal* as well.

Every day as we travelled around that beautiful island, often well off the *tourist route*, we had experiences that can never be forgotten, and possibly can never be repeated. Civil war with the Tamil Separatists meant that until 2009, Sri Lanka was not a safe tourist destination. The Tamil forces occupied the northern provinces for 26 years.

After a tour of the central highlands, including the sacred city of Kandy, and the misty, cold tea estate township of Nuwara Eliya (*Little England*) at above 6,600 feet, we had already seen more of Ceylon than most. In the far north of the country, we travelled for miles on corridors of rutted red dirt roads with low-lying tropical scrub on either side, just high enough and dense enough to prevent seeing any large hills or landmarks.

In that northern province area, in one day of driving, we came across a band of nomadic stone-age men standing in the middle of the track (they were *Veddhas*—thought by the Sinhalese to be the original indigenous occupants of the isle); a band of *Devil Dancers* scaring off evil spirits from a nearby village; and we also ran over the tail of a sizeable monitor lizard that scampered across the track. The tail ejected itself with no loss of blood, and it flapped around crazily in the red dirt for some minutes, while its saurian owner escaped into the scrub, presumably to grow a replacement tail later on.

One site worthy of its local status as *The Eighth Wonder of the Ancient World,* was the amazing fifth century *Lion Rock* at Sigirya, where a megalomaniac *king* built an impregnable fortress atop a sheer-walled granite rock that juts 660 feet above the surrounding jungle plains. The engineering was so good that many of the original water cisterns still functioned, after 1500 years. There were many ancient temples and ancient cities we saw, and we really didn't want to leave Ceylon.

Farewell to Serendip

We soon flew out from Colombo, this time headed for Singapore, on a Vickers Viscount Electra, which was a propeller aircraft.

I don't remember much about the layover in Singapore at all, but I do remember the next stop: Darwin, in the northern territory of Australia. The airport runway sat right beside a mangrove swamp. I remember seeing RAAF jets in camouflage colours sharing the airport runway with passenger aircraft in Darwin, and we disembarked into a very large aircraft hangar that had been modified to accept passengers. One of the friendly immigration officers asked me where I had acquired my 'Mexican hat' from, and I remember politely informing him that it was a 'Panama' hat, and that I had been given it in Kenya to protect me from sunburn.

The next stop was Melbourne, where we met up again with the Potgieter family, who had bought a small farm acreage just outside Castlemaine, in Central Victoria, not far from where my family now lives in Bendigo. Melbourne's main airport then was in Essendon, which is these days considered an inner suburb. The original airport is still there, hemmed in by freeways and housing estates, and a large shopping development built with the *Concrete Monstrosity* aesthetic. Predictably, a nasty fatal plane crash several years ago promoted calls for the closure of the airport that was there in the first place, before the local authorities legislated that it was safe to build a high-density shopping centre right by a medium-level commercial airfield.

With Caroline, Anne and Smartie Potgieter and visitors in Castlemaine.

We stayed for a week or so with Anne and Smartie and their family at the Reckleben Street address; the three girls were all *grown up*, and they had a younger brother, Ian, or *Potty*, who was about 16, and who was later to become a very good friend when I was studying in Melbourne in the 1980s. His older sister, Sue Milne, still lives in Castlemaine, and another, Georgie, lives in country Victoria.

At Reckleben Street, the day after we arrived, we managed to almost cause a bush-fire one blazing hot afternoon that was described curiously by locals as *110 degrees in the waterbag!* I remember this extremely well. This would be the equivalent of 43 degrees Celsius *in the shade* today. The adults were all engrossed in conversation in the living room of the house, and I'd discovered a box of matches nearby.

Outside, I shared this new find with Colin, and showed him how to strike a match, which I'd learnt by watching the adults lighting their cigarettes a few minutes earlier. I demonstrated the newly-observed miracle of striking a match to start a flame; in Kenya, the *grownups* we knew used heavy ornamental metal cigarette lighters, which we had mastered already.

I chose a paddock beside the house, unseen from the living room, to show Colin my skill with the match. When he had a turn, he successfully lit the match at the first attempt, however he was startled and managed to drop it somehow and a small patch of tinder-dry grass started burning. We tried to stamp it out, however it spread too quickly, so I decided to walk around to the house, where I very politely asked *Aunty Anne* for the use of a hose.

I remember the look of horror on Anne's face. All the adults were *up in a flash*, and before we knew it there were bells ringing, and neighbours and friends all over the paddock putting the fire out with shovels, blankets, boots, and buckets of tank-water. The local Country Fire Authority engine soon turned up, and the front of the paddock was a patch of steaming, blackened earth and grass stubble when they left. We were not very popular after that, but I'm sure we were suitably punished.

New Zealand

After that little adventure, we flew *across the pond* (Tasman Sea) to our new home of Auckland. We landed at Whenuapai Airport, which is now the RNZAF base for Auckland, and, as in Darwin, we were processed in a converted aircraft hangar. I remember the immigration men being very kind and friendly to me and Colin, asking where the passports for our koala bears were. We were so used to the *Queen's English* that the pronunciation of basic English words in New Zealand (pronounced *Noo Zild*) made it hard to understand exactly what was being said for the first few months. Eventually we spoke *Noo Zild* at school and *Queen's English* at home.

We stayed for a week or so with another Kenyan family, the Watsons, in a beautiful home at the top of View Street in Mt Eden; a very nice part of inner Auckland. Mum and Mrs Watson took us to look at potential accommodation a couple of miles further away, in Owairaka Avenue, Mt Albert. This was before seat belts, and when Mrs Watson turned left into a street called Hallam Street, off Owairaka Avenue, a few houses before our eventual *new home,* I rolled out of the back door onto the road, but I only suffered a few cuts and grazes. I was always fiddling with things.

Mum secured a teaching job at Auckland Girls Grammar School in downtown Auckland, catching the No.7 bus to town every morning. We moved into Flat 1, 92 Owairaka Avenue, Mt Albert, which has hardly changed in appearance since 1965, although the identical block of flats next door has long since been replaced, and several neighbouring homes have been replaced by high-density living units.

Colin and I were enrolled at Owairaka Primary School, around the corner from the flat, on Richardson Road. One day I said "Jambo" to a Maori boy, Jerry Mahouri, thinking he might understand Swahili somehow. He didn't. Another day, a white kid named *Jeffrey* got a few boys to surround me at *morning playtime,* all yelling "Kenya boy! Kenya boy!" while pushing and shoving me.

I gave him a good dose of *Kenya boy* in return, hitting him repeatedly while he cried incessantly. The more he cried, the more I hit him, on the ground, until the junior school headmistress, Miss Nicholls, stopped me. "Why are you hitting him?" asked Miss Nicholls? "Because he keeps on crying!" I said, which she found very puzzling. As I was new to New Zealand and the school, she gave me a stern warning about fighting at school, but no punishment. I still can't stand 'cry-babies' to this day, of any age.

The Vesey's house was over the fence from our front door.

When the large wooden crates with our possessions eventually arrived, there was sea-water damage to quite a few books and some linen. Colin and I converted the crates into a 'hut' at the rear of the flats, under some pine trees. I remember day-dreaming about turning them into a live-on raft that I could sail down the local creek.

The *hut* was where I stashed my collection of *preserved* wildlife ; namely little nestlings that had plummeted from the upper branches of the pine trees along the fence line. I put them in water with eucalyptus oil, not having access to ethanol or formaldehyde, or even knowing what to do. I had a stash of little sample bottles in a cardboard box in the hut, however the cardboard box rotted out eventually, and I dropped a bottle when I was transferring the contents to a plastic tub.

The stench was indescribable, and prevented further visits to the *hut* for months.

CHAPTER 12

Growing Up 'Kiwi'

We soon made friends with the young family over the fence; Doug and Rose Vesey had four children; Michelle, Grant, Anne, and Greg. The Vesey family were our introduction to the beautiful wild outdoors of New Zealand. The males of the family were real outdoorsmen, good with a rifle and keen on hunting deer. (Michele was a gentle-natured *tomboy* who was probably the strongest kid in her class at primary school.) The Veseys were stalwarts of Muriwai Surf Lifesaving Club, and had a little *bach* near the beach, at the base of a large sand-dune.

Michele and her husband Steve now live a blissfully simple life in a tiny *bach* with an outdoor toilet, on acreage far north of Auckland, now their boys have flown the nest.

Rose Vesey was a tiny Irish lady, who passed away a couple of months ago at 102 years of age. Rose played Bingo with a group of much younger *girls* in Auckland's Casino several days a week right until she was ready to pass. Her hundredth birthday at the Casino made national television in April 2016, as she was a guest of Honour in a reception room provided by the Casino. The visiting President of Ireland held a special reception for Rose in honour of her 100th birthday, also at the Casino.

In 1930, when she was only 14 years old, Roseanna Fitzpatrick left her family home in Bunnahow, County Clare, to escape depression-era Ireland for London, where she soon got a job in a hotel as a maid. She followed older siblings to London. Her sheltered upbringing in a large Catholic family didn't prepare her for the seedy side of life in London- especially when she had to prepare a double bed for two gentlemen guests, one of whom she found murdered in the same bed the next morning. Within a few days of moving to London, Rose had been interviewed as a witness in a murder case by detectives from Scotland Yard!

Colin and I had every reason to love Rose and the Veseys. We used to spend an hour or so at their house after school each afternoon, until Mum came home from a big day's teaching. Mum was very strict and, perhaps because she was tired, could be quite hard on us. She definitely had no time to hear about things like fights with the school bully, dismissing hard-won victories as 'senseless fighting', whereas Rose was a stay-at-home mother who was very keen to hear about what had transpired during the day, warts and all.

After one good whipping I gave my nemesis of the time, Rose was all ears; enthusiastically asking "Did you whup him good, then, Keet, did yer? Good boy! I'm proud of yer!" Small boys like us needed that validation.

Early in 1965, Colin and I were put into separate classes, and in my Primer 4 class with *Miss Powell*, I got to know my life-long friend Gavin Harris. There was a class excursion by bus to the nearest local beach, *Walker's Beach*, which would more accurately be described as *mangrove-covered rocky foreshore with tiny areas of shell-covered beach*. I can still recall that trip in great detail, especially the sea anemones and crabs in one rock-pool that had me entranced for quite some time. When I came out of my *trance*, I saw the school charter bus driving off without me! Evidently, I hadn't heard a thing while I was watching the action in the rock-pool, which is something that still occurs when I'm in deep concentration.

A New Friend

I wasn't too worried, as I thought it would be quite an adventure to walk home *all by myself*, but I didn't get the opportunity, as a blonde kid called Gavin, and his mother, appeared on the *beach*, and Gavin told me to come home with them. So I hopped into their Austin 1100 and went home with them. My clothes were absolutely filthy, so Mrs. Harris ran a hot bath for me and Gavin, and chucked everything in the wash. She put me in to some of Gavin's spare clothes, and gave me an early tea, before delivering me to our flat, where she had a nice long conversation with Mum. Culturally, they had a lot in common, as Mrs. Harris was a London-trained drama teacher and highly educated.

Gavin's Dad, Norman Harris, was a great guy; a very encouraging, easy-going man. Although Norm and Edna married in December 1945, Gavin was their only child to survive pregnancy, so Gavin loved having *two brothers* to hang around with. Norm was a paramedic in the North African campaign in World War Two, serving in the famous Allied withdrawal from Alexandria as well as having served in the Siege of Tobruk, a 241-day epic resulting in the first Allied victory of the North African campaign against General Rommel, the *Desert Fox*. As a paramedic, he must have seen the very worst of the action, possibly under enemy fire, but he never discussed it much as far as I know. No wonder he enjoyed his peaceful civilian life when he returned to Auckland after the war.

Norm was an early member of *Auckland Joggers*, Arthur Lydiard's jogging club he created to get sedentary middle-aged men active and healthy, which eventually inspired the founder of Nike, Bill Bowerman, to do the same in the USA, and start the world-wide jogging boom.

I have fond memories of Norm and my Dad sharing a cold beer while watching the classic movie about the desert campaign, 'Ice Cold in Alex', on our black and white TV.

Over the years, Gavin and I did many things together. Gavin got me involved with the Boy Scouts, or its junior counterpart, *cubs*, at St Judes Scouts, and his father Norm often drove us to scout camps. Our first cub-mistress, 'Connie *Akela* Crooks, passed away recently at 97 years of age. Her late husband Harold *Rata* Crooks was in charge of the Boy Scouts, and never brooked any nonsense. Apparently, soon before she passed, Connie said that she'd "do it all over again" with the involvement in scouting. It would be true to say that Boy Scouts was exactly the thing I needed growing up; especially the camping and extremely long hikes in Auckland's verdant Waitakere Ranges.

With other scouts at the National Scout Jamboree, 1972.

Some of my favourite memories are of the *Wide Games* held from our annual camp at *Hamilton's Farm* near Muriwai. These were wide-ranging tactical affairs over open farmland, played from hilltop to hilltop, with red flags on hilltops about a mile apart but still quite visible, where a team had to get inside another's area, steal their flag, and safely get it back to their home base.

The founder of the Boy Scout movement, Lord Robert Baden Powell, was a former British military hero who successfully defended the town in the 1899 Siege of Mafeking during the Second Boer War, and it is thought he started the Boy Scout movement as a way to *train* boys and young men in the skills and attitudes necessary in order to survive in a wartime situation. As I was a good runner I could usually evade capture even if I had been seen, and usually no one had a chance of getting near me on the return to our base.

With the confidence instilled in us by organized Scouting adventures, Colin and I frequently took off on our own hikes with school friends, carrying heavy packs up and down very steep hills and setting up tents by crystal-clear streams. A popular point of entry into the vast Waitakere Ranges trails was along the Karamatura track, which climbed vertically from a beautiful glade of semi-bushland In Huia.

A favourite destination was the gloriously isolated and hard to get to Pararaha Valley. This idyllic spot was nestled at the base of a huge volcanic rock 'dome' with a near-vertical 600 foot descent from the Karamatura track at the top. The Pararaha stream was crystal clear, and spread out to form a perfect lagoon at the base of large ironsand dunes that eventually gave way to steep cliffs and the constant high surf waves of the Tasman Sea.

In later years, Gavin got keen on running with Wesley Harriers, and was Mt Albert Grammar School sprint champion as well as cross-country champion in his senior years. He got me involved with running, to which I took like a *duck to water*. One memorable afternoon in February of 1976, I won an Inter-counties under-18 3000m race at Porritt Stadium in Hamilton, kicking away from the front, while he *came from behind* to beat the New Zealand under-eighteen champion of the time, over 400m, in a slick 50.1s.

Even though our little family were strange creatures to the local Kiwis, we were made to feel very welcome by neighbours generally. Very early on, in around 1965, there was a lovely older couple who lived over the back fence from our block of flats, and Mum, Colin and I were invited over for cups of tea and home-made cakes with Mr and Mrs Service quite often. In the house between our flats and the road, the Knowles family resided, and we were friends with their kids Geoffrey and Susan.

In the identical block of flats next door, we got to know Mr and Mrs Crause, and their daughter Linda, who was an apprentice hairdresser. Mr Crause was a Cockney man with large ears and a large nose, and he used to entertain us by wiggling his ears either individually or together, without involving any facial movements.

Our first landlord in New Zealand, Mr Grattan, was a kind, understated man who was probably very well-off. Mr Grattan lived with his wife and daughter in a beautiful home surrounded by native bush in Green Bay, overlooking the Manukau Harbour; the property has since been turned into a wildlife sanctuary, and was not far from where Mum and Dad eventually bought our first house in New Zealand, in Cliff View Drive in Green Bay. Mr Grattan and his wife had us out for dinner several times at their beautiful home.

The Veseys had a lovely Labrador retriever dog named *Flash*, who we often used to see on his solo walks around the neighbourhood years later, when we had moved to another bigger home nearby.

To hear Grant Vesey talk about *Flash*, he was the *Top Dog Genius* of the retriever dog world, which was undoubtedly true. Grant's room-cave was a fascinating blend of opossum skins in various stages of preparation, fluorescent pop-art posters, surf gear, hiking boots, pin-up girl posters, air rifles, Bowie knives, back-packs, and his prolific drawings.

Grant was quick on the uptake, and a man of action, even at only ten or eleven years of age. One day, when he found me bailed up a by a much bigger neighbourhood bully in front of a hedge, he broke a twig off and jabbed it hard into my assailant's rib-cage, saying "Leave him alone, Addison! He's much smaller than you! Get the point?"

Almost **Catholic**

Around the age of eight, soon after my father had arrived in New Zealand, Colin and I managed to miss out on our First Holy Communion ceremony at Christ the King Catholic Church in Owairaka. I think it was on a Saturday, which was inconvenient for a start.

We were there for all the preceding rigmarole, and had been doing complicated preparations for weeks, but when Irish priest Father Quinn gave the kids a short break, we thought the whole thing was over, so took off on our next mission, which was to climb the steep scoria cliff on the old quarry site up La Veta Avenue, nearly a mile away.

Dad went to his car to retrieve his binoculars, which he always had with him in case he saw something interesting to photograph. What he saw when he sighted his binoculars on the Mt Albert hillside to the north were two small missing figures in bright white shirts struggling manfully up the quarry face through thick fennel.

I was pulling Colin up by twine rope tied tightly around his wrist, and I used my deceased grandmother's antique silver mascara knife as a climber's pickaxe in miniature. My climber's pack was the BOAC *Junior Jet Club* bag from our big trip. As far as I was concerned, I was conquering Mt Everest, just like in the Edmund Hillary documentary we'd been enthralled by on TV.

At the very end of the climb, I remember becoming aware that Dad was there waiting for us. He wasn't angry. He pointed to the church on the opposite hill to the south, where the ceremony was still continuing, and more or less swore us to secrecy with his usual "Not a word to Bessy" comment when referring to Mum's potential wrath.

Somehow, Dad got us into the tail end of the ceremony, and we were presented with our medallions just like all the other kids who had actually sat through the whole thing. We even had smiling photos taken in the back yard with our First Holy Communion badges afterwards.

I well-remember being dosed up with a spoon of fish-oil each afternoon after school, which *Aunty Rose* dispensed by saying "You want to grow up big and strong like Peter Snell, don't you, noo, Keet?" The bottle had a worrying image of a young, bronzed guy on it, surrounded by healthy children with glowing rosy cheeks.

Peter Snell had at that stage just retired from a glorious international athletics career, and had assumed a mythical status in my mind, resembling an amorphous blend of the Fish-Oil Adonis and Superman. After all, Rose said he was the "fastest man in the world- like Superman". You can imagine what images were conjured up by that sort of benevolent coercion. Peter Snell lived over the hill, and was coached by Arthur Lydiard, the *world's greatest running coach*, who lived less than 400 metres away as the crow flies, in Wainwright Avenue, in a state house, with his wife and 4 children, although we knew nothing of him at that age.

Arthur Lydiard's home-spun endurance training philosophy turned talented neighbourhood kids, mostly from the same state housing background, into absolute world-beaters and record-breakers. He was the father of the jogging boom too, founding the first jogging club in the world: *Auckland Joggers*. He and his philosophy would feature far more prominently in my life in later years as I aimed for an international running career.

We moved after a couple of years to another house about 600 metres away, and yet again we were blessed with a very pleasant landlord, who was extremely fit for his age. Frank Slevin was a widower and a veteran of the awful Somme campaign in World War One. He couldn't abide the sound of fireworks as it stirred up horrible memories, so we didn't celebrate Guy Fawkes Day in that home.

He lived with his sister in a stylish two-storey home he built across the rear of the block. Formerly a headmaster at Auckland's Kowhai Intermediate School, he had strong memories of teaching a child maths prodigy named Robert Muldoon, later to become New Zealand's prime minister.

Colin and I settled well into Owairaka Primary School, and I have no particular memory of thinking I was *clever* at anything except for drawing, or having much of an ego until I was about ten years old. I enjoyed what I enjoyed, and did what I did, especially going to the Pt Chevalier Public Library with Mum and Dad on Thursday nights and coming back loaded with beautiful books on great Renaissance artists, or books on archaeology, but something in my neurology must have exploded into action around that time without me being particularly aware. Colin was much the same.

Money was very scarce for several years, however we had a very happy childhood, and what money couldn't buy was made up for by Dad's resourceful *recycling* of salvaged materials into toys for us. On one birthday he presented us with two pedal cars he had salvaged from the tip, and converted into World War One aeroplanes, complete with noisy mounted Lincoln International plastic machine guns. Colin had a three-winged red Fokker triplane based on the Red Baron's plane (Baron von Richtofen), and I had an RAF Sopwith Camel to pedal around in.

Unfortunately, the wings couldn't take the use we gave these pedal-planes for very long, but we had a lot of jealous boys at school whose fathers had 'only' bought them expensive regular toys. Dad must have fabricated these toys in the pokey open-air carport, and somehow kept them from our sight until the birthday. Our first shared two-wheel bicycle was an ingenious miniature *Penny Farthing* affair which married the front end of an old tricycle to a rear wheel from a motor mower, using *Handy Angle* steel bracketing. We then had a *real* second-hand red quarter-size bicycle which we shared. It's hard to align the waste of materials I see in my own children's lives with my upbringing.

I have no idea why we were so short of cash, but I do know that female teachers in those days were on a vastly reduced scale of pay compared to men. This prompted Mum to bother the Minister of Education quite a bit, and eventually *equal pay* was instated. In those days, women who married automatically relinquished any long-service pay or superannuation, in the civil service in Kenya and in New Zealand and presumably in the UK too. Whereas my Uncle Tony Stanley got a very handy *golden handshake* from the Kenyan civil service when he emigrated to South Africa, Mum got nothing, because she was a married woman.

In my final year of primary school, in Standard Four, Colin and I had an excellent teacher named Alan Lawn, who was probably the most encouraging, sensitive, and to-the-point teacher of my whole school life. I had a bad habit of speaking over the top of Colin in class, which Mr. Lawn bailed me out for in front of the whole class. That was a lesson which I never forgot.

One day, at the end of term, Mr. Lawn placed my term report on my desk, open, and asked me what I thought about it. There were a lot of 1As, and *first in class* comments, and *excellents*, but my attention was drawn straight to a mark of *only* 2A for hand-writing: 2 for attainment, and A for Effort. I said "It's OK", to which Mr Lawn said "OK? It's the best darned report I've handed out in 25 years of teaching!"

I thought differently about myself after that, and had a lovely year as I was so far ahead of the rest of the class in some subjects that I was given things to do outside of the classroom, like being a library monitor, where I read to my heart's content and did all the filing and stamping for borrowed and returned books. I was also placed in the school office, answering phones, and running errands for the principal, Ron Erwin. That probably saved the school budget quite a bit on staff costs.

Around that time, I had also entered an art competition for *Father's Day* with the now-defunct Auckland Star newspaper. Colin didn't enter for some reason. I was extremely upset when my oil pastel portrait of Dad wasn't reproduced in The Auckland Star's lift-out of entries. Clearly, the pictures which were reproduced from my age section were nowhere near as good as what I had done, I thought. I was almost inconsolable at the *injustice* of being overlooked. The lift-out, in fact, featured just a cross-section of pictures drawn at random from all the entries, but that wasn't communicated well at all.

However, we were contacted by the Auckland Star on a Wednesday, saying I *had* won my age-group, and the prize-giving was in the central city department store, *John Courts*, on the following night. I won ten dollars for myself, and a *Whitmont Permanent Press business shirt* for Dad, which was still in circulation when Dad eventually retired in about 1980. Ten dollars went a very long way in 1969; I bought a chemistry set for myself and several genuine lead soldiers for Colin. There was a small article with a photo in the Auckland star on the Friday evening.

By the following Monday at school, after a full weekend spent mostly on the *mountain* looking for ancient shells or artefacts, and playing with friends, that art competition result was ancient history. I remember Mr. Lawn asking me "Did you do anything special late last week, Keith?", to which I said "No! Mostly exploring on the mountain"; his look of surprise as he had to prise the art competition result out of me was priceless. I had genuinely forgotten about it. To me, then, it was not a big deal; I was drawing all the time, and would have been more surprised if someone else out there did better.

When I was about ten I started to develop nasty attacks of colic where I was completely unable to move, especially after vigorous exercise, and had to recover for hours each time in a foetal position.

Adult doses of the morphia drugs codeine and pethidine made absolutely no difference to the horrible pain in my gut. I was very surprised to learn in later years that these are regarded as very powerful analgaesics, amongst the most addictive of the prescription morphia drugs known. They didn't even *touch the sides* as far as I was concerned at the time. I know why horses with colic get shot.

This problem was caused by adhesions of scar tissue from the initial surgery 8 years earlier, causing the intestines to gradually adhere to the abdominal wall and peritoneum; these adhesions were removed by surgery when I was eleven years old. The surgery was successful, and I never suffered from colic attacks again.

I made up my mind when I was hospitalized to get as strong, fit and healthy as I could, and *never* go back to hospital again. I never did, for another thirty-seven years. However, my childhood was still plagued by frequent sore throats and respiratory infections, which were treated with antibiotics prescribed by a medical doctor who always had a full ashtray on his desk! I never enquired what brand our doctor smoked, but I'm sure it was the one that doctors recommended at that time.

If I wanted to take a day off school, I could rely on citing a sore throat and *temperature*; I'd put the thermometer tip into a cup of tea to get it up to an impressive figure, and that was often sufficient. Mum usually had full-time work teaching during the day, and Dad was at work in the city, so I was my own master. During the day, I'd cycle down to the Dominion Road shops, which had trinket stores and curio shops, where I'd barter small canvas board oil paintings and portraits for a few dollars, before cycling home. Once, when I was cycling to school, I kept on going to Dominion Road, and handed in a fake absence letter from *Mum*, the next day.

Mount Albert was a suburb in which there was a definite divide between the *haves* and the *have nots*. There were grand Victorian mansions and stately homes near the top of Mount Albert, but a kilometer or so away there was the sprawl of *state housing* that had been created to house lower-income households after World War Two.

The post-war state housing in Mount Albert has always looked drab, and what is left of it (a great deal, unfortunately!) has the innate ability to stay looking the same year after year, just for my visits. It's like driving through a crazy time-warp for me when I visit old haunts. In one area, a huge steel shed roof, covering acres of motorway construction works, has been plonked straight over former paddocks, immediately behind state housing which sits there unchanged as always.

Our local shopping centre in Stoddard Road, which was the model of typical suburban Kiwi life for many years, now looks like it's located in the third world, with all the familiar shop names gone and replaced by Asian or Islamic names. Some shop fronts are boarded up, and others have cage-fronts pulled down after-hours. Across the road, the state houses still look the same as they ever did!! The state houses which used to house the *white trash* gangs and their dysfunctional families are now occupied by more peaceable immigrants from all over the world. There's even a mosque!

Beyond the suburban banality and twenty-first century *progress* lurks ancient Maori legend and mystery. Owairaka is the traditional Maori name of Mount Albert, and means *place of Wairaka*. *Wairaka* was a very great Maori queen and tribal leader. There is still obvious evidence of the hill fortification that crowned the summit of the small dormant volcano; one of many Maori forts in the Auckland region to have crowned hilltops with their strategic outlooks.

If you know where to look, there's still a big horseshoe-shaped pond that sits in a sheep paddock hidden from view near a main road, where *Queen Wairaka* bathed several hundred years ago, and there are underground lava caves that were used as escape routes for women and children between several of the volcanic hills, during the raids that apparently were common amongst rival tribes centuries ago.

The Maori hill forts closely resemble what's left of Iron-Age British hill-forts, which were also similarly palisaded with vertical sharpened timber posts. When I was a young teenager, I'd often dig around near the summit, surfacing quite a few large semi-fossilised marine snail-shells from what I presumed was the original seabed of the isthmus. My science teacher thought I must have been digging into Maori middens. I'll have to find out one day.

CHAPTER 13

The Great Kiwi Outdoors

We spent an enormous amount of time exploring the bushlands surrounding regional Auckland as teenagers and young adults. My fondest memories of New Zealand all involve being outside in the bush or in the surf, or in the mountains of the volcanic plateau in the central North Island region and, later, the foothills of the Southern Alps. As an elite endurance runner in later years, I was always outside, running over big hills in the bush or countryside whenever possible.

When we were eleven years old, Colin and I were both given brand-new three-quarter-size Raleigh bicycles, which my parents bought by hire purchase from the old *Vague's Cycles* store in the Stoddard Road shops. My bike was blue, and Colin's was red. Within a month or two, Colin had bought a carrier rack at Vague's Cycles, and he tastefully covered the supporting uprights with fluffy woolskin, and painted the rest of the carrier rack *metal-flake red*.

We had *direct-drive* flexible cable speedometers with bright red dials that went as high as 50 miles per hour, and the only place where our tiny bodies could get those un-geared bicycles up over 30 miles an hour was on the many long downhills around Auckland. Those bikes got used regularly, and when we attended Wesley Intermediate School for the pre-secondary part of our state education, they provided our transport to and from school.

Because the brakes were controlled by reversing the pedals, it was possible to ride the whole two–mile journey to school without touching the handlebars. That included quite a bit of hopping up onto footpaths and off again onto the road.

On one occasion, we teamed up with a couple of other boys from school to see if we could get out as far as Huia, near the Manukau Heads, and then get back, a very hilly round trip of about 50 kilometres or thirty miles. Colin decided to see how fast he could go on a big downhill section that went past the Nihotupu dam, and I think he reached a gravity-aided top speed of over the magical 30 miles per hour before his chain came loose and he did a massive slide into some gravel, taking quite a bit of bark off. We reattached the chain and kept on our mission, eventually making it to the general store in Huia, famous for its massive whale rib out the front.

After a few bottles of *Lemon and Paeroa* soft drink we turned back for home. Up a long uphill slog on the ungeared bicycles, approaching the hilltop community of Titirangi, one of our companions, a reddish-haired boy called Pierre, insisted on knocking on the front door of a charming little white house with a beautiful garden and a white picket fence.

The door was presently answered by a lady we all knew as *Alma Johnson*, who was a TV presenter for Broadcasting New Zealand at the time. She was a manicured, very gracious host to several sweaty, dirty little boys, after Pierre asked her "Aren't you Alma Johnson?" as he stood in the doorway. She was *TV royalty* in Auckland, and way above our league we thought, but she said "Yes! I am! Would you like to come in? I can make you some cordial or a cup of tea if you'd like, or give you some fruitcake..."

We were ushered into an exquisite lounge with mahogany antique furniture, while our congenial hostess wanted to hear all about our road trip. She cleaned up Colin's wounds with Dettol and Elastoplast, and once suitably refreshed we took our leave to commence the mostly downhill trip back home, where Dad had been in his model railway room all day and hadn't noticed our absence, and Mum had been marking school exam-papers, so was not concerned much either.

In 1972, we commenced secondary school at Sacred Heart College, Auckland's preeminent Catholic Boys School. In my first week I got into a tussle with a senior student of about 17 or 18, who was trying to push his way into a bus-line ahead of all of the younger kids who'd been lined up for minutes. One thing led to another, and after he had slammed me into the side of the bus and removed my glasses and spat on them, before standing on them ; I hit him as hard as I could; flattening his nose across his right cheek. There was blood all over his face. I then proceeded to give him more again, until several senior students managed to pull me off.

The next day the headmaster, Brother Julian, asked for the *third former who'd been involved in a fight at the bus stop* to see him in his office. He nearly guffawed out loud when I presented, at about 68 pounds and 4 feet 10 inches, clearly expecting someone much larger than me; apparently my assailant told quite a tale to his own parents to explain it all, and they complained to the headmaster about me. I didn't get picked on after that.

In my mid-teens I became a boarder at Sacred Heart College, so that I could study properly. I discovered a talent for running, and would train by myself on *long* runs along the waterfront, or to the top of Mount Wellington, an extinct volcano that had been a Maori hill fort a few centuries ago. Occasionally I tried running in bare feet along the waterfront on the light scoria paths, to *toughen* my feet. I'd go as long as 9 miles on roads after school in my sixth-form year, when I was 16, and on *free Sundays* I'd often run from school to home in the morning, then run back again at night, which comprised two runs of about 9 miles (or 14.4 kilometres) each way.

I won quite a few cross-country and track races at school, continuing on to win several titles on road, track and cross-country as a senior athlete a few years later. In my first official Auckland Championships, I won the Under-18 3000m title in bare feet in 8:54.6, winning by over 11 seconds. Although probably more gifted academically than physically, the successes I had at school exceeded my loftiest ambitions, so I was described in the School magazine as *Athletics First, School second!*

I also managed to swim 50 metres underwater in the School Swimming Championships, completing one and a half laps of the $33^{1/3}$ yard pool when I was 15, earning the title *Frogman* for a while at boarding school. I believe that this would still be a school record, over 44 years later, as I won the title one more time before the event was deemed too dangerous to be repeated.

Our forays deep into the bush continued unabated for several years, and long weekends or holidays nearly always included long hikes of several days with friends. We were very independent, catching buses to the start of our hiking destinations, and catching a bus back if necessary. Sometimes, when we lived in a suburb called Waterview that backed onto coastal estuary and mangroves, we'd explore the upper reaches of the Waitemata Harbour in the painted canvas kayak Dad had made for us.

When I left school I was extremely fortunate to earn a cadetship with Radio New Zealand in Auckland, where I was exposed to all the different occupations and departments that are necessary to keep a radio station humming along. I stayed with Radio New Zealand for five years, working as a production copywriter creating commercials in Auckland, Christchurch, and Wellington.

My first day at Radio New Zealand had to be delayed by a fortnight as I'd acquired dysentery from a bowel parasite infection named giardiasis while camping and tramping in remote parts of New Zealand's gorgeous Bay of Islands in the far north. Colin and I, and our great friend Peter Matthews often took off on long weekend hikes in various parts of the northern region of the North Island; we'd unknowingly eaten shellfish that were taken from a large, sheltered bay near a Maori settlement, where safe effluent disposal was definitely not a high priority. Only I took sick; Peter and Colin must've had cast-iron intestines.

On this trip we experienced everything that nature had to offer. The weather that was on offer was the tail of a tropical cyclone that hit suddenly, following on from a glorious spell of summer weather. About a 30–minute walk away from the Maori settlement, we encountered the early rumblings of a wild storm that later completely washed away a 100 metre stretch of sandstone cliff that jutted above a beautiful little inlet. With the storm brewing, we chose to weather it out by sheltering in a solid little shed by the nearby road. It was a very violent storm that only abated in the early hours around sunrise the next day. When we looked back over the paddocks we saw that the top of the cliff had disappeared. All that was left after the overnight storm was the fence, hanging in space, with just a couple of larger uprights missing, but all its spacer bars intact.

Peter whooped with delight when we saw the washed away cliff face, noticing several distinct layers of sediment that were now exposed to the elements. He said "We might be able to find something interesting here", then he whooped again soon after as he prised a greenstone jade *tiki,* (a valuable carved Maori amulet or *charm*) from a promising dark layer of earth which must've been an ancient midden.

Peter's father was Professor Richard Matthews, New Zealand's first scientist of Maori ancestry to be accepted into the Royal Society, for his work in cell biology. As per his Maori ancestry, Peter was big and raw-boned, with Maori skin tones but blondish hair. He almost always got around in bare feet. As per his father's influence, at just 17 years of age he had a major grasp of indigenous culture and anthropology already.

These days, Peter is a well-respected Professor of Ethnology at Osaka's National Museum of Ethnology. Ethnology is a form of anthropology that tracks foodstuff origins and diversification across migration routes of ancient peoples. He has specialized in tracing the spread of food staples like taro (a yam plant), across the Indo-Pacific, and is married to a Japanese lady, with a young son.

The solid little shed turned out to belong to a very helpful local *Pakeha* man (European ancestry) who was a *charcoal-burner*; he had a license that allowed him to cut down light scrub timber or *tea-tree* in kilometer-long swathes through the thick, hilly bushland. These long swathes were several metres wide, and he converted the cut timber to charcoal by a series of controlled burns in special steel ovens recycled from 44-gallon drums he'd installed in *our* shed, complete with chimney pipes. He told us that the local mountain was known for having the biggest population of wild Kiwis in New Zealand, and that at night you'd hear them running around and chirping loudly from metres down the track. Judging by how isolated this region was, even though in reality it was only 190 kilometres due north of central Auckland, it could well have been totally true, because the region was very hard to get into without hiking in or driving a Land Rover in. It seemed a century removed in time, and there was nothing on that long five-day hike that harked at early 1977 at all. It could as easily have been 1877.

When we left the coal-burner's shed early in the morning and made moves to march all the way back to the Matthews's holiday house near the historic township of Russell, I fell very ill, vomiting violently and dropping into a semi-conscious stupor while Peter and Colin decided to keep on going to see if they could rouse Peter's family to drive back along the dirt track to pick me up and get me to a doctor. I chose to rest up by a beautiful little stream in a fern glade, and at one stage in the early afternoon I could hear Maori children giggling as they swam naked in the creek, speaking in Maori. A few of them came up to inspect me while on the back of their little black pony, but I was so tired I probably made no sense to them, and they soon lost interest and rode back to their community, leaving me in my sleeping bag to drift off to sleep.

I was woken in the late afternoon by the Matthews clan, who'd all piled into the car to come and retrieve me. Once I had returned to Auckland, I saw my medical doctor, who arranged lab tests to identify the agent of infection, which was an impressively named one-celled organism; *Giardia intestinalis*; that was able to rapidly colonize the large intestine, utilizing whatever foods were there for its own purposes.

The *giardia* parasite was knocked off with a specific enteric drug I had to take for a week or two, but it took about 6 months for my muscle mass to come up to its usual level again, so my running went into a gentle build-up stage for several months.

The dysentery and inactivity depleted whatever lean muscle mass I had and I lost a stone (about 6 kilograms) from an already lean runner's frame.

CHAPTER 14

Radio New Zealand

Radio New Zealand was a great place to work for someone like me, needing intellectual stimulation while still undecided on and unable to self-fund any university course, while I concentrated on athletics in the interim. From memory, the years 1976-1977 were not good years for young people seeking employment, and I managed as a school leaver at 18 to grab the only cadetship going in Auckland, from about 600 applicants. Les McCathie, the General Manager of Radio New Zealand in Auckland at the time, was a very pleasant and astute man who had young guys like me figured out pretty well. He said that I was the only applicant who didn't fancy himself as a potential radio announcer in my application. My high School Certificate and University Entrance marks did not go amiss either. I was more interested in the journalism and production-writing (radio advertising) opportunities.

My journalism experience ended abruptly after a couple of youthful misadventures; one included drinking at lunchtime with a veteran journalist named *Les*, during New Zealand's longest Supreme Court Criminal Trial of the day, the JBL Enquiry. I was guilty of banging loudly on jury-room doors shortly afterwards. *Les* the veteran journalist didn't turn me in, but the Clerk of the Court made it his business to find out who did it, as if his life depended on it, and he was rather successful, hounding every newsroom editor in Auckland until he got names, ages, and descriptions that matched what he'd been told. I remember him threatening to do the same in an extremely high-pitched, purple-faced squeal to the amassed journalists in the Press room, guiltily and anonymously hiding amongst the mass of journalists. Our chief editor, Ron, asked if it was me, and when I admitted it he told *Les* that he shouldn't start me off with bad habits in the job, and that was about it.

Another incident included phoning in with a live radio report from a newsroom car, when I was only supposed to be taking the car 600 metres to the Radio New Zealand garage for servicing. Instead, I went for a spin on the Southern Motorway and inadvertently drove above a derailed train incident at Newmarket Railway station. I pulled the radio-car over and phoned the report in over the car's radio transmitter for an initially well-received *live* report.

Another time, I made up a story about a love bird at Auckland Zoo being in love with a lyre bird, and I did this in cahoots with the manager of the Auckland Zoo at the time, who was up for a quick interview. That last stunt was necessary as I got bored with the routine of continually ringing the various emergency services asking about accidents and deaths, so I rang the Auckland Zoo instead with a view to a different sort of story going to air.

The story got heard around the country, and the next thing I knew my name was being proffered as more suitable for radio production writing, which was far better in terms of work-hours for a young athlete. There were no smokers in the production writing team, whereas newsrooms of the day looked like chimneys when their windows were open, and smelt like smoke-filled breweries after-hours.

I was then put to work in the accounts department for a couple of months, until I was practically begging for a transfer to any major city with a vacancy in production writing. I got a job rather quickly, in Christchurch, but because of my previous sins, Mr McCathie made me sweat a while, doing the Radio New Zealand Imprest Account figures, and payments for contracted staff and actors, keeping the Chistchurch production-writing crew waiting a whole month for my arrival.

I was not popular with my accounting colleagues, as I'd apparently acquired an *attitude*, and I was often 5 minutes late in starting, which meant that a black line was ruled through my name. Rarely, if I was ten minutes behind schedule, I'd get a red line ruled through my name as well; this caused the lady responsible for monitoring our public service attendance records in the office to break into tears once, terribly upset at my cavalier attitude. All this preoccupation with time was lost completely on me at that age.

There were all kinds of crazy people working for the Government under the auspices of Government-funded broadcasting, and the amazing thing about the New Zealand public service of the day was that once someone had got past the probationary period of about two years without major incident, they had a job for as long as the NZBC (New Zealand Broadcasting Corporation) existed.

In Wellington, we had a Breakfast Show Host, Lindsay Yeo, who was as mad as a hatter. One morning I arrived at work in the bowels of Broadcasting House where Radio Station 2ZB was sited, to the sounds of a revving two stroke minibike being ridden inside, up and down the corridor outside his studio door in the basement. The whole floor reeked of two stroke fumes for hours afterwards. That was fairly typical. Another morning, Lindsay managed to accost the Labour prime minister of the day, Wallace *Bill* Rowling, as he walked on the lawn directly outside the basement level of the studios. From inside the eye-level peephole windows in the basement floor where the studio was sited, we could look out between plants in the garden bed at people walking past, or see their knees and feet at least.

Lindsay managed to spot *Bill* walking to Parliament, which was right next door to our building. So we had to poke a microphone attached to a very long lead out through the peep-hole window, as *Bill* obligingly bent down into the roses and talked to Lindsay on air, having to rely on the third-hand sound of the studio speakers coming out through the open studio door and corridor, via the peep-hole window behind the garden bed. *Bill* was so obliging that he really didn't seem to notice when we called his name with a squeaky voice from deep within the garden bed. *Bill* was known all around New Zealand for his high pitched *jockey voice*.

In Auckland it was not unusual to have world-famous entertainers roaming in the building, and on one occasion I nearly knocked *Dolly Parton* off her feet when I came charging out of a recording studio's firmly sealed soundproof door by booting it open with my foot, as usual. She was on her July 1979 New Zealand tour, and was taken to the spare studio for an impromptu interview because studio space was short on supply in a busy commercial radio station.

I'd grabbed the same studio to do some post-production work on some commercials, and my main memories of that incident are that she was totally unfazed, and very tiny. I said "Oh... I'm so sorry!" to this *random* small lady in a grey-suited skirt who I'd nearly hit. I remember the top of her bright platinum wig, and her voice coming from below, simply saying something like "*Wahhhh, that's orl raaght*!!". Her escort on that visit was a small effete man with a waistcoat and a silver-tipped cane. He was Darrel Sambell, who was an Australian music impresario, and he looked at me as if I was something he'd just stepped in.

Another person who was rather interesting was William Christopher, the actor famous for playing *Father Mulcahy* in the MASH series. He was in Auckland for a long season with a pantomime, which ran at nights, so he was occupied during the day in an arrangement where he'd spend time in our programming department. I have no idea what the reasons were for his presence in our workplace, but he blended in nonchalantly. I gave him directions so that he could take his wife and young children out to our beautiful west coach beaches and bushland, and he was very appreciative.

In Christchurch, at 3ZB, in the old Gloucester Street building's rabbit warren rooms, I made a cup of tea in our staff canteen for a very pretty and polite English girl who was about my age at that time, (nineteen).

She was left just sitting there by programming staff while they sorted out where they could slot her *impromptu* interview in. I didn't follow music closely, so I made *Kate Bush* a cup of tea, and I only twigged that she was the girl who'd sung *Wuthering Heights* when I got back to my production writing office while she was being interviewed.

Radio New Zealand still exists as the nationwide radio broadcaster, and the glass ceiling I envisaged occurring when I was younger doesn't seem to have taken place. The major assets have all been sold off though, and Radio New Zealand ekes a profit from studios in leased premises all over the country these days. Two absolutely classic art-deco period Broadcasting House buildings have now disappeared completely; the one in Durham Lane West in central

Auckland was sold to a developer who illegally knocked it down, and now there is a five–storey carpark on the site.

Broadcasting House in Auckland had an amazing spiral staircase and full symphony orchestra concert recording studio based exactly based on the original in the BBC's 1930s–era Maida Vale studios in London. All gone due to the corporate greed and mismanagement which defined corporate New Zealand in the 1980's and 1990's. The other Broadcasting House, in Wellington, was knocked down completely and now only a pleasant rolling green lawn with agreeable statuary occupies the site, which sits directly behind the iconic *Beehive* Parliament building.

I still know a few of the sports broadcasters for Radio New Zealand who pop up now and again commentating on rugby and cricket tests between Australia and New Zealand, and I keep up with Karen Lloyd, a former radio journalist who was in the same intake of radio cadets that I was with in 1977. By now I would have been able to have taken an early retirement after 40 years of service, if I'd stayed, but I doubt if I would have had the fulfilment that studying for and completing a hard degree course gave me, and my life is all the more full for my time in Chiropractic and what I have chosen to *give back* to it.

CHAPTER 15

Running Becomes My Life

In my running life, I had ambitions of making it to Olympic level, however when I was only 21 years old I suffered very bad sciatica after wrenching my spine while avoiding an out-of-control car on a wet road while running home from work, in Auckland.

The nerve irritation progressed to the point where I couldn't eat, and I was coughing up blue-green bile. I thought I had some form of liver or pancreatic cancer. Every time I bent my head forwards, I felt a sensation like ants crawling over my rib-cage, and had lancing pain right down to my big toe. I had to walk backwards down stairs.

No one could help me; the New Zealand Olympic team doctor wanted to inject cortisone into my spine, and the team physiotherapists told me that I had a *C-shaped spine,* and to forget about ever approaching the training mileage I was doing till then; this was consistently around 200 kilometres a week of the steady aerobic running vital to reach the highest levels.

This advice went down like a lead balloon, and in desperation I asked my friend Lorraine Moller, one of New Zealand's great female athletes of the time, for advice. Her reply was this: "Just see a chiropractor! Dr Jim Brownlie is excellent!".

I duly visited Dr Brownlie in his offices, and his approach was confident and sensible. The first thing he did after localizing the area of focal irritation with his strong thumb was to take X-Rays of the whole spine. Then he showed me on the X-Ray exactly where the spine was unlevelled the most; even my untrained eyes could see that the 4th lumbar vertebra was rotated and unlevelled, and that the mid-thoracic spine was unlevelled in compensation, as well as a compensatory upper-neck rotation.

Dr Brownlie had told me that it would "take about 14 weeks" to get back to my previous level, with chiropractic care. Suffice to say, I improved rapidly over the next 14 weeks, in which time I moved cities to Wellington, with a new job in Radio New Zealand as an advertising production-writer. I saw Dr Brian Kelly, a chiropractor in Wellington, who used the same technique as Dr Brownlie. I scheduled in a chiropractic visit every Friday night, as part of my training schedule.

"Just Another One in the Sausage Factory"

Dr Jim asked what my occupation was. When I told him I was writing radio commercials, he looked at me intently, saying "Oh…just another one in the sausage factory! Here…have a read of this!". He then handed me a brochure about the newly started Chiropractic degree course in Melbourne, with the intriguing title *In a forest full of trees…*.

CHAPTER 16

Wellington Days

Fourteen weeks after I first saw Dr Brownlie, after securing work in Wellington as a copywriter with Radio New Zealand again, I romped away with the Wellington provincial 10-mile (16.09 km) road running championships by about 21 seconds, with a lead which I'd opened up on the last of four circuits from three other national-level athletes.

I ran 49:33 for a demanding course with a challenging hill-climb on each circuit. A few weeks later I was 4th in the NZ road-running championships, in a time 20 seconds faster again, closing very quickly over the final 800m.

In Wellington, I got to know Lorraine Moller's brother, Gary. Lorraine said she thought we'd have a lot in common, and she was certainly right about that. Gary became one of my life-long friends. Gary was always an athlete looking for an event; he was not quite smooth enough as a runner to make it to the top like his sister, but he had vast reservoirs of endurance, tenacity and patience.

Gary took me on some almost terrifying long *runs* a few times; the most adventurous one involved an ascent and descent of the highest peak overlooking Wellington city, Makara Peak, overlooking the city and harbor on one side and Cook Strait and the South Island's snow-clad peaks on the other side.

Gary in habitual position on the top of a sheer cliff

At the very top of the climb, above steep cliffs that descended up to 400 metres, the wind was so constant and strong I could lean 15 degrees into it with my arms outstretched; then we clambered down the southern cliffs overlooking Cook Strait, right down to the rocky shoreline, past colonies of barking seals. (I clambered down the southern cliffs, while Gary scampered like a buck rabbit.) We then ran back to Gary's place, following the shoreline around the bays. One of his hidden skills was mountaineering, from his days at Otago University.

Me surviving descent of same sheer cliff

Gary first stated carving a niche for himself in run/bike/kayak events. Paul MacDonald, New Zealand's celebrated Olympic kayaker was at secondary school with me, and like Gary he was also an athlete looking for a sport until he discovered surf lifesaving and eventually surf-ski and kayak. I remember Paul finishing third in our school cross-country behind me and my brother, but several years later he'd packed on great slabs of muscle in his upper body and was an Olympic kayak champion. He seemed twice as wide across his shoulders as he was at school.

Gary Moller was ahead of Paul MacDonald right to the closing kayak stages of a multisport race in Wellington years ago, before Paul got him in the very last stretch. That's how hard Gary could push himself. At times, Gary used to amaze me by his ability to go out in the surf in his kayak, flip upside down and *eskimo–roll* his way upright again, using his paddle. He could also do *The Cross* on the rings, in the gym, which takes superb neuromotor recruitment (aka *strength*)

These days, Gary is undefeated in his age group in Australia or New Zealand in his favourite sport of mountain-biking. In the UCI world age group mountain biking championships in 2016, in Italy, a marshalling error at the start cost Gary a front-line start, however he overtook many cyclists from deep within the field to finish a close second in his 60+ age-group to the winner, an Italian of some repute. Next time, the outcome will be different I'd say.

Wellington is one of the world's windiest and hilliest cities, sitting upon Cook Strait, where the winds of the Tasman Sea and the Pacific Ocean meet those coming from far away over the Antarctic waters of the Southern Ocean. Nevertheless, I kept up my 200 kilometres a week for 18 months in Wellington, winning many more races along the way. I never got ill once, or suffered any injury other than a mild arch strain. The upper respiratory tract infections and sore throats of my teenage years never emerged again. This I believe was testimony to the benefits of chiropractic to a healthy immune system and overall body balance, despite arguably *over-training*.

Later that year I was second in the national athletics trials for the Pacific Conference Games, to 1972 Olympic 1500m medallist Rod Dixon, and in the ensuing season I had several breakthrough performances including a win against Japanese opposition over 3000m in an international track meeting in Wellington, as well as a debut 10000m track performance on a very windy afternoon, where I was 4th in the New Zealand rankings with a solo run in 29:41.9, winning by 58s, and lapping all athletes except the second place-getter, Dave Hatfield.

The following winter I embarked on a very ambitious training programme where I amassed well over 200 kms a week, for weeks on end, with my Sunday runs being just over 40 kilometres, over a massively hilly course. Arguably, I was *over-training*, however I never got even a cold or flu, or running niggle, despite Wellington's weather being notorious for its strong southerly gales straight from the Southern Ocean. The consistent factor was my weekly chiropractic check-up, keeping my biomechanics, neurology, and immunity in good shape.

The best race of the winter was a huge win in New Zealand's hilliest cross-country race, the Vosseler Shield, run on the steep slopes of Mount Victoria, which looms above Wellington on one side and the waterway to Cook Strait on the other. (This was later the venue for the World short-course Mountain Running Championships, in 2005). In that race in 1981, I dug very deep, running through nausea and dizziness at halfway, and won by 27 seconds, ahead of Derek Froude, who came second in the National cross-country championships a few months later. I suspect that this one huge effort *turned* my season because I didn't do enough easy training to recover from it. If I had just run easily for a few weeks to fully recover I daresay my winter season may well have included a few national championship medals. Instead, because of the volume of training behind me, even though I didn't realise at the time that I was *tired*, I was able to stay high up in national championships without necessarily winning. That's unfortunately how I learnt about my body's responses to training and racing: hard experience.

I held the course record for 8 years, until the course was changed slightly. Derek, later a New Zealand cross-country champion and double-Olympian at the marathon, eventually got to within one second of my course record, and told me so years later. I said "It's an extremely long second, isn't it?". The second-best race for that winter was a defense of my Wellington 10-mile road title, beating Derek by over 10 seconds after opening up a big lead earlier on, and then cruising in to the finish.

The chiropractic care continued apace, every week, scheduled in as part of my *training*. I also ran some very fast road relay championship legs, reeling in national-level runners from minutes behind, on several occasions.

I was lucky to be sharing a house with Diana Reeve, a dietician, and Vicky Russell, a town planning trainee, and as they enjoyed cooking, and I enjoyed eating, we had an arrangement in the flat where I would do all the dishes each evening when I'd finished my running, and eaten their gourmet meals. The flat was ideally nested very close to several other households of younger people and university students in Central Wellington, and was only an 800 metre walk from my workplace.

CHAPTER 17

University Days

In the interim, I had applied to study chiropractic at Phillip Institute of Technology (PIT), in Bundoora, Melbourne. PIT is now known as RMIT University, Bundoora. This course was the first chiropractic degree course in Australia, and was the first federally-funded Chiropractic course in the world.

In Melbourne, I ran with Glenhuntly Athletics Club, arguably one of the strongest distance running clubs in the world in those years, boasting members such as multiple world record-holder Ron Clarke, and 1983 World marathon champion Rob de Castella. I have fourteen state gold medals in a jar in my shed from state team championships in various winter cross-country and road events, as well as state track running medals over 5000m and 10000m.

The six years from February 1982 to 1988 were taken up with full-time chiropractic study combined with part-time evening jobs, fitting in my athletics training and study where I could. In 1984, I obtained interesting employment as a gym instructor at Broadmeadows Leisure Centre, alternated with being a sessional supervisor for *pre-release* and *attendance centre* prisoners for the Victorian Office of Corrections. That last job involved dealing with some pretty hard-nosed characters, but I got on fine with most, and one major difference between them and me was that their Dads used to steal cars for a living, and my Dad didn't.

With the gym job, I applied on the strength of my chiropractic studies and athletics background, and was accepted for the position of gym instructor/aerobics instructor. I knew nothing about aerobics classes, so Geoff Downey, a fellow-worker who was a Physical Education student at my university, copied off several of his own aerobics tapes, and offered to guide me in the various movements from the back of the room, while all the attendees were watching me at the front, possibly thinking how uncannily alike my session was to Geoff's. He did that for a few weeks until I felt I could do it by myself, doing the *Jane Fonda* with large classes of ladies in lycra and leg-warmers.

With the Corrections Centre job, they were looking for a Social Work student, but somehow I convinced them that I was the man for the job. There were two classifications of attendees: *Pre-Release* and *Attendance Centre*. The *Pre-Release* men I was dealing with had completed significant jail time already, for relatively serious crimes ranging up to manslaughter, while the *Attendance Centre* clients were those with minor records for things like car theft. The *Pre-Release* men were distinctive for pacing up and down when they were talking to each other, much as they must have when they were behind high fences in jail exercise yards.

Initially, I was required to drive a minibus on Tuesdays and Thursdays to the Latrobe University gymnasium and swim centre, a few kilometres up the road. They required an *endorsed* licence for me to drive up to a dozen low-risk clients across town to work out.

I did not have a Victorian driver's licence at that stage. However, I could legally drive a car on my New Zealand licence for a few months, but it was expected that a new resident in the state would sit for a Victorian licence in

due course. An endorsed licence for a bigger transit vehicle was another thing on top of a regular car licence. The only thing that stopped me was my limited student budget and the affordability of driving lessons for light passenger transit vehicles, and as *endorsed* also meant *signed* in the broader understanding of the term, I surmised that my signature on my New Zealand licence also meant that I had an *endorsed licence*. Every few weeks one of the supervisors would ask me if I had presented my licence yet, but I rode it out with vague answers, and after a few months on the job, no-one asked anymore.

I managed to get three of my university friends similar employment at the Attendance Centre, and one of them, the late Johnathon *Jack* Crosbie, amazingly got the nod despite a *record* in earlier years himself. He first came to the attention of the law when he was a seminarian priest at a seminary in Brunswick, and intervened when he saw two policemen beating up an aboriginal. Jack, who was one of the great *characters* I've known, apparently gave the cops such a belting that he was *done* for *assaulting a policeman* on two counts. His superiors in the order wouldn't support him, so Jack left the seminary in disgust.

Working with people on the wrong side of the law was not without its hazards. One night as I was driving the minibus back to the attendance centre, a very long white saloon with darkened windows pulled up alongside at traffic lights in Bell Street, a major thoroughfare. One of the clueless attendance-centre boys behind me started yelling abuse at someone he thought was staring at him from the elongated car. When a sawn-off shotgun barrel emerged from the front passenger window, aimed vaguely in my direction, I took immediate action, turning straight from my lane into a convenient side street and turning all my lights off at the same time. The white saloon couldn't follow, as the lights had turned green and other cars swept it along.

About 100 metres down the side-street, I turned right into one of the numerous old service alleys behind homes in Northcote, and, with the lights off, continued to emerge from alley after alley till we neared the Attendance Centre. Needless to say, all of my passengers were extremely impressed, with a couple saying I was a *natural* as a *getaway man*.

Working with *the crims* was incredibly funny on occasion, and there were several hilarious Saturdays spent supervising *community service* gardening and landscaping projects at schools across the Northern Suburbs. I got on so well with the guys that I might have missed my calling.

At one school in Thornbury, an inner-city area, our task each week was to weed gardens, mow lawns, and create a playground. Motivating the guys to meet the required work rate proved easy once I'd worked out that a lot of them were *rev-heads*: –I set up a reward-system where as long as all our set tasks for the day were done by lunch, we could *race* the ride-on lawnmower in the afternoon. The school playground was handily not able to be seen from the main road, being totally enclosed by large red-brick buildings. Competition got very tight very quickly, with circuit rankings recorded to tenths of a second. As skills improved, the final limit to improvement was power output.

One of the guys decided to remove the standard Briggs and Stratton four-stroke low-compression cylinder-head and *take specifications*. The next Saturday, having sourced an identical item at his own expense, he had shaved it down and created a high-compression replacement which was fitted each Saturday afternoon before time-trials commenced. After racing was done with, the mower had its original cylinder-head put back on, and it was parked innocently in the shed. By the time we'd done our month there, the engine-block had been re-sleeved and re-ported, and had new gaskets. I wonder if anyone noticed.

Getting Past Road Blocks.

Sooner or later, for anyone who doesn't fit the mould, nature will throw up an obstacle or an annoyed person for no other reason than to push you back into *the mould*. This will occur 100% of the time for anyone who feels destined for greater things. The obstacle could take the form of a freakishly random run of minor set-backs, or, in an institutional setting, the obstacle could be a person in some form of authority.

Ironically, even though I loved chiropractic from personal experience, and had more academic ability than most, I found it difficult to get through the Chiropractic course, perhaps because I was too busy with outside activities and *life* generally. Definitely I wasn't studying *hard enough*. Perhaps my sheer zest for life was unsettling? I was made to do an extra year of study on the basis of failing one exam.

Cooperate and Graduate was the saying most heard around the chiropractic course in my undergraduate years, sagely passed on by cowed undergraduate students in senior years to those they felt were *rocking the boat*.

Feeling that I had little chance of being given a fair chance of finishing the course, I applied for a job as a copywriter at an advertising agency in central Melbourne, and made it through to the last two applicants. I rang my mother in Auckland. She was well aware of my travails with the chiropractic course. I told her that I was very close to getting a high-paying job as a copywriter again, to which she responded icily with *"What? I didn't bring you up to be a quitter! You finish that course and ignore those people who say you can't!"*

Suitably chastened, I also was not allowed to leave the course by my house mates, who regarded me as a bit of an older brother at that stage, and they made it very clear that they wanted to see me finish my course.

(This experience of being *not allowed to leave* was what I experienced many years later when I first collapsed with the *little brain* issue. I had many cards and letters from people, some of whom I barely l knew, telling me that they *knew* I was going to make it. All I can say is that one in particular, from a church friend and former client named Tracey Shadbolt, was so strongly insistent that I would survive that I had very little choice except to fully absorb it. I'm sure I've kept her card somewhere.)

So I stayed at Chiropractic College, and decided to have a big year of running and working part-time. Even though I had only failed one exam, by one mark, in biochemistry, a ruling was invoked that I should have submitted a certain green form detailing my illness, straight after the exam. As I was normally never sick, I had no idea about this *ruling*, or the need for a green form, and certainly wasn't advised of it by staff in all the numerous exams I'd had over the prior two years. My biochemistry professor happily said that I could sit a supplementary exam, given my good course-work results, however he was *over-ruled* by the Chiropractic College Board, who'd taken a collectively dim view of my prospects.

It wasn't all bad; I had plenty of time to review areas of anatomy and physiology that I'd already passed comprehensively, and I learnt to love the intricacies of biochemistry, which is a hobby interest for me to this day.

In 1985, as I wound my racing down, and my study load up, I hooked up with Kate, a nursing student with a sunny disposition, a zany sense of humour, and a huge work ethic. We met through the *Pitiful Plodders Running and Social Club*, which, in my enforced repeat-year, I had formed as a vehicle for PIT students to get out to wilderness areas to enjoy healthy outdoor fitness pursuits. Kate's family were based in the lovely little country town of Warragul, south-east of Melbourne.

Holiday times were often spent at the family's holiday house on Lake Glen Maggie, further south-east again, where I learnt to water-ski. I later stayed with the family for several months while I did internship hours with a local chiropractor and running enthusiast, Dr Doug

Emerson. My time with Kate and her family helped me knuckle down to the demands of completing my heavy course-work in a very supportive situation.

When I had my final clinical practical exams, in 1987, I bought a brand new suit and shoes, so that I *looked a million bucks*. I was in the position of having to know everything inside out and back to front, and I certainly did, having made very detailed notes while listening to classical music most nights when I wasn't working.

There was *no way* that I was going to fail. One subject called *Clinical Practicum* was a review of many chiropractic techniques taught during the curriculum, taught by a man who took a very dim view of me. The funny thing was that many in my year were relying on my very detailed notes, and while I was being *failed* in practical tests by my nemesis, the rest of the class who were using my notes had good passes. In the end, to take direct pressure off me, and send a shot across the beams at my perceived oppressors, I resorted to joining the Victorian Tertiary Students Union, known to be able to escalate trouble on behalf of its members rapidly, like many other unions.

My relationship with Kate ended in 1988, a couple of months after my father passed away, probably because I was very affected by my Dad's passing and very self-preoccupied. I was a bit of a pig, really.

We lost contact for many years, until recently, when we caught up again. I'd always hoped that her life had panned out well. In the years since I'd last seen her, she'd steadily moved on with her studies to the point where she earned a PhD in psychology, and became Chair of Organizational Psychology at Deakin University. She is now CEO of a Psychology Institute in Melbourne, happily married, and the mother of two children who appear to have inherited their mother's work ethic.

In 1988, having completed my chiropractic studies, I tutored anatomy for a year to chiropractic and osteopathic students, supervising human dissection sessions and helping with practical exams. Ironically, my former nemesis complained extremely vigorously when it was announced that I was to be the new senior anatomy tutor. Dr Chandraraj, our anatomy professor, informed me with a mischievous grin that he had tried to *block* me from the job. What he thought I would do, I cannot imagine.

CHAPTER 18

Swan Hill Beckons

In 1989 I was offered an opportunity to buy Mid Murray Chiropractic Centre, in sunny Swan Hill, where I had spent a couple of months of field-work after my final clinical exams in 1987, away from Melbourne's moody winter weather.

I attended a small church group in Swan Hill where I was made very welcome, and became firm friends with Pastor Russell Treloar and his wife Sharon. Russell's *day-job* was plumbing, however he was also a fanatical fisherman and duck-hunter as well. His sermons were first-class; prepared with hours of work, week after week.

I was a lonely young bachelor for a year or so in Swan Hill, chasing one *false lead* in particular, until I was directed by Sharon that "there is only one girl you should go after, Keith: I've known her since she was 12! She's just right for you, so don't go chasing after anyone else!"

Sharon was quite right, and one night when I visited the larger 'sister church' to our small church in Swan Hill, in Bendigo, I was introduced to Joanne by several women who I later named *The Pastors' Wives Committee* at a dinner after the main service one Sunday night in May of 1990.

As it turned out, I had already met Joanne a few months earlier, in Swan Hill, just before I was to fly home to New Zealand for Christmas in 1989. We met at a 21st Birthday Celebration for a mutual friend who was from Swan Hill but attending university in Bendigo. We had talked amicably for a few minutes before she was whisked away from my presence by another girl, who mistakenly thought I was someone else with *a reputation*.

As she hadn't made her way back across the hall on the first night to talk again, and as I left early to get a good sleep before flying to New Zealand the next day, I assumed she was not overly interested in talking further, so I went home.

Anyhow, our *official* courting started on 1st June 1990, when we visited the Bendigo Art Gallery together. To cut a long story a bit shorter, we were married in Bendigo a year after our first date, on 1st June 1991. Colin, Tony Alessi, and Gavin Harris were my grooms-men, and my housemate of the time, Wayne Dyer, a talented singer, as well as a very talented athlete, sang at the service.

The next few years in practice were years of much learning and change. We got very involved with the Chiropractors Association of Australia, and with Joanne started publishing the inaugural Victorian CAA state magazine, *Your Voice*, with Joanne doing layout and me being editor. By nature I'm not a *committee man*, however I was asked to help out by a couple of friends on the state Public Education committee who knew I'd had experience in radio advertising, and my involvement grew from there.

Your Voice was printed in Swan Hill for 6 years, and in 1999 I was awarded *Victorian Chiropractor of the Year* by the CAA for *outstanding service to the chiropractic community*. I helped establish a *multi-media* advertising campaign for the Chiropractors Association of Australia nationally, for which I received another *pat on the back award* nationally in the same year.

In July 1994, the first of our five children was born. A foyer full of teddy bears given by delighted practice clients heralded Annabel's arrival. Together, Joanne and I built up Mid Murray Chiropractic Centre to be one of the busiest solo-practitioner chiropractic practices in the country, winning a practice management award in 1995. In February 1998, Miranda, our second daughter announced herself a few hours before the starting gun of the Swan Hill Triathlon, which Mid Murray Chiropractic Centre sponsored. We had a new baby at the same time as a few house guests who'd come up to help out with running the triathlon.

In June 2001, Conrad was born after the quickest and easiest delivery of all our children; one hour from *waters breaking* till a child was in our hands. Conrad required emergency lower bowel surgery at one day of age, and possibly had the smallest colostomy bag in Victoria for a month while he was in the Royal Children's Hospital in Melbourne. He needed follow-up care every morning and night from Joanne till he acquired full function a couple of years later. By November 2001 we secured the services of a recently-graduated married American chiropractic couple, who later bought the practice from us. Dr Josh Cutrell and Dr Kimberley Elliott are now naturalized Australians, with two young daughters, and at present they have two associate chiropractors working full-time as well.

Over the years in Swan Hill our practice sponsored several triathlon events, and I took up road cycling to keep fit, riding in several very long group rides for charity a couple of times each year.

In 2002 we purchased Cohuna Chiropractic Centre as a secondary practice, and built that up to a good level over the next five years.

In June–July of 2002 I went on a 31-day round-world-ticketed *bucket-list* trip by myself, taking in a chiropractic seminar in San Diego, a trip down to Tijuana in Mexico, and a good stay with my friend Lorraine Moller and her husband Harlan in Boulder, Colorado, before getting across to Boston to stay with my friend Eric Lammi, and his child-bride Mary. Eric is a former US decathlete who shares my sense of the bizarre, and we get up to no good if left together for too long. Eric and Mary took me around some of Boston's fantastic historic precinct, as well as spending a night at their lake house near Boston.

I then went down to New York for a few days before heading over to Glasgow, where I picked up a hire-car for a sojourn through the highlands, to meet the head of my clan in Argyll. I then caught up with my brother in Wales, and visited Kenya to call on my childhood *ayah* Grace Wambui Kenyatta, who was 100 years old. I also saw what was left of my childhood home, visited my old primary school, and went up to the high country to locate my Mum's childhood town, Kakamega, and find her father's grave. There were 18 flights and umpteen car hires in those 31 days, and I never missed a flight or a scheduled visit. My last night in Africa was spent with my cousin Tim Stanley in Richards Bay, near Durban in South Africa, where he had a role in management of the port.

CHAPTER 19

The Inland Sea Change

In early 2004 we left Swan Hill and purchased *Moira Lakes*, a 14 acre historic property in the Barmah Forest, a 400 metre walk from the Murray River. I could kayak from my property border on the Broken Creek out into the Barmah Lakes in a few minutes. The *plan* was to run a bed and breakfast in the spare cottage, (a restored 1870s wooden cottage), as well as run a part-time chiropractic practice for *locals* in an office off the cottage verandah. The plan was thought out in great detail, but we forgot to tell God. He had other plans it seems. We signed for the property without realizing Joanne was several weeks pregnant, so that put a spanner in the works.

In June 2004, *Henry the Fourth* came along. We had planned a home birth for our fourth child, and for three days we had a midwife on call in our guest cottage, waiting for Henry to get going. Those few days cost over $3000, but we had to have the delivery in the Echuca Hospital, forty kilometres away, as Henry's umbilical cord was twisted in a loop around his neck, preventing the delivery from proceeding naturally. When Henry finally did arrive, the poor little guy looked like he'd been in a street fight, with a swollen purple head and black eyes. He later turned into an adorable little platinum blonde kid with blue eyes and big dimples.

For about 18 months, I played hobby-farmer with the 1956 Massey Ferguson tractor and a ride-on mower, attending mostly to watering the 3 acres of lawn and gardens near the two houses, and pruning the fruit trees. We had a water-right that enabled me to pump water from the Broken Creek, a tributary of the Murray River. The Broken Creek formed the eastern border of the property for 700 metres, before it opened up into the Barmah Lakes.

In 2006, Joanne's parents, Graeme and Junette Phillips, returned to Bendigo after a long stint of service at Yirara College, a Lutheran-run secondary boarding school for aboriginal youth from all over the Northern Territory, sited in Alice Springs.

We decided to move to Bendigo so that the children could grow up with their grandparents very close by. We thought we could lease the property out in the interim. We bought a large old home overlooking a park, in Bendigo. We also decided to start a new practice in Bendigo, and had a goal of making it a centre of excellence in chiropractic. We sourced an old brick house on a street corner, in a main thoroughfare in Bendigo just a short walk from our home. This was to be our *twenty-year* practice, with a view to putting the children through an education at an excellent local grammar school, and eventually running it with associates who we could mentor to a high level.

It was not to be. After many delays with builders and planning permits, we eventually opened our amazing new clinic in September 2006. Right from the start, we had difficulties getting established. Often this is an *energy issue* with practitioners. In my case, I was extremely tired, and getting to bed very early each night didn't help.

CHAPTER 20

The Beast Starts Lurking

When I drove on the long, dark straight stretches of flat road on the plains between my clinic in Cohuna, and Bendigo, I often had premonitions of an *early death* awaiting me. I imagined that it might come about from hitting a wandering farm-beast or large kangaroo in the dark at high speed in my sapphire-blue 1998 Jaguar X300 Sports. I leased this feline monster second-hand for a bargain price after some former high-flying corporate owner had paid all the *brand new* costs. I called this very pleasant saloon *Chester* in honour of my father, who would have approved.

I had already inadvertently cleaned up native wildlife, when a beautiful teal duck flew straight across *Chester's* path while crossing a bridge over an irrigation channel, in bright summer daylight. The duck was flying along the length of the channel, and the collision was a collection of 90 degree angles and velocities that were very high. The last thing that went through the duck's mind was my safety-laminated windscreen. The extraordinary physics of the collision meant that there was not even a blood-soaked feather on my windscreen afterwards, or a crack in the windscreen. I'm pretty sure the teal duck vaporized instantly into the atmosphere, on the resultant vector of the z-axis, because I saw no remnant in my rear-vision mirrors. A remnant may well have reached the stratosphere before re-entry burnt it to a crisp.

Death occasionally taunted me by digging his bony fingers into my left upper trapezius (shoulder to neck) muscle, invisibly pincering the muscle upwards before letting it spring back to its normal tone. This would happen quite spontaneously for no apparent reason. I thought it might relate to a neck problem irritating the pathway to the accessory nerve, and got checked on several occasions chiropractically to chase this up. I definitely felt as if my time was limited, but kept it to myself and pretended it wasn't there. You can imagine anything into existence if you keep at it, so it's not a good idea.

At one stage several weeks before I collapsed, I had a constantly running nose, just like there was a tap of clear water above my nostrils: it took a couple of weeks before it stopped dripping, but there was no infection. This, in fact, was possibly very close to the fact, as expanding tumours within the cranium can increase intracranial pressure to the point of forcing excess cerebrospinal fluid out through the nostrils. This is called *cerebrospinal fluid rhinorrhea.*

Neurologically, the right pre-frontal cortex above the expanding tumour was possibly firing off bizarrely into the motor pathways of the accessory nerve which powers the upper trapezius muscle. The accessory nerve, (also known as the 11th cranial nerve), can sometimes be affected indirectly by neck problems. The neuroscience term for this errant nerve conduction is *dysafferentation,* which is akin to *interference* in a radio signal or *eddy currents* in an electrical circuit.

This sort of *nerve interference* is the sort of common problem that chiropractors deal with many times a day. I was adjusted for several weeks by colleagues with no noticeable change in the spontaneous twitching. Because I had none of the usual *red flags* like double vision, nausea, headaches and vomiting, and was functioning at a very high level, I assumed I just needed a long holiday!

I had no energy to put into the clinic or clients in my brand new practice in Bendigo. The practice started very slowly. On the first day, no-one showed up, despite an advertising campaign beforehand. I might as well have been broadcasting "Go Away! Practitioner Too Tired!" The reason for this lack of energy became apparent in late July of 2007, when I collapsed in my clinic with a massive *tonic clonic seizure,* which by now you'll know all about!

CHAPTER 21

Turning Lemons Into Lemonade

I'll share a story with you about how I've tried to turn every possible negative into a positive. The main thing I've found is if you can still enjoy yourself or laugh, then the cancer entity can't *win*. Fear and worry are the killers.

One week when I was going OK, nearly a year after my first collapse, I was driven up to the little isolated farm property we had at the entry to the Barmah Forest, by the Murray River. I hadn't seen the property in all the time I'd been ill. The *tenant* we somehow acquired when I was *away with the fairies* in Bendigo was a chain-smoking bachelor with one lung who smelt of car gearbox, old dog, stale sweat, fusty beer, nicotine and musty marijuana. He also had no idea about paying rent or doing the basic maintenance we asked of him, in exchange for the modest rental. Watering and mowing were conditions of the rental.

He'd held a week-long *clothing-optional Hippy-Fest* with over 200 *invited guests* on the property, and the locals never informed us because he'd told them all in the pub that he'd bought the property from us. So we'd had the whole *Woodstock* thing going on; the communal mattress in the middle of the paddock, the bongo drums, and the old iron water-tank stand bodily lifted and moved 200m to the edge of the creek for the bongo-drummer to sit on top of. It must've resembled the building of the pyramids.

He'd also arranged thirteen stolen Council wheelie bins (1000 litre rubbish containers on wheels) in a circle around a large gum tree out of sight of the house and the road, and these were all chained to the tree and each other. The wheels had all been removed just in case someone else decided to *steal* them off *him*. The bins were joined at their bases by an ingenious sequence of large PVC pipes and brackets, and filled to varying degrees by sawdust, water, human excrement, and toilet paper. Each bin lid had a hole cut into it for *communal* defecation purposes.

Anyhow, you get the picture. Once I'd seen and heard about what he'd done, I left him a note requesting he vacate immediately, with the promise that if he wasn't gone within two weeks, I'd start moving all of his accumulated junk to the edge of the property to be put into a big dumpster.

When I was dropped off on the appointed day, early in the winter, he and his mutt were nowhere to be seen, and several of his trucks had gone, but all his accumulated scrap iron and junk still filled a formerly empty large shed. Old fridges, freezers, washing machines, beds; copper pipes, galvanized iron, crappy wires; anything that didn't having a hope in hell of resurrection was hoarded in my shed! It was crammed to the edges and overflowing with his treasures.

He'd also let a little paddock right beside the gardens go to seed, and I had no hope of clearing it all up quickly with the tractor and blade because he'd taken my big petrol cannister and left the tractor battery stone cold dead. The same situation applied to my big ride-on mower; dead battery and no petrol. Luckily the kangaroos and the long dry summer had made long grass a non-issue.

I didn't have a car, and the local mechanic was away for that week, so this presented a bit of a problem. I was preparing the property for sale, but it was unpresentable in the state my tenant had left it in.

It so happened that the major weed that had taken over my little paddock was a very nasty one that bore a remarkable physical and physiological resemblance to my then-nemesis, the oligoastrocytoma.

A tangled new growth of Tribulus Terrestris (Caltrop) with its central tubers. The star-shaped green thorns harden quickly. This growth is only a couple of days old.

Tribulus Terrestris is a spiteful weed of uncertain origins that is endemic in parts of the Southern Mediterranean, North Africa, and Asia. Its grotesque multi-spiked seed heads look like the horned face of Satan, and when they mature, they harden and can puncture bicycle tyres, or Nike Air running shoes. The seeds can lie latent in dry sandy soils for years, and can come to life within a day or so of any decent rain. Bizarrely, the central fleshy tap-root or tuber has been used for centuries as a source of male aphrodisiac tonics.

It has gone by many common names in different countries, including cat's head, devil's eyelashes, devil's thorn, devil's weed, goathead, puncturevine, and in Australia: *Caltrop* or *bindii* (pronounced *bindy-eye*).

So I had several problems to solve in my time at the property. Any of these problems could have been solved by paying someone a bit of cash to help out. But at that stage, after months of going without any form of income, all reserves were gone, and cash was in poor supply.

In the interim I decided that I'd use this opportunity of being totally alone for the month to work physically all day long from dawn to sundown, and sleep with the cycles of nature. Joanne arranged to visit once a week and top up my food supplies. I'd had enough of becoming a flabby, soft, middle-aged convalescent.

So I decided to use the lack of tractor as an incentive to exercise hard instead. I've found, nearly always, that the reason *not* to do something is nearly always the same reason to *do* something!

I'd get woken up at dawn by the cacophony of thousands of cockatoos flying overhead, and after preparing a hot cooked breakfast with coffee, I'd get stuck into the work at hand. I prayed a prayer of thanks for the immediate problems all being solved for me, too.

The weeds were the first major obstacle to overcome. The second was the disposal of all the wheelie bins with their human manure. The third major problem was the disposal of all the junk in my shed.

With my garden gloves, a good rake, and a sharp spade as my major tools, I set about digging out every single clump of *caltrop* I saw. This was easy, because I told myself that with each one I plucked out by the long tuber, I was destroying yet another projection of my tumour. The subconscious mind apparently cannot distinguish between a vividly imagined event and *reality*, so you can see how that whole paddock got cleared up completely within two days.

It is a fact of physiology that one can perform intense exercise without incurring major fatigue as long as the bursts last less than 10 seconds on average. This intense activity, with reasonable recovery intervals, exercises the most powerful muscle fibres we possess, the Type IIB, using an intramuscular fuel called creatine phosphate that keeps replenishing itself when given a suitable recovery. It also produces none of the lactic acid that slightly longer bursts of very intense activity would produce. For this reason it is known as *alactic* exercise.

I'd very vigorously attack the centre of each large weed clump for the alactic exercise burst, then recover with far easier aerobic activity as I raked the large fronds in to the centre of the clump I'd just attacked.

This constant aerobic recovery/ short alactic power burst activity really woke up my whole body, and by the time I'd plucked all the weeds out and placed the *tumour fronds* into thirteen large gatherings I'd made around the paddock, I felt as strong as I ever have in my life. I only stopped for a quick lunch of fruit and toast with marmalade, and a cup of tea. I drank rainwater from a bottle I had with me in the paddock.

Each one of the thirteen wheel-less 1000 litre wheelie bins was at least half-full of wet sawdust and faeces, and weighed several hundred kilograms apiece. Without my tractor, it would be very difficult to get all of them 200 metres away, up the slope of the paddock and across to where I was hoping to empty them in a ring where I could rake them over and make them into a very large compost pile to stack beside the cottage gardens.

So I cut the chains with the large bolt-cutters that my tenant *hadn't* stolen, undid the crude plumbing connections, and allowed the stinking liquid in each bin to seep into the sand where it stood.

While that slow process was happening, I removed myself from the stench and attacked other parts of the garden with a hacksaw. However, the sawdust in the bins was still absolutely sodden, so I set about dragging these massive weights in very short distances with the resistance of the sand to contend with as well.

This was an ideal exercise to build back in some whole-body strength and power. I dragged each wheelie bin to a position beside the *removed tumours*, and emptied the bin beside it.

Then I raked and shovelled the *tumour fronds* into the empty bins at each clump, and dragged these much lighter bins to my planned cremation site.

I'd already dragged hundreds of pruned branches from my long-suffering fruit trees to the cremation site, and I gleefully shovelled all my amassed tumour material onto the funeral pyre. The blaze was magnificent, and I stayed patrolling the embers until darkness came, hosing down the earth on all sides of the fire, and turning the earth over, so that it couldn't spread.

"Keith! Get to bed—*Now!*" said a voice above my head. It had such calm authority that I did exactly that and lay down just as the aura of a large seizure came, hovered threateningly for some minutes over me, and then went. I'd gone all day without taking my anti-seizure medication, and with only my breakfast and light lunch. Whatever entity was attacking me certainly hated what I'd just accomplished, but I knew I was being looked after by a far more powerful force.

The next morning, after a very large breakfast, and feeling very happy, I set about the task of gathering up all the drying compost piles back into the wheelie bins. These I then dragged up to the area I designated my compost heap was going to be, beside the cottage gardens.

I had asked the *dumpster* delivery man to leave two of his biggest dumpsters beside my shed full of my former resident hoarder's junk. The dumpsters were massive steel bins I could walk around in, with about 30 cubic metres of capacity each.

There was a cold thick winter mist creeping up from the creek. The sun was a vague yellow orb I could just make out through the fog. I gazed at my very large shed, and set about heaving and shoving several large ancient electric stoves and refrigerators into one bin, when two men I did not know ranged up from the end of my property and suggested that I'd be far better off ringing up the scrap metal dealer from Rochester, another country town an hour or so away. They told me that all the metal would fetch good money as scrap metal prices at that stage were sky-high. They also said he'd bring his loader with him and do the whole clean-up on-site.

I thanked them warmly, and then they wandered away, but not before they insisted on helping me remove the items I'd just shoved into the big bin. "What good fellows" I thought, then considered how odd it was that two ordinary-looking men I'd never seen before would stroll up on my remote property proffering such good advice, in a winter mist, before most people were out of bed.

I rang the dealer as advised, and he duly came and cleaned out all of the shed of anything with metal in it. He and his work partner had it all done in a couple of hours with his special forklift and various useful tools. He said he'd weigh all the different items back at his depot, and pay me the next week by cheque.

While the men from Rochester were emptying my shed's contents for me, I dragged a long lump of concrete I'd tied to an old thick blanket, up and down the paddock to pick up any stray heads of *caltrop* thorns from the dust. The blanket I then burnt as well.

In the interim, I had the problem of getting rid of thirteen *stolen* council wheelie bins. I'd been told by an officious council employee that as the ratepayer on the property, I was responsible for the *safe disposal* of these bins, not the council. He also helpfully informed me that I was personally liable should the Environmental Protection Agency find that I had allowed a portable septic system to be built without permits on my property, which was located in a *national park area*.

So, I filled all the bins equally with other detritus I found around the property, then neatly stacked them at the base of the two big dumpsters. These I then covered with enough loose junk to disguise the whole lot.

A cheque for over $1300 arrived in the mail at home, and this was enough to pay for the hire of the dumpsters, and give us a much-needed cash injection at the same time.

I'll finish up this particular chapter now as it's getting late in the day and I need to get out on my evening walk. Needless to say I am fit and well, and continue to believe I will be so for a good time yet.

I sincerely hope I've inspired someone out there with strategies for dealing with tough situations. Life is just a series of problem-solving exercises, really. You keep going until you decide you can't solve any more problems: —and then you pray in gratitude for having them solved, from your future stance.

To quote the German philosopher Nietzsche;

He who has a *why* can live with almost any *how*.

CHAPTER 22

Enthusiasm!

Don't ask what the world needs. Ask what makes you come alive, and go do it.
Because what the world needs is people who have come alive.

Howard Thurman

If there's one word that can best describe me, it's *Enthusiast*. According to an online dictionary, the origins of this word are described as follows: from French *enthousiasme*, or via late Latin from Greek *enthousiasmos*, from *enthous* 'possessed by a god, inspired' (based on *theos*: 'god').

So wherever you see an enthusiast, bubbling away while she or he pursues his or her favourite pursuit, you have a little sampling of God's nature. The *Great Enthusiast*. Enthusiasm is contagious; I love being in the presence of enthusiasts; whether it's people who pursue an interest with excellence, or people who are less talented, but enjoy themselves nevertheless; it doesn't matter.

It's the JOY of creating something I most associate with Enthusiasm. In my family, enthusiasm expressed itself in different forms; my father was an absolute enthusiast for model trains and planes, full-scale trains and planes, fast veteran classic sports cars, as well as an enthusiast for film. His war diaries have frequent annotations about the latest movies he had seen.

One of my favourite memories is of the time I was staying with Mum and Dad on a visit home from Australia. I was leaving the house to go for a run, when Dad informed me that he'd be "having a couple of friends around to look at the *layout* (model railway) later". When I returned, I noted a small bicycle parked against the house, alongside a late-model Mercedes Benz.

Sure enough, in Dad's hobby room, there was Dad, and his good friend Merv Smith, Auckland's famous breakfast show radio host of the time, both engaged in enthusiastic conversation about their shared hobby with a twelve year old boy. Perceived differences in age and status evaporated away, as the two older men were 'twelve' again.

My mother was always reading books, or writing letters to friends overseas. I counted 120 Christmas cards on her walls one day, which is about 120 more than I've received for some time now. She loved to know about people's origins and backgrounds, and made friends everywhere, scrupulously filing away their personal stories, which she always found fascinating. Even the week before she passed away, she had a palpable frisson of enthusiasm about the prospect of her impending *trip of a lifetime,* saying to my brother late one night "How exciting! Everyone's here now! It won't be long!"

What she was seeing or experiencing is up for discussion, however even in the last few days of her life (and she was absolutely aware of this fact) she was *forward-focusing* her psychology into her *death* with her words.

Physiologically, there's no measureable difference in heart rate or activation of the *central excitatory state* between states of anxiety or enthusiasm. So I think my mother discovered an important principle for herself which is now starting to be explored by psychology in concert with the science of epigenetics.

By re-framing what could be termed a very anxious time, at the end of her life, as *exciting,* she was taking her psychology from a possible depressive state associated with the depressive sympathetic response of the autonomic nervous system to the calming parasympathetic response associated with elevated mood and expectation.

She could discuss any topic with anyone at any level, but she would never, ever gossip. If someone tried to go there, they were soon forcefully told "I'm sorry, so-and-so, but I won't listen to gossip! I've seen too much harm done over the years!" Mum made it her mission to find what made people *tick*; this ability made even the *dullest* of people seem *remarkable* in her eyes.

My own twin brother, Colin is enthusiastic about his creative pursuits, and martial arts, and ancient history, and is also one of the most talented illustrators in the United Kingdom. I regard him as one of the most multi-talented people I've ever met in my life, being an extremely gifted writer and cartoonist. His work is frequently seen in the DK Books series, and currently he helps with the coaching of an athletics squad in Shrewsbury, as well as being the father of three young adults aged between 18 and 24, with his English wife, Diana.

As an athlete, he had immense natural ability; more than my own I'd say, however his incredibly creative and artistic nature couldn't be corralled enough to go with the tedium of consistent training, day after day after day. Too boring. I do remember, when we were both about 19 years old, him beating me by about 20 seconds in the Howick ten-mile road race on a hot day in Auckland, where he finished only 2 minutes behind the legendary *Ancient Marathoner* Jack Foster, and ran neck and neck with senior athletes with many more years of training under their belts.

Like my brother, I was absolutely enthusiastic about running and creative pursuits. So much so that in my last year at school, rather than star academically as was deemed likely in earlier years, I was described as *Athletics First, School Second* in the school magazine, and won the inaugural *Best Sportsman* cup at the School prize-giving. Rather than consider university, which would've been another financial drain on my parents, I managed to gain a cadetship with Radio New Zealand, which enabled me to train as much as I liked while still holding my head up financially.

Eventually it was nothing for me to run over 125 miles a week (200 kilometres) regularly, winning quite a few races in the process, and several provincial titles over cross-country, track, and road as a young senior-level athlete. I thought I had the ability to get to the Olympics, as I beat several people quite handily, along the way, who eventually did make it to the Olympics.

At 23 years of age I moved to Melbourne, Australia, to study chiropractic. While studying I had to curb my enthusiasm for large training loads somewhat in order to maintain enough ready energy to study effectively. My enthusiasm for racing didn't disappear, though, and on less than half of my previous training load, I was usually high up in races, winning quite a few. A serious Achilles tendon strain forced me out of serious competition by 1988, and in the interim I purchased a chiropractic clinic in Swan Hill, a border town sited in the sunny Murray River region of Northern Victoria.

I married my wife Joanne in 1991, and in the years since we have had five children; all quite different to each other in their interests. My enthusiasm for learning as much as I could about the physiological, psychological, neurological, nutritional and biomechanical aspects of health and exercise increased over the years, even though I no longer trained at a high level.

About twelve years ago, I got it into my head that I would write and self-publish a book on how to properly train for running events further than 800m, based on the training philosophy of the great New Zealand Olympic coach, Arthur Lydiard. I grew up in the same suburb as Arthur Lydiard, and eventually was coached by one of his star pupils, 1960 Olympic marathon bronze medallist Barry Magee.

At first the book was a 20-page summary of basic principles, but as I fleshed it out it grew to become quite a large document, complete with photographs and diagrams. My rough draft of 90 pages, which I shared by email with running friends in North America for the purpose of fact-checking, was forwarded without my knowledge onto Dr Daniel E Martin of the University of Georgia, who had been exercise physiologist to English middle distance great Sebastian Coe for many years.

Dr Martin, then about 68 years old, emailed me to call him, and I rang the laboratory number on Dr Martin's email one Sunday at about 1pm, which would've been about 10:30 p.m. on

Saturday night in Atlanta. I rang to leave a call-back message, however Dr Martin answered the phone himself, despite the late hour. We had an amenable chat for about an hour, and I thought it was remarkable that he was so engrossed in his on-going physiology research that he was still in his laboratory late into the night on a weekend. I'd say Dr Martin was a *total enthusiast*!

He suggested that I forward my document to Meyer and Meyer, Europe's biggest sports book publishers, who had already asked him to write a book, subsequent to his previous best-seller on training for middle distance track events, co-written with Peter Coe, Sebastian Coe's father and coach. David wrote an enthusiastic email to Meyer & Meyer saying that the book was "90% complete, and very good, but not written by me."

He asked me what I intended to do with the book, and I said I intended to self-publish about 3000 copies and sell it online, to which he responded in his raspy voice "No! No! No! Don't do that! It's too good to be self-published! Go for gold! Try for 30,000 copies, or more!"

Eventually it grew to become my first published book, *Healthy Intelligent Training*, which acquired a publisher almost without my needing to do anything. Meyer & Meyer took on my book more or less *as is*, and it is now very popular amongst the distance running fraternity, and in its third edition, with an updated edition due shortly.

The adage that "all a man needs is someone to love, something to live for, and *something to do*" was true for me, and I applied myself with zeal to the ambitious task of writing the best running training book I could, answering the exact questions I wanted answered during my own career. I started writing the book about a year before my sudden first collapse, however it gave me a huge focus while I was recovering. In a way it was *rehab* of sorts, and good for my concentration; especially alphabetically and numerically indexing the whole 276 pages.

Since the book has been published, I have given talks on the principles in Ireland, England, New Zealand, and the USA, as well as in Melbourne and Tasmania. I have invitations to speak in a number of other countries now, but as I have a young family I need to be with, those possible trips will have to be put on *hold* for a few more years yet. It'll all happen when the timing is right. It's nice to be wanted and appreciated, though.

There's too much fascinating stuff to do, and too many interesting people to meet, to contemplate an early departure date. Some of my friends from schooldays are living overseas, and I'd like to catch up with them over the next few years.

I have done so much since my *little issue* first surfaced that I could write another book again. The craziest stunt was a two-month solo locum residency in the only chiropractic practice in the Solomon Islands, in 2014. That only ended when Honiara suffered its worst torrential downpour in recorded history, and a main river split the town in two, after floods had washed away a steel bridge that had been emplaced by the US military in 1942. It didn't help when the *trained staff* who lived within walking distance chose not to show up either, the day after the major flooding.

Put it this way; this *little issue* hasn't stopped me planning more adventures; the more exotic, the better.

CHAPTER 23

Where There Is No Vision The People Perish: (Proverbs 29:18)

One translation of this very ancient adage is "without a vision the people go *astray*". Another similar interpretation is "without a vision the people run *amuck*". Clearly, an insightful vision of a compelling future keeps people *on purpose* with their lives, or the path laid out for them by their Creator.

This proverb, attributed to King Solomon from about 1000BC, is possibly several thousand years older again, drawing on the wisom literature of the Levant, the ancient food bowl and cultural centre of the Middle East. I consider the Book of Proverbs to be a summation of the world's longest-running observational study based on behaviours and outcomes; a prelude to what is now called the science of *psychoneuroimmunology*(PNI): the study of the interaction between psychological processes and the nervous and immune systems of the human body.

My great 'hero' in the psychology of survival is Dr Victor Frankel, who was a leading Austrian psychiatrist and neurologist before he was incarcerated in three consecutive prisoner of war camps, including Auschwitz, during World War Two. Frankel not only survived his incarceration, but flourished in later years, living to the grand old age of ninety-two years.

His seminal work, *Man's Search for Meaning* can be read in one night, and my take-home point from the book was that as soon as a prisoner started to dissociate himself from his fellows, or *give up* on his future, he was often dead within a few days from whichever infection was prevalent in the camp at that time. The prisoner who had given up hope would give away his possessions, stay in his bunk, and not react when camp guards would beat him on his bed. Frankl reasoned that if a prisoner had a reason, or a meaning, to live for, then he could survive all indignities he was put through. Frankl observed that if a prisoner had a life goal to achieve, a religious faith, or close family members he could *live for*, then his chances of survival were much greater.

Problems? Why Not Use Time Travel to 'escape'?

The answer to this was for the person to *go forward in time* to a vantage point where he could accurately describe what was going on to a future perceived audience; this technique of *forward-focus* is essentially the same quality of *vision* referred to in Proverbs 29:18.

When Frankl endured his many beatings by camp guards, he *forward-focused* himself to a lecture theatre many years in his future, where he objectively described the pain and degradation he was suffering to a large group of imaginary psychology students. This technique *protected* his psyche from total immersion in the brutality of the beating.

This self-created *forward-focus technique*, which Frankl had already created in his research work, was honed to absolute perfection in the cauldron of Auschwitz. There's a special division of science devoted to the psychology of survival, and Frankl's *logotherapy* takes pride of place in my opinion.

When we think of things like self-control and vision, one startling tale comes to mind. It's about being *caught between a rock and a hard place*, literally.

You may remember that in 2003, in the USA, an outdoor adventurer got caught in a canyon, and ended up amputating his own arm with a pocket knife before walking many hours to safety. His name is Aaron Ralston, and his biography is called *Between a Rock and a Hard Place*.

However, what I'm about to share with you comes from an interview he did on Australian TV, where he revealed to interviewer Andrew Denton just what it was that got him through his fifth night in a lonely canyon, with his right arm and hand pinned by a massive boulder, and gangrene starting to set in. He was reduced to drinking his own urine, which was now a black tar, and the nights were terrible as below zero temperatures combined with his thirst and hunger.

He'd recorded his goodbyes to the world on his video camera, and had decided he was going to savour his life to the very end, and not kill himself. In other words, Aaron was the ultimate example of *Hanging In There*.

Here's what happened, in his own words...

> "As it worked out, I survived that fifth night. And it came about, I think, through a vision I had - the vision that came to me at about two on Thursday morning. This was now my sixth day since Saturday... I walked through the canyon wall into a hallway that came to a doorway. Looking through this into a wood-floored room, a living room, there was a little boy playing on the floor.

STARING DOWN THE BEAST

"As I entered the room, he became aware of my presence and turned and looked up at me. He smiled and came running over, this little, blond-haired, red-shirted three-year-old, and practically leapt into my arms. And I saw myself bend down and pick him up, using my left hand and my right arm. I looked to make sure that I was picking him up properly - and I saw that I didn't have a hand on my right side.

"And the way that we interacted told me that this was my son. This was a vision of a son that I was going to have some three years down the road. And we danced around this living room and I looked up at him and he smiled. And that vision totally changed my perspective on what was happening at the canyon. It told me that there was a future outside of that canyon, that I was going to get out of there to have a son. And it gave me the strength, I think, to get through that most terrible night."

Wow! The power of a vision. Was he hallucinating? Possibly. But wait till he tells you what happened later, when he used a knife that was only good for buttering bread, to amputate his arm. Although Aaron had managed to cut away the decomposing and living flesh that tethered him to that place in time and space, his bones were still largely intact and holding him under the boulder. Again, he received intuition…

"In those few moments that I thrashed myself around, an epiphany came to me. In my opinion, this was a divine interaction. I heard, as if from an outside voice, but inside my head, the idea that I could use this boulder to break the bones in my arm. And this voice just yelled out repeatedly, "That's It! That's It! Break the bones." And I went about it."

Aaron could've so easily died in that canyon if he'd chosen to be overcome with the *reality* of his situation. But he prayed it through to a power he didn't really know was there…he hung in, and *acted,* and literally removed the thing that was going to hold him back from his destiny…and boy did it hurt! The problem, of course, was nowhere near as big as the reward for *overcoming*: a son, a future, a book contract, and world fame.

CHAPTER 24

Teachable Moments

I get great pleasure from recalling incidents from my childhood where the *iron* in my kind and gentle parents was tested. The funniest was in early 1966, when we still lived in our tiny flat in Owairaka Avenue, and Dad hadn't arrived in New Zealand as yet. There was an extremely-persistent door-to-door vacuum-cleaner salesman who wouldn't take *No!* for an answer. Once Mum had eyeballed him out of the doorway, and started to shut the door, he wedged his foot into the gap. She then opened the door a little more, before slamming it as hard as she could on his ankle, saying "There! Now *Go Away!*". He howled very loudly, and Colin and I giggled as we watched him limp away up the drive, from behind the Venetian blinds in the living area.

Another occasion was probably in 1968, when our tiny blue 1956 Austin A30 car was being rocked and blocked by a large mob of unruly Auckland University students outside the Auckland Town Hall. The very hairy, raucous crowd was in a frenzy, chanting and yelling and waving anti-Vietnam War placards. They had no intention of letting anyone get past.

Valerie Livingstone tugged the driver's door window pane down manually, with its glass tab handle, then, honking her horn and revving t4he accelerator, she poked her head out and yelled *"Baaaaaaaa"*… *"Sheep!"*… *"Get out of the way!"* as she barged the little car through the stunned flock, with the horn honking loudly.

The car's mighty 850cc 4-pot engine, smaller than a lot of modern ride-on mower engines, was taken to maximum revs, but Mum ably graunched the car into 2nd gear with the usual clunk with the non-synchromesh gearbox.

Once well-clear of the throng, she said something that still chimes down through the years; "Wherever you get a crowd like that, you have mass hysteria. And wherever you can get mass hysteria, you can create another Hitler!"

Another hilarious incident comes to mind in recalling my Mum's character. For a number of years, our family rented a lovely little weatherboard home in Mt Albert that was only a block away from an *urban ghetto* of *State Housing*, replete with gangs of *white–trash* youths who had nothing better to do than make trouble.

On one occasion, on a weekend, a local gang was haranguing us from their bicycles as we played within our yard, with a younger kid called Peter, who made the big mistake of jeering at them from our yard, while he still had to negotiate the 200 metres to his own home later on. This led to a stand-off, where about six young teenagers swore and carried on for an hour or so, stating their intentions about what would happen to Peter. The young gangsters, led by their *alpha male, Cooper*, wouldn't enter our yard, as they knew my mother was at home, so they just chose to waste their time yelling abuse from outside.

My mother went out and told them to leave, or she'd ring the police. They laughed at her, so on the spur of the moment, Mum grabbed *Peter* by the hand and declared that she'd walk him home. As soon as she left the property, *Cooper* swooped closely at her with his *Easy-Rider Ape-Hanger bicycle complete with banana-seat*. He suddenly found himself dumped onto the concrete, with Mum standing over him with her hands on her hips, and even his gang-members laughed at him. *Peter* made it home safely, while the gang disbanded, leaving *Cooper* to get over his psychological scar on his own.

One cold winter night when we were twelve, our father took us to see a movie in the city at Auckland's legendary Civic Theatre. Afterwards, it was raining and dark when we got deliberately splashed by a *hoon driver* who drove into a puddle near the crossing lights we were approaching. Dad was furious.

While the hoon driver and his friends laughed amongst themselves, waiting for the lights to go green, former Staff Sergeant Livingstone marched round to the driver's still-open window and grabbed him by his jacket collar. He then pulled him up so hard from his seat that he hit his head on the top of his door. We heard the *thump* from the other side of the car. Dad was using British Army adjectives and verbs we'd never heard him say before. The communal jollity stopped abruptly, but straight afterwards Dad said "Not a word to Bessy!", meaning we weren't to tell our Mum a thing.

So very early on, in those teachable moments, I learnt that *departure from convention* is probably a good thing in the bigger scheme of things. Surprisingly, my thoughts and experiences with *departure from convention*, now closely parallel those of avowed atheist and secular humanist Bertrand Russell, who accurately described the phenomenon this way: "*Conventional people are roused to fury by departure from convention, largely because they regard such departure as a criticism of themselves.*"

Needless to say, *Departure from Convention* could almost be a family motto, as none of us really gave a hoot about public opinion.

It is amusing to note that Bertrand Russell was proof in himself that miracles can and do happen. With an appearance that closely resembled the head and neck of an ostrich, he managed to marry four times!

Many years later, this *departure from convention* became very apparent one day when I was advised that my optimistic long-term outlook was *unrealistic* in the face of my dire prognosis by a medical oncology radiation specialist, with my wife also present.

CHAPTER 25

Don't Worry! Be Happy!

On a beautiful morning in early September, 1988, I found myself at Lihue Airport, on Kauai, the *garden island* of Hawaii, with my great friend Tony Alessi, having made the sensible decision to upgrade our hire car from a VW Golf to the latest Ford Mustang Convertible.

We were enroute to England for my brother's wedding to Diana.

Looming offshore was a long Pacific cloudbank waiting to disperse and reveal the sun.

Having picked up the car, the first thing we did after flipping the automatic roof back was turn on the radio. A song came on that synched perfectly with the Pacific breeze, the emerging sun, and the wafting scent of frangipani.

We'd never heard it before, but pretty soon we were humming Bobby McFerrin's new hit song *Don't Worry, Be Happy*, and as we turned onto the Kapule Highway towards our hotel, our song was rudely interrupted by the blaring horn of a very large truck bearing down on us *head-on*, on *our* side of the road.

After swerving onto the correct *right* hand side of the road, as was apparently the driving custom in the USA, we continued on our way as our hearts re-started and descended back down into our chests.

We both learnt the USA road rules in a few fractions of a second.

That song's lyrics have never been far from my consciousness ever since, having been seared into my permanent memory with a lightning-like jolt of adrenalin and noise.

Like so many one-hit wonders this simple song embodies a scriptural truth, best enunciated by the disciple Matthew when he cites the Master's advice in Matthew 6:25-27;

Do Not Worry

25 Therefore I tell you, *do not worry* about your life, what you will eat or drink; or about your body, what you will wear. Is not life more than food, and the body more than clothes?
26 Look at the birds of the air: They do not sow or reap or gather into barns-and yet your Heavenly Father feeds them. Are you not much more valuable than they?
27 Who of you by worrying can add a single hour to his lifespan?

CHAPTER 26

Why Me? Why not Me?

I've had a thoroughly enjoyable life, so life doesn't owe me a thing. I'm happy. I've done a lot of things, I have a loving family, I've met a lot of interesting people, and I've travelled quite a bit. What more does one need? In my case, quite a bit. I still want the lot! I feel I still have lots of work to finish before I move on. Do I deserve a longer life? I have no idea, and we'll see how that pans out. But for now I'm still here, and have stuff to do. LOTS of stuff. Not for my sake, but for those who come after me. I want to leave my story for future generations of my own family, *and* I want to share some of my hard-won knowledge about outlasting metabolic challenges to the brain, which is what I now consider my little brain tumour issue to be; a lifestyle challenge to the normal metabolism of healthy substrates in the metabolic furnaces that power the brain - the mitochondria.

How does one 'reverse-engineer' one's life, with respect to the particular qualities, life experiences and traits that ensure survival from an insidious *fatal* illness? Well…. that's what this book aims to do, so you'll have to excuse me if I make it *all about me* for the duration. In sharing my story, I'm mindful of the way in which I was brought up, which was that talking about oneself or *blowing one's own trumpet* were not good qualities to have, however the bigger picture is that my story is likely going to be useful to many others, and in order to get it out there, a certain amount of trumpet-blowing is necessary.

> *"When one man, for whatever reason, has the opportunity to lead an extraordinary life, he has no right to keep it to himself."* — Jacques Costeau

I know I'm not the only person to have survived something insidious and terrible; far from it! However, I feel it's my duty to share my story with people who have been or are going to be in a similar position. There have been many survivors of terrible happenings that I greatly admire, and I have read many biographies of these people. In a sense, you really don't know what is in you until it's squeezed out, and I feel that my years of avid reading from an eclectic range of authors who write on such things has helped me enormously to reframe my reality and re-position my thought-life strategically, more or less from the beginning of my health challenge.

In addition, I derive a great deal of *inner strength* or *calm* from my family, including my late parents, and the very many generations of ancestors who shaped family attitudes before them.

Friends are extremely important, and although I live overseas from many of them, they all know who they are in my life, and in one way I live for my friends and friendships, even though I'm reasonably introspective and enjoy my own company.

I have a personal belief that what we say is extremely important in either surviving or being defeated by the inevitable challenges in our lives.

From Victor Frankl to Winston Churchill to Cicero to Marcus Aurelius to Victor Frankel and Sir Edmund Hillary, and virtually every running and sporting legend of the modern era, I have been inspired all my adult life. Never in a *month of Sundays* did I expect or suspect that I would come down with with a 'terminal' brain tumour.

No one seems to know what causes the brain tumour type I have been diagnosed with. One of the *new* concepts in medicine that is not going away is the concept of *chronic inflammation* leading to disease.

I was very reckless physically until well into my 20s, getting into all kinds of scrapes. *Perhaps glioblastoma multiforme*, which is really an overgrowth of the glial cells in the matrix which supports the brain matter, could find an *inflammatory cause* in mild head trauma. If that's the case then a fall onto the back of my head onto concrete, through the upper branches of a lemon tree when I was 21, was a 'smoking gun'.

As one does when one turns 21, I was walking on a narrow steel railing that served as a barrier on a back patio bordering a lemon tree and the back lawn. It was dark. There was a party going on. I'd had a few beers and was trying to walk the length of the patio, but I slipped when stepping over a branch of the lemon tree that was resting on the railing.

When I hit the concrete path nearly 3 metres below my feet on the railing, I literally *saw stars* and deliberately moved my hands and legs straight away, to make sure that my brain was *still* connected to my body. Once I'd sorted myself out, I got myself upstairs to see if I needed further help. People started screaming as torrents of blood seeped out from beneath my long hair and torn scalp. My friend Gavin had just arrived at the party with his new girlfriend (and now–wife of 38 years, the long-suffering Dianne).

Gavin drove me straight to the Emergency clinic at Greenlane Hospital, where I was checked out medically, stitched up, and sent home with no apparent ill-effects. Not even a headache. There's a noticeable scar that is still present to this day, best observed when my hair has grown a few millimetres from its normal closely-shaved state.

The scar is diametrically opposed to the location of the original tumour site and the recent incision scars. This doesn't surprise me, as the many fine bones of the cranial vault are all able to transmit direct and indirect (oblique) forces along the very tough fibrous connective tissue (the dura mater) that holds the cranial vault together. This connective tissue matrix also serves to separate and suspend various compartments and ventricles of the brain.

Ninety percent of all brain cells are 'glia'. Structurally, they create the matrix that suspends the nerve cells in the brain, much like the extruded glass fibres in fiberglass weave fabrics act to support the epoxy or plastic resin that is poured over them. Their purpose does not stop there. The glia coordinate function, facilitate communication between brain and body and monitor and modify input and output.

The glial cells also support the transport of lymphatic fluid into and out of the brain cells; for that reason they have earned the nickname of the *Glymphatic system* from neurology researchers. The *glymphatic system* (or *glymphatic* clearance pathway, or *paravascular system*) is a functional waste clearance pathway for the *vertebrate central nervous system (CNS)*.

The term *glio*blastoma refers directly to the involvement of new or altered *glial* cells in the brain in this tumour, as opposed to the neuronal cells that depend on the glial cells for their nutrition and metabolic needs. Nerve cells do not generally form tumours, but the glial cells that support them certainly do. So a *brain tumour* is often not a tumour of nerve or neuronal tissue, but merely has the capacity to inhibit the function or metabolism of existing neurons in the brain and nervous system that it supports. The inter-relationship of neurons and the glial cells that support their metabolism is so complex that the tissue types cannot be separated biochemically or surgically, in my opinion; this tends to call into question the purpose of the hardline therapies of chemotherapy (entailing whole-body poisoning) and radiation (the localized *burning* of brain cells) that are used in conjunction with surgery (excision) to effect a *cure*.

I think perhaps that the one hard *whack* in October 1979 served to give a jolt to many of the attached glial cells within the local connective tissue framework, the *dural* sheath, including those that eventually came to support my right frontal cortex on the other side of the skull. The mystery is to how I was not immediately affected; this was around the time that I started having chiropractic care so it's possible I was having correction of the underlying *dural* torsion done through the upper neck adjustments I had initially, and as I'd never stopped having reasonably regular chiropractic care since that time, this may go part of the way to explain why things took so long to emerge in the form of a glial cell overgrowth, or tumour. Who is to say I'm wrong?

Other possible causes for me personally are long-term exposure to formaldehyde fumes in human anatomy labs when I was a student and later a tutor in anatomy. Another possible cause could be long-term exposure to various agricultural poisons like Roundup and the other ubiquitous glyphosate weed killers that Monsanto foisted upon the population as being biodegradable after spraying, and *harmless* to humans and livestock. That was in the 1990s. At the end of the day, the entity has appeared and been diagnosed medically, and no one can tell me the cause, and there's no medical expectation of the long-term survival I expect and seek.

No-one is rushing around right now giving bold answers, so as someone who has relentlessly lived with this brain health challenge for over eleven years, with a degree of success unmatched by the current medical approach, I've decided to help people out without having to wait yet another decade for advice on the lifestyle approaches that work. Most of the supportive literature for the approach I advocate comes from established research that was all done well before 2006, and as far as I can see, my all-around lifestyle approach has given me a decade of reasonable health when the original prognosis was only months at most.

The only longer-term medical expectation for glioblastoma multiforme which has been successfully resected or stabilized, is further recurrence, and eventual death. Great! I think we can do a bit better than that, and all you'll have to do is exercise pleasurably, eat delicious fresh food prepared with healthy saturated fats, and bolster your thinking a bit with attitudinal shifts along the way!

The expectations and treatment modalities when I was first given my *terminal* prognosis have not changed one tiny little bit in the interim, despite a mountain of research having been done on a number of different safe nutritional or supplemental options that could improve post-surgical outcomes immediately for patients who suffer any kind of brain trauma (I include brain surgery as *brain trauma*). They should all be on *magnesium* supplementation.

As I said earlier, prior to my latest invasive surgery, I'd gone a decade in good health since my first *terminal* diagnosis. A decade of survival with glioblastoma multiforme placed me at *Population Survival Rate*, which is apparently achieved by a tiny minority of patients under the age of 40, (I am 59 years and ten months old at time of writing).

Population Survival Rate specific to glioblastoma multiforme grade IV simply means that one's chance of surviving the *cancer* are the same as someone of the same age and gender who does not have the condition. So that's where I thought I was a few short months ago, and ready to write a book about it because of that milestone. As I write, I have just returned from the gym, where I had a good strength circuit workout, so I rate myself as being about 95% as far as normal neuromotor function goes.

After having been channeled into the rough currents of the medical oncology system yet again, due to the unforeseen complications of my third and latest surgery, I am not eager to go that way again, especially since I ended up so confused, and so dissociated, from my young family for so many weeks. Since I've been at home again, and eating my beautiful brain-healing foods, every day, and I am able to get outdoors in the fresh air and walk on bush trails again, I've been improving with balance, concentration, memory, and general happiness every day.

CHAPTER 27

Chiropractic: The Vital Difference

In 1903 Thomas Edison was concerned about the healthcare of his time and stated: *"The doctor of the future will give no medicine, but will interest his patient in the care of the human frame, in diet and in the cause and prevention of disease."*

Chiropractors work with the spine and central nervous system, which together have the capacity to influence the whole body. Chiropractic is a health science that was founded in 1895 in the USA by D.D. Palmer, and was developed further by his son, B.J. Palmer.

In its early years, chiropractic was lionized by its advocates and pilloried by the medical authorities, mostly because it was so simple in practice and had undeniable results that orthodox medicine was unable to achieve. Medical doctors were told by their *political arm*, the American Medical Association, not to refer to members of an *unscientific cult*, or their licences would be revoked.

Many of the early chiropractors like *Herbert Reaver* were routinely jailed for *practicing medicine without a licence*, and as recently as November 1990 the American Medical Association, after a fourteen-year process, was found guilty on appeal in the US Supreme Court, along with ten medical organizations as co-defendants, of attempting to eliminate the chiropractic profession. (1)

If imitation is the sincerest form of flattery, then chiropractic is flattered by the open use of its philosophy, terminology, techniques, and world-view by many other professions these days.

To quote the philosopher Arthur Schopenhaeuer: *All truth passes through three stages. First, it is ridiculed. Second, it is violently opposed. Third, it is accepted as being self-evident.*

So what is this truth that chiropractic exemplifies? It's pretty basic really; the brain and nervous system coordinate the whole body. The most direct conduit of information from brain to body and back is the spinal cord, protected by the cranium, the twenty-four spinal vertebrae, and the sacrum, and the coccyx, which are all mobile. As your body is usually a self-healing, self-regulating organism, anything that compromises the normal integrity of the skeletal framework and spine has the capacity to compromise normal nerve function elsewhere in the body. Simple enough?

If these joints become stiff or hypo mobile, this can create a *hyper-excitable central state* in the nervous system, known as *nociceptive noise*. This is akin to background noise in a poorly tuned radio, but in the case of the nervous system, it has the effect of *scrambling* information being received or sent by the brain.

According to what is compromised in each individual case, symptoms are often very predictable, but some may be completely unpredictable, especially if they compromise the autonomic nervous system that regulates our organic function, hormonal systems, and our neurochemistry.

A chiropractic analysis system developed in Australia by Dr Wayne Todd, called the SD Protocol, (*Sympathetic Dominance* Protocol) cleverly ties together basic postural findings and under-functioning regions of the central nervous system and brainstem with hormonal and metabolic dysfunction, and has methodologies to correct them.

It is thought that gentle and subtle correction of such mechanical derangements by chiropractic adjustments can reverse the *hyper-excitable central state* and explain a myriad of symptoms that will not respond to any other therapy.

These days, a great deal of exciting chiropractic research is being carried out in universities around the world.

In October 2002, a paper presented on a long-term asthma study by researchers at Sydney's MacQuarie University indicated steady reduction in blood levels of the stress hormone cortisol accompanied by an increase in salivary levels of the immune complex IgA following chiropractic care [2],

This effect on the hormonal system is thought to be a reason why asthmatics seem to have fewer attacks when under chiropractic care, even though no major differences in breathing power or *forced expiratory volume* (FEV) were noted following chiropractic care.

Another very interesting study published in May 2005 indicates that there is a link between the number of dysfunctional regions (subluxations) ascertained in the spine and reaction time. The more regions of dysfunction, the slower the reaction time.[3]

One study published in May 2006 indicates improvement in cursor movement time of 9.2% for a chiropractic group following chiropractic care, compared with 1.7% for a control group [4]. This has implications for motor control.

For me, regular chiropractic care has been enormously important in keeping my spine, and cranium, and the central nervous system they protect, in good shape. There has been a lot of fascinating neuroscience research coming out of New Zealand in the last few years that demonstrates that chiropractic *adjustment* (specific manipulation) of spinal vertebral joints has a positive effect on stimulating the frontal cortex of the brain, as well as providing demonstrable benefits with improved coordination and neuromotor skills[5].

Chiropractic seems to assist the brain and the body to communicate more coherently, for want of a better expression [6].

One study showed that chiropractic care can *make you stronger* [7]. The amazing thing was that the changes seen within the central nervous system seen in this study were very similar to what has previously been shown after three weeks of strength training, demonstrating powerful changes in the brain and spinal cord.

Six studies show that chiropractic care improves spinal function. One of the mainstays of our 123-year old chiropractic profession is a specific method of analysis and care known as S.O.T., or sacro-occipital technique. This technique looks at the parameters that associate the movement of the sacrum (large tailbone) with the occiput (the cranial bone that comprises the base of the skull that also attaches to the top of the neck). The association of cranio–sacral motion with proper neurological function has been studied intensively since 1924, primarily by Dr *Major* (yes, *Major* was his Christian name!) Bertrand de Jarnette, an early chiropractor with an engineering background who continually refined his methodologies and research with his team for over 60 years.

In a nutshell, de Jarnette postulated a very close relationship of coupled cranio–sacral motion with the unimpeded flow of cerebro-spinal fluid along the length of the spinal column, within the confines of the dural sheath that protects the brain and all of the spinal cord down to the level of the first lumbar spinal nerve root, from where the sheath spreads thinly over the remaining lumbar nerves, and also attaches strongly to the coccyx in a thin but incredibly strong ligament called the filum terminale.

From this conceptual platform, you can see how disruptions of normal spinal, cranial, sacral or coccygeal motion can negatively affect brain and central nervous system function and internal ventricular and vascular fluid pressure dynamics. Form affects function, with direct and indirect effects on the complete organism.

The unimpeded motion of CSF is imperative for the nutritional and metabolic support of all the neuronal and glial cells that it bathes. With each breath, there is a corresponding flexion–extension motion of the sacrum and the occipital bone, that exactly corresponds with the desired *pumping* action of the cerebrospinal fluid along its intended course.

References:

1   *Wilk v. American Medical Association*, 895 F.2d 352 (7th Cir. 1990), was a federal antitrust suit brought against the American Medical Association (AMA) and 10 co-defendants by chiropractor Chester A. Wilk, DC, and four co-plaintiffs. It resulted in a ruling against the AMA.

2   Effect of Chiropractic Treatments on the Endocrine and Immune System in Asthmatic Patients. *Proceedings of the 2002 International Conference on Spinal Manipulation*, Toronto Ontario, Canada, Oct 2002: 57-8

3   The Effect of Chiropractic Adjustments on Movement Time: A Pilot Study Using Fitts Law. Journal of Manipulative and Physiological Therapeutics, Volume 29, Issue 4, Pages 257-266 D. Smith, M. Dainoff, J. Smith

4   The Relationship Between Spinal Dysfunction and Reaction Time Measures. Journal of Manipulative and Physiological Therapeutics, Volume 28, Issue 7, Pages 502-507 L. Lersa, C. Stinear, R. Lersa

5   Lelic et al. Neural Plasticity 2016:3704964

6   Haavik Taylor & Murphy. Chiro Journal Australia. 2007;37:106-116

7   Niazietal. Exp Brain Res. 2015;1165-1173.

CHAPTER 28

What It was Like to Have Cranial Surgery While Conscious

I have had three neurosurgeries; two over 10 years ago now, and one just three months ago as I write. I've had completely different experiences with each one. The first surgery I can't tell you a great deal about, except that I do remember every step of being prepared for surgery, then being put under, on my back, while looking up at several masked faces below a bright light, then 'straight away' being wheeled backwards in the opposite direction.

All they were able to do on the first occasion was take a biopsy of my tumour in a couple of small slices and ascertain the tumour type; in this case an aggressive grade III /III mixed anaplastic oligoastrocytoma, which was considered inoperable as it was a bit like a small octopus with a central body and many small projections throughout the brain.

This tumour statistically takes people out of commission on average in about 18 months. In some cases, this tumour type could regress into a far more life-threatening type, the full-blown *glioblastoma multiforme grade IV/IV.* It was thought too risky to do more in case *eloquent tissue* was affected that would harm my left motor pathways.

The second neurosurgery, about a year later, was done with me being fully conscious. It was deemed necessary, because I'd suffered a vicious escalation in tumour size that made me nauseous, upset, and emotionally *all over the place.* Whereas the monthly MRI scans of the initial tumour showed that it had been successfully shrunken by the radiation and chemotherapy, and that it was sitting there *unchanged,* I was put under incredible stress when a young locum in my clinic quit on me with two days' notice to work for someone else, and I was forced back to work.

In one day in a little country practice I saw 58 people between 10am and 5pm; (in earlier years this was just an *average* number of clients that was easily handled, because I had complete examination and X-Ray histories for each client, and knew exactly where to position each person in order to give them their specific adjustment each time). The concentration required with an inflamed brain was all the stress my tumour needed to *shape-shift*; talking was incredibly tiring for my fatigued brain, and a practitioner needs to talk with every client about their concerns.

I remember bawling my eyes out to my parents-in-law and Joanne, apologizing for being so ill and unable to earn an income any more.

My oncologist arranged for an MRI and the tumour had grown to be about the size of a small potato, whereas before it had been shrunken to something the size of an olive. It had only taken a couple of weeks to grow that much, with all the sudden stress and worry.

Anyhow, to accurately describe what goes on with a brain tumour operation, I'll take you back to the MRI imaging procedures. The initial imaging located the tumour very accurately by flushing my brain with a solution of the heavy metal gadolinium, after several prior scans of the normal resting brain. (Even now when I get an occasional MRI, I can taste the gadolinium in my mouth a few seconds after the cold-feeling solution has been pumped into a canulus in my arm!). To me, the taste is something like the smell of nail-varnish remover, or acetone. The information gained from the MRI enables the surgical team to set up for the surgical excision with millimetre accuracy.

Making a phone call the night before surgery, with the corn–pads on my noggin!

To get this repeatable accuracy, an MRI is done the day before the surgery, with the skull clamped tightly (and rather uncomfortably!) into a steel halo for the half-hour imaging. Small Plastic tabs that are held in place like corn pads are put on anatomical landmarks around the proposed surgical incision site. These remain on overnight, and then when the surgery is started the next day, the skull is clamped into the exact same position again, with pinpoint accuracy so that only the *non-eloquent* or tumour material is excised.

To be extremely sure that *eloquent* material was not removed, it was decided to operate on me while I was still conscious. That was a fascinating experience for me.

The first preparations for cranial surgery are not unlike preparations for a tooth extraction, where several little pin-pricks of local anaesthetic are placed around the eyebrow on the affected side, so that one cannot feel one's own forehead at all. (Maybe that's what it feels like with Botox injections!)

The next stage involved reclining me down into the exact position for surgery, with the steel brace clamped down. At this stage I could move my eyes and speak, but there was no way I could turn my neck, or even reach to scratch my nose.

The next stage after that was amazing! The anaesthetist took me right to the very edge of consciousness, taking me right down to where I was aware only of my own self (albeit a *self* who felt as small as a particle of dust): the noises of the room and all the activities blurred away to a noiseless background, and I felt as if I could stay in that state for hours. I was *all of me,* reduced to this tiny speck of perception, feeling as if I was floating at the bottom of a pond of consciousness in serene bliss, with a big smile. The sensation was almost womb-like. Then the anaesthetist said he was going to bring me back to full consciousness, which I found disappointing. I now know why anaesthetists as a group are alleged to be the most likely recreational drug users in medicine. If it's true, I don't blame them! The *Fentanyl* drugs are said to be many times more powerful than heroin.

I have no idea how one measures or compares the narcotic power of different drugs objectively, because someone who is *stoned* doesn't have the power to be objective enough to rate their experience, but I read recently in a newspaper article that the Fentanyl drugs are considered to be several hundred times more powerful than heroin, so it may be true.

The final part of the preparation was draping a green canvas over my upper body and head, totally restricting the right side of my field of vision where the clock was on the wall. I'd wanted to time the whole procedure, but this precluded me from doing so. I'd long since decided that if this brain tumour thing was to be the path laid out for me in life, I might as well get interested and enthusiastic about the whole process. This was based on what the amazing Dr Victor Frankel did during World War Two, when he was a prisoner in Auschwitz for the crime of being a highly educated young professor of neurology and psychiatry.

In his short but powerful book *Man's Search for Meaning*, Frankel recounted his observations that whenever a prisoner *gave up* in the camps, he'd usually smoke his last remaining cigarettes, and withdraw from the others. Frankel noted that if the prisoner had a strong religious faith or family members to live for, or a dream of a life after the war, survival was much more likely, despite the daily brutality of the camp. Men who'd given up hope soon died of whatever infectious disease was doing the rounds of the prison.

When subjected to routine beatings, Frankel's default psychology by disassociation was to project himself years into his imagined future, or *forward-focusing* mentally, trying to describe what was happening to him in a talk he was giving to a lecture theatre crowded by students many years in his vividly imagined future. As Frankel's approach saw him survive well past the war, to the age of 92, it was an approach that appealed. I took careful note of everything that was happening.

Anyhow, I spent the next hour or so talking with the anaesthetist, a former state-level steeplechase runner with Old Scotch Harriers in Melbourne, who asked me if I was the same Keith Livingstone who was a good runner in the 1980's. We regaled each other about our best exploits; occasionally he would ask me to do something like sequentially opposing my first, second, third, and fourth digits with my thumb; fingertip to tip of thumb; on the left hand. He also asked me to flex my left knee and wiggle my toes.

At this juncture I'll go back a step or so; my anaesthetist friend was asking me to do these things while the neurosurgeon was busying himself with a small electrical probe in my head, lightly touching amorphous appearing areas of my right frontal cortex; the tiny local electrical charge had the effect of taking the region probed out of commission for a second or so, with no harm done. So there were an incredible series of checks, stops, and balances during the procedure, all the while making sure I lost none of my fine motor control.

Going back about half an hour before this, after my right forehead from eyebrow to crown was numbed, the surgeon made a crescent-shaped cut into the shaved skin, and lifted the scalp up as a flap, securing it out of the way to be stapled back down later. The next part was getting a small drill-like oscillating buzz-saw that was designed to cut bone (but not skin) by vibration of a fine serrated edge, to make the major crescent shape excision out of the temporo-frontal bones. (We used identical instruments in the human dissection laboratories in Chiropractic College. Similar oscillating devices can be bought at any hardware store to cut ceramic tiles.)

The small amounts of bone remaining as bridges from the major cuts were severed with an extremely fine chainsaw held by hand, with the surgeon pulling to and fro with a v-shaped action against the remaining bridge of cranial bone. The fine chain was inserted similarly to a thread under the tab of bone from one side, and pulled out from the other.

How do I know this? Because I was asking questions all the time, at each juncture, until I was more or less told to shut up, because Professor Murphy, the neurosurgeon, was concentrating. All I could see was a green canvas framing a triangular view of the outside world, which now and again would get filled by the anaesthetist's enquiring face, or various theatre staff shuffling about in the background.

Anyhow, the crescent-shaped bone was lifted free and put aside while the talented Professor went to work. I couldn't feel a thing directly, because the brain itself has no pain-sensory nerves. However, I could feel the very light probing and cutting and tugging *second-hand* via other motion-sensory pathways. It was like being worked on with a bike helmet diffusing the sensation, with the incisions and surgery being done on the surface of the helmet. In other words, I hardly felt a thing. The official term for the procedure on the discharge sheet was *Awake stealth-guided craniotomy*.

Time passed quickly, and before I knew it the professor was apparently satisfied, and had left the operating theatre while his assistants replaced my bone flap in its nest, and stapled my scalp and underlying bone into place with 17 small titanium-alloy staples. He didn't even say 'hello' or 'goodbye'!

Then I was trundled out to a room where there were a few other people on their own surgical gurneys, recovering from their surgeries done in other operating theatres. It was as busy as a cattle yard in there that morning!

Another half-hour later I was trundled up to my own bed on the tenth floor, ready for family and friends, and the post-surgical assessment team.

CHAPTER 29

What having a Seizure Feels Like

You may be interested to know what it feels like before, during, and after a *seizure*. There are many different types and severities of seizures; most of which can be prevented by ample sleep, good nutrition, anti-seizure medication, and quite possibly just magnesium supplementation and Fish Oil, in my case.

Most of the seizures I've had have been small affairs, and I just wait for the activity to settle down while the rest of my brain functions absolutely normally around the mostly left-sided hyper-activity, which I usually cannot over-ride. This left-sided hyperactivity in the upper and lower limbs often coincides with stuttering, and an inability to get words out; it is expected that the left limbs will be affected most by a lesion in the right motor cortex of the brain.

My very first seizure, which forcefully announced a burst sub-arachnoid blood vessel above the frontal lobe tumour, was *tonic-clonic*, or *grand-mal*.

I lost all consciousness, and went into full extension at full power, over a chiropractic bench, to then lie on the ground with my left leg and arm thumping hard on the ground while I bit down hard on the inside of my left cheek. Eventually I woke up, after voiding my bladder during the seizure.

The first seizure I have conscious memory of *riding through* like a surfer on a wave was probably a *tonic* or *petit mal* seizure, where my left upper and lower extremities went into rigid extension, and thumped up and down very hard, while my left inner cheek got macerated by biting down hard with the left molar teeth.

I was lying on my bed on a Sunday morning, the night after a very late night out, where I'd stupidly had some alcohol. A few seconds earlier I had been holding my newborn daughter, and knew just enough as the aura came to roll to my right and dump her on the bed-cover before my body started thumping very hard up and down with the left limbs. A new-born baby would have had no chance if it was struck by a limb flying around violently during a seizure. Even though I was fully conscious there was nothing I could do to stop my seizure, so I just *relaxed* into it until it ebbed away in about 60 very long seconds.

On another occasion, I had a very unusual experience, a *crumple seizure*, or *atonic seizure*, after staying up too late. I recall falling in what felt like extremely slow-motion spirals to the carpet in my study, and as I fell through cardboard storeage boxes without any sensation of pain whatsoever, I remember thinking, somewhat disappointedly "Am I dying now? Is this all it feels like?" before everything clouded over.

I awoke at about 5 am, having filtered oxygen into my nostrils face-down through dusty old carpet for several hours, and went back to my own bed to sleep properly for another six hours.

On one occasion I remember very well, I'd been working hard on my house all day, preparing it for sale, and then at sun-down went for a hilly three kilometre walk. I'd only gone a kilometre when I started to have a seizure, which was unusual because I very rarely get a seizure if I'm doing something physically active.

What happened on this occasion was that my head tilted and rotated to the left, and I was stuck to the spot with my left arm hanging floppily, still upright, as I consciously tried to fully right and de-rotate myself. Cars were driving past, but no one noticed enough to stop. There is nothing any other person can do to speed up recovery from a seizure once it's started going. It just has to play itself out. Eventually the seizure abated, and I walked the remaining two kilometres home.

On other occasions I just lose the ability to speak clearly, stuttering in staccato fashion, while my left hand will shake quickly.

Sounds Inside My Head

After my second surgery, which removed a considerable portion of the tumour, I was often awoken in the middle of the night by sounds not unlike the dripping of water inside a cave, complete with gurgling sounds like a toilet cistern emptying. These sounds I believe were the cerebrospinal fluid dynamics re-establishing themselves within the ventricular system of the brain after the big lump of gristle which had been blocking the cistern had been removed.

This *flushing of the cistern* phenomenon was surprisingly similar to what former American football great Jim McMahon described after care from cranio-cervical chiropractor Dr Scott Rosa.

McMahon, an all-time great who was known for his hard-hitting style on the field, had experienced years of debilitating migraines and was entering early progressive dementia when Dr Rosa cleared out an area in his upper neck where most normal motion had been lost.

Once specific care for the purpose of restoration of normal spinal joint motion was underway, McMahon heard his own cerebrospinal fluid dynamics restore themselves, and his progressive debilitation ceased soon after, presumably because the areas of the brain that were being deprived of normal cerebrospinal fluid flow were now receiving normal supplies. He was soon able to play golf again, whereas before his outlook was very bleak.

Warning Signs

I know I have to particularly look after myself if I start to stutter slightly, or find my morning crossword or cross-code word puzzles difficult. The cause is often that I've forgotten to take anti-seizure medication. I've never been a pill-popper, but it appears for now that I need to stay on this medication to stay out of trouble. One protracted seizure may well have the ability to over-excite neurons in my brain to the point of cell-death, and certainly after 'BIG' seizures, my brain feels as if it's a wrung-out rag, and it can take up to a month to recover my full battery life.

Sometimes, I stutter slightly even though I'm well-rested and well-fed. If I have company when that occurs, I know I usually have another hour or so of useful battery life before it becomes a concern, so I just state the obvious, saying "excuse my stutter- it's part of the deal", and make preparations to get home and take it easy, or take extra medication. If there's no medication, I usually buy or scrounge some fish-oil capsules.

Pre-Seizure Auras: I feel very strangely disconnected from everything around me, with a sense of impending doom.

Loss of Thought: For me, I become aware that I can't generate a proper thought; this has the potential to be be quite terrifying sometimes, as I have to wait for just a spark of thought to enter a vast void of consciousness surrounding me.

There's no hint where my consciousness might have gone to when in this void, or that it will even come back at all. One has to be calm throughout the void of consciousness, much as one would wait for a gas burner to light with a pizo-electric switch. Sometimes a rational thought *clicks* alight, and I make straight for my anti-seizure medication or do my *inter-hemispheric activity scrambling exercises* which involve stimulating both hemispheres of the brain at the same time, to divert electrical activity away from the franticly short-circuiting area causing the seizure.

If I can't get to it in time, I just *ride the seizure out* till it abates. On a couple of occasions I have apparently gone completely unconscious, with no ready memory of the seizure, however most times I am well aware of what is going on, and it's a bit like being pulled out to sea by a *rip* in the surf; you just wait till it has pulled you out as much as it's going to, then swim aside and paddle back in.

Stimulating electrical activity away from the injured right frontal lobe of my brain can be achieved by provoking the left hemisphere; doing fine-motor finger to thumb exercises with my right hand, or scratching the scalp over my left frontal lobe with my right hand.

In the early months of recovery, I could stop a seizure by yelling out loud, but this has not worked lately.

There is an eerie empty feeling, or *aura*, which can be short-circuited if I'm aware of things early enough. I am getting better all the time, but several years ago seizures were reasonably common. As I write, it's well over a year since I had my last major seizure, and prior to it I had to cease working in my country clinic and ask my staff to arrange for my family to take me home. I had a minor seizure earlier in the day, followed by a period where I walked down near the Murray River for a couple of hours just to calm my nervous system down with gentle activity in the beauty of the nearby national park.

When I was safely back with the family in Bendigo, I went for a walk around my favourite bush circuit with my beautiful son Henry, saying next to nothing and just enjoying his calming presence. Later, I took exception to being told by Joanne and Annabel, my oldest daughter, to get to bed and sleep, and to her great credit Annabel stood her ground and gave as good as she got when I got agitated with the idea of my daughter telling me what to do. I made a quiet, cunning getaway into the dark winter night while they were in the kitchen, eventually necessitating my being rounded up by police who took me to hospital for assessment.

In my agitated and confused state, I had enough common-sense to make it over the hill to Joanne's parents' home, where I planned to confront them about some imagined misgiving, and although there were any number of ways to get back home without being trailed easily, I chose to emerge from the house and cooperate. That was the first time I've been handcuffed and put in a cramped paddy-wagon. That's not to say I've always been a good law-abiding citizen; in my less-responsible years no-one would've been able to get near me.

The police were very good with me, even removing my handcuffs because they were uncomfortable. I thought I was being taken to the police lock-up to calm down for a while, but they delivered me straight to the local hospital, where I apparently had a massive seizure soon after admission, but was totally unaware I had. I remember telling an orderly to stop whistling loudly while I was resting on a bed, and Joanne being there while I was given a number of cognitive tests. However that hour or so flowed seamlessly in my memory, and I was amazed when I was told later that I'd had a huge seizure in the middle of it.

This was a totally different experience to February 2015, when running my Chiropractic Clinic in Cobram, over two hours' drive away from home and family. For some reason I was unable to sleep for 4 nights in a row, and had managed to lose my car, house, and clinic keys while shopping for vegetables at a supermarket. I eventually recalled where I had spent some time in the vegetable section, and a shelf-stacker was able to find my keys, well after midnight.

CHAPTER 30

Into The Abyss

One night I rang my mother and her husband Brian in Auckland, quite late at night. I asked if I could have permission to beat up my longest-standing friend, Gavin, on their back lawn, thinking he was somehow inveigled in some dark and deep plot to worm his way into my family.

This was sheer delusional madness, as they had no back lawn, only a steep drop covered in thick native foliage. My poor mother, who was 89 at the time, was quite shaken up by that, not to say Brian, whose sage advice to me was to "let him stew in his own juice if you feel there's a case to answer."

An older lady who was working for me as a receptionist on the front desk had stormed off in a fit of pique, after informing me how sure she was that my venture could not succeed, and questioning my integrity and honesty. I *had to let her go* as *Arnold* would say. I was down to running my clinic by myself, on very low battery life. I reverted to default survival mode, soldiering on in extreme slow-motion. I didn't even think to ring Joanne, such was my state. She would've been up in a shot.

One poor man watched in disbelief as I took a huge amount of time to process his payment on the computer, asking me if I was OK and saying "should you be really working in this state?" I assured him I was fine, kidding no-one but myself.

My brain was operating at minimal capacity, behind a filthy, greasy windscreen to the world, and when I found it beyond my ability to find the number for the local hospital to admit myself, I knew I was in trouble.

I decided to abandon the rest of my day at about 10 am. Mercifully, as happens when things aren't quite right in the ether, no further clients were booked in at that stage. A lady who knew me helped me out by calling the ambulance, who eventually arrived. The advertising manager of the local newspaper drove my car back to my flat, while I awaited medical help at my workplace.

The para-medics duly arrived, having come from another small town because the local ambulance had another call they'd responded to. I explained that I wanted to be taken to hospital so that I could be sedated, and all was proceeding OK until one of the men decided I was about to cause trouble, saying "Now calm down, mate!" while firmly trying to make me sit on a low brick wall by pushing me down. That just fired me off into a truly agitated state where I pushed him off and another man, as they tried to restrain me.

This is the way I remember it, and in my mind if they had just treated me calmly, I would never have started pushing back. As three of them started to push me on my back down onto the ground, I saw a burly middle-aged former soldier I had been caring for come into the fray.

"Great! Bob's going to help me out here!" I thought, however he also held me down. I felt let down by that, but really he was looking out for me.

The biggest of the paramedics, a jiujitsu exponent apparently, put me in a neck and shoulder lock. He was the one I'd tried to push backwards over the low brick wall while I was pushing up under his chin, and I don't think he appreciated it.

Unable to do much while the big man had me zipped up, I chatted with the guys, but as far as I can remember I wasn't taken to the local hospital. A lot of the rest of that day's events are a complete mystery to me, including how I was put into the ambulance.

Someone phoned Joanne in Bendigo, and she drove up towards Cobram as fast as she could get there. When she had reached the small country town of Nathalia, she received another call saying I was now being assessed at Goulburn Valley Health, the public hospital in the large regional centre of Shepparton, so she changed direction and caught up to me in Shepparton in the early afternoon.

She caught up with me in the A & E department. For reasons that defy all logic, I was kept awake for hours and not given a bed till after midnight. I was moved around from booth to booth. At no stage was I sedated, which is all I wanted in the first place. I remember Joanne being with me when they gave me a 'cognitive function test' after midnight, and she says I was *awful to be with*, talking non-stop, with my eyes twitching everywhere, and my head jerking quickly.

By this stage, having been awake for nearly 5 days, my brain was in extreme fast-forward, and my thoughts came at rapid-fire speed, like a machine-gun. Despite my issues, I was able to score 29/30 in the cognitive function test. One of the questions required me to draw a clock face showing *ten minutes past eleven*, so I obliged by making all the numbers into Roman Numerals just to show that I could, as well as giving the dial a happy smile.

I was then *admitted* to the Mental Health Unit, walking the short distance from the hospital exit with Joanne. She told me later she felt as if it was *a bit like taking you into Auschwitz*, in the gloom. It was well after midnight.

I can't recall how I was taken away from under poor Joanne's watchful eye, but she had to get back to Cobram to get some hard-earned sleep. I recall being frog-marched like a criminal down a hall, after struggling when I saw a beefy security guard pull on gloves while smirking at me. I thought I saw plastic ties in his hand.

Somehow I made my way through a flurry of arms towards his smirking face, which turned to shock-horror when I snotted him right on the extreme tip of his snout. If it was in a movie, it would've been in slow-motion with a delightful 'ting' sound-effect at point of feather-light contact. I also decided to stomp down hard on the top of someone's foot with my heel, and the yelp accompanying that confirmed I'd been successful. I felt like a confused trapped animal, and behaved accordingly.

We turned a corner, and I was still surrounded by about five men as a large steel door was opened hurriedly. I was half-carried inside, still struggling. I think I felt a sharp pin-prick administered by a diving hand into my left buttock as I was struggling in the doorway. I knew there was no real hope of *escape* there and then, but I just wanted to make it as difficult for them as possible, as what should have been a simple admission was turned into a travesty.

As soon as I was tossed inside, the *hit-squad* scrambled out and slammed the door behind. I was in a dark room with a foam mat on the floor, five white plastic cups of water, and a cardboard container to pee in. My watch and belt had been removed, as well as my glasses, socks and shoes, wallet and phone. There was a tempered glass window in the door letting minimal light in.

I lay down on the mat, and my brain was going unbelievably fast as I spoke loudly in metronomic verse, going on and on about a crazily obsessive vision I had about ending the ISIS occupation in Mosul. It was a matter of *extreme* urgency that I got this vision to then-serving prime minister Tony Abbott. (Prime ministers tend to swap around a bit in Australia).

I ranted on my back in that dark room, as I outlined my vision in a 'tick the dotted line' form of metronomic verse. I was speaking out loud in the form of brief statements followed by the word 'Tick' to affirm each statement.

One line I remember is: *"Is She, who is dedicated by God, to evict this Evil from earth, present? Tick!"*

It was not a dream or nightmare, because I was still awake. It was rampant delirium. In my normal state of mind, there'd be little hope I could churn out line after line of pre-worded statements anywhere like that. The sentences came to me as if off a metaphysical conveyor belt, pre-framed and complete, pulled down from the ether, and in rhyme.

If it was possible to have a functional MRI scan while that was happening; the electrical activity would've resembled hot oil spitting off an overheated frying-pan.

The vision involved three grand old ladies, all born in 1926, walking up a main street in Mosul, northern Iraq, towards an ISIS stronghold, with several hundred Australian light-horse infantry in World War One uniform, behind them with sabres drawn. The ISIS stronghold was on the opposite bank of the Tigris from the site of the ancient Biblical city of Nineveh.

Behind the three old ladies, all walking purposefully and defiantly, was the immense, muscular frame of Australian Victoria cross winner Ben Roberts-Smith, resplendent in his uniform and many medals, cradling the oldest and tiniest Victorian cross winner in the world in his massive arms. The ancient old man, highly bemedalled as well, held a ceremonial sabre raised and pointed directly at the enemy.

One of the three old ladies was Her Majesty Queen Elizabeth herself, and two were the two Valerie Livingstones I've known- one my mother, and the other, the wife of the late Alastair Livingstone, Head of the Clan MacLea (same clan as the Livingstones–long story!), also named Valerie, and unbelievably, also born in 1926, and also speaking with the same Oxbridge accent.

At some stage, the door was opened slightly, and I yelled "Leave me alone! I'm having my rant!". The door was politely closed.

Back in my alternative reality, Queen Elizabeth would stop every few steps and read from a declaration of intent on an ancient scroll, to the stunned Islamics.

The pinnacle of the vision was when the Queen, hearing no repentance from the Islamics, after delivering several strong warnings, plunged *Curtana*, the *sword of justice*, downwards with two hands into the dirt in front of the stronghold, vocally condemning the stronghold and all the evil in it to the pit of hell, with the rights given to her as head of the Church of England, and as monarch of the Commonwealth of Nations.

What happened next I cannot say, except there was light of an impossible golden intensity that was blinding.

Wooohhhh!! The urge to get the vision to Abbott by any means whatsoever was huge, and as I write, over five years later, I consider myself *very sane* again, but it took every bit of two months to get back to normal. I did very little for those two months, imagining my exhausted neuronal pool needed every bit of time and good nutrition it could get to heal and function properly again. Amazingly, through all this, there was *no change* to the remaining tumour mass on MRI, yet again.

As I've said elsewhere, the feeling after a fairly massive seizure can be described as being like a wrung-out rag, and it can take quite a while to fully return to normal. However, all of these experiences certainly raise questions about what's real and unreal in the world of spirit, where black and white increasingly become multiple shades of grey.

In the morning, I was given a secure room with gloomy lighting and an all-steel bathroom. It was like showering in a submarine. There was a nice touch with a corner window view of garden and lawn outside.

I partook very little of the communal breakfast in the dining room. It was not the best nutrition for people with brain chemistry issues, comprising standard issue corn flakes, sugar, instant coffee, tea bags, milk, white bread toast with jam or honey, or orange cordial. All I had was a cup of tea in the mornings, or perhaps a little toast and marmalade. Eating utensils were white plastic, for safety purposes I suppose. Lunch or dinner were where I obtained my best nutrition, with decent serves of vegetables and sliced roast beef with gravy, and ice-cream or apple crumble for desserts, for those who wanted them.

It was interesting how rapidly I got better in the next few days, having been given tiny orange tablets which helped me to sleep. I was able to observe what it's like to be in an acute mental health unit quite objectively, although it was quite challenging to experience loss of agency to the point where I had to explain why I needed my watch and leather belt back to a young nurse who talked to me as though I was actually quite stupid.

There was a comfortable TV room in the unit, and a large common-room where there was a large table tennis table, and desks for drawing or painting. The TV lounge opened out onto a lawn with pleasant shrubs bordering it, and a not-so-challenging high fence to keep residents in. I did briefly consider an escape, but decided against this for a number of common-sense reasons.

In the TV lounge, there was often a small tanned lady in her 60s, with jet-black hair and piercing eyes. She claimed to know or be related to any of the featured people in the news bulletins, fixing a stare on other people present just to reaffirm her claims.

One morning, a friendly, graciously-mannered older lady, who was meticulously dressed, appeared for lunch. To look at her she had no business being in the mental health unit, however I heard some staff discussing her case amongst themselves over their meal, and it turned out that *though the lights were on, no-one was home,* as she had dementia and her family couldn't look after her at home any more. Extremely sad.

STARING DOWN THE BEAST

I got talking with an extremely tall, dark Somali boy I'll call *Abdul*, who was 19 years old and was very keen on soccer. He was friendly and intelligent, and expressed keen interest in learning how to get really fit for soccer again, after he was released.

A couple of nights later, as I settled in to sleep, I was awoken by terrible, anguished howling coming from a room up the corridor from mine. I heard "Mummeeee!... Mummeeee!". It was heart-breaking. I walked past the room, and through the partially open door saw *Abdul* being cradled in close by his mother, who was a magnificent, beautifully-dressed, extremely tall woman.

Apparently he'd been given electro-convulsive therapy (ECT) earlier on, and was inconsolable after that intervention. The ECT room was not hidden, being off the corridor to the dining room, labelled as *ECT ROOM*, with a window in the door enabling one to see which of the practitioners was in there making case notes. (I have since read that ECT can be useful in certain cases that are poorly managed with drug therapies, which is why ECT is still in use).

Each night around 8:30 p.m., the serious young nurse came around to deliver my tiny orange tablet with a glass of water. Most of the time I was just content to read books, or do sets of push-ups with my hands on the floor and my feet on the mattress to keep in shape as much as I could while incarcerated. I also took the time to memorise the Twenty-third psalm by heart, and I still recite it each night while on my regular bush-walk near home.

I still have the notebook Joanne gave me to write or draw in while incarcerated. It is written with a secretive intent, leaving cryptic messages for certain people to decipher should any imagined harm come to me. Having just re-read those cryptic messages as I write this chapter, I cannot make any sense of what I had written then, so any intended *recipient* of my messages would conclude I had flipped my lid totally, which was absolutely true.

I thought I could see future events and people's hidden intents- but they were all behind a dark fog which had nothing good about it. If you believe in demons, then I had one, or several, desperate to rob me of my sanity. They nearly got there, too.

While my brain was slowing down to normal speeds, I got obsessed with what I called my *Unified Theory of Consciousness and mass*, and how if we put Einstein's never-disproven equation of $E=mc^2$ to its furthest limits, to a level whereby the speed of light was infinite (∞) at some stage we'd quickly reach a balanced equation where the mass of the whole cosmos was equal to the total Energy in existence divided by infinity squared, which would be written as $m = E/\infty^2$. In other words, if or when the speed of light was infinite, the mass of the whole cosmos was zero, regardless of the fact that E represents the sum total of all energy in the cosmos.

(Even if E could be expressed as infinity, *infinity* divided by *infinity squared* is best expressed as *zero*.)

I drew a parallel from a similarly expressed and similarly famous equation, first discovered in the 3rd century BC by Archimedes, where the area of a circle (A) was expressed as A= πr2. This served as a two-dimensional platform whereby I made the area of a circle analogous with the *area* of a two dimensional slice of a three-dimensional cosmos exploding uniformly from a central source, so that $E=mc^2 \cong A = \varpi\, r^2$, with *r* representing the speed of light exploding out from a single infinitesimally small source.

As with the famous $A = \varpi\, r^2$, ϖ has only one value, as a constant ratio of 22/7. My mind was coping with the possibility that the *mass* of everything in existence may also be just a ratio, with the variables being the amount of energy being expressed as matter, or the speed of light.

I was thinking about my experience when taken under anaesthesia, to the edge of consciousness, prior to my *awake* neurosurgery in 2008, and how I was *aware* of everything around me even though I felt *no body* around me. I write about it elsewhere in this book as being like a *speck of self-awareness floating blissfully on the bottom of a pond of consciousness.*

Then, I concluded that the problem of maintaining the balanced equation while including the existence of consciousness in either an original singularity or an expanding cosmos could be done by ascribing a mass of zero to consciousness while in the singularity. Even so, the possibility of everything in existence, including a consciousness that pervades the whole cosmos having exploded out of something definable only as *zero* is pretty awesome and one that kept me fully occupied while incarcerated.

Interestingly, it is held that a photon of light has no mass either, so the correlation of light and consciousness in an expanding cosmos arising from a singular entity is something to think about: when you're in a psychiatric unit, anyhow.

Everything you can imagine is real – Pablo Picasso

I imagine that because I'm not a physicist of any sort, that there could be any number of *impossible* roadblocks to the scenarios my mind conjured up, while it calmed down from its frenetic ascent into *manic psychosis of no known cause.* However, this all showed what my sped-up-brain chose to occupy itself with, protecting itself from any form of self-pity or depression; and why couldn't something that a guy dreamt up out of nowhere be *possible*?

Eventually, after 9 days, I was deemed well enough to go back to my normal life, however it took quite a few weeks more to get back to what I would consider a *normal healthy state of mind*, in the safe nest of normal family life. For a good 15 months I was fine; even going back to work for that time, until, as I mentioned, my exhausted brain let me know that it needed complete recuperation with my family around me.

CHAPTER 31

Is There Anyone Else Out There?

For a number of years I was the only person I knew of who had survived as long as I had with a glioblastoma multiforme tumour. That was until recently, when a plethora of books surfaced on Amazon by long-term survivors. Yes, there are others!

Over the years, I have heard of several people who had a similar diagnosis to mine, and unfortunately they've all since passed on. I thought mistakenly that I could encourage them to stay alive, however each case is unique, and there is absolutely no judgement from me. Some people must *let go* because they don't want to put their families through months and years of struggle and expense. Even I felt that way early on with my *little issue*, before I decided to accept the challenge and keep turning up. I know in my heart that some of the people who *succumbed* were fighters to their deepest being, so it is a source of wonder that I am still here, relatively whole in function and comparatively un-harmed.

I now have an incredible sense of gratitude that the possibility of the full and adventurous life I always envisaged is now more possible than ever! For a while, I thought I must have been the longest-surviving GBM patient in Australia, at least, however I was informed by a physiotherapist in the hospital system that there is a man in my own town who is still alive after 15 years with the same condition. Medical ethics prevent my being able to contact this man, and check his story out., but it goes to show that by the laws of probability, there must be *many* long-term survivors out there in the larger world if a country town of only 100,000 people in rural Australia has two long-term survivors, or *thrivors*.

However, there are remarkable stories out there in the public domain which shade mine by quite a margin. One of the most remarkable of all is that of Chery Broyle, who in 2012 published her account of overcoming glioblastoma: *Life's Mountains: What a Brain Tumor Survivor Learned Climbing a Mountain and Battling 'Terminal Cancer'*. She took to climbing high mountain peaks as a metaphor for conquering her challenges.

Unlike me, Cheryl has had challenge after challenge during all this time, with the latest being in October 2017, with a nasty inoperable pituitary challenge that has really knocked her around. Cheryl seems to be an incredible survivor and I sincerely hope and pray that she will keep on living for a good number of years yet!

There is one amazing story of the *complete disappearance* of a glioblastoma multiforme tumour with one lady called Heather Knies, who made national news in the USA a few years ago. As well as following the *orthodox* routine of chemotherapy and radiotherapy, Heather had an intense Christian faith that allowed her to know she was going to live and survive.

Mrs Knies said God *had a plan* for her and never once thought she would succumb to the disease. Remarkably, all evidence of her tumour as seen on MRI disappeared completely, and she went on to have a baby girl named Zoe, with a viable egg that wasn't affected by all of her chemotherapy or radiotherapy, via a surrogate mother.

She told ABC News "The mind is so much more powerful than anyone can imagine. I never once thought it would be the death of me."

CHAPTER 32

Manuel's Story

I was by chance introduced to Manuel Fernandez, a Spanish-born man who was raised in Australia, and lives in Melbourne. He, too, has survived a number of years; over nine years; and he's going well.

I believe that after a few years without major issues, it's entirely probable that one will make it to the statistical landmark of ten years, where one hops off the terminal brain tumour survival data-base to the normal population survival database. Does this mean there will be no further issues? No; as I've found out, there will always be reminders that the body and mind has been hit really hard.

Whereas I owe my current excellent health and fitness and strength to a lifetime of interest, practice, and study in those areas, as well as very strong support from my wife and children, Manuel has had none of those advantages. Manuel's elderly mother lived in Sydney until very recently, and she is his only remaining close family.

Manuel's survival story is extremely impressive to me, as he lived alone for many years, and still ran his consulting business in Melbourne.

I'll start from the beginning, as told by Manuel.

Over nine years ago, in September 2009, Manuel had a life partner who was a medical practitioner, and life and business were going very well. He was bothered with an ache in his neck that *wouldn't go away*. He thought he may have strained it at the gym. His partner ordered a CT scan of the area involved; the *Guiding Hand* must have been at work even at that early stage, as his partner ticked an extra box on the CT scan form.

Whereas she would normally have only ticked the regional examination box for C. spine (cervical spine, or neck) she also ticked the box for *Head*. She herself remarked later that she *never normally would tick that box for a neck problem*.

Whether the *Guiding Hand* was at work or not, it was an amazingly fortuitous stroke of *sheer dumb luck*. The radiologist reported a tumour, and within a few days Manuel went from being a busy guy enjoying life on all fronts to a man being faced with a *death sentence*. He was operated on within a few days, and was more or less advised by his neurosurgeon that the tumour would *kill him*.

Manuel was infuriated that this man could tell him so bluntly about his life expectancy when he didn't even know him personally. Manuel then asked the neurosurgeon "When, exactly, will this tumour kill me?"; a declaration of defiance and absolute intent. As he has shared with me, he adopted the position of *never accepting any possibility of defeat*.

Manuel was accepted into several trials for promising new chemotherapy agents. In one, from 15 participants around the world, he was the *last man standing*. In another one, he was placed on a placebo, but he still *got a bit better*.

He took up meditation practices and yoga, which he found enormously beneficial. When he was having his regular MRI scans, he used that time to visualize all his brain tumour cells being destroyed by his white blood cells. A further operation was deemed necessary at one stage, and the neurosurgeon warned Manuel that he could *lose 70% of the sensation in his arm*, however after the operation, he didn't lose sensation like that. Instead, his left hand and forearm experienced numbness.

Finding it hard to cope with all the *busy-ness* of the city, Manuel decided to take a long break at the delightful Mornington Peninsula, an hour's drive south of Melbourne. This sojourn was short-lived, as he missed his friends too much, so he returned to Melbourne. He decided that he only had one intention for each day: to get better. Manuel also decided to help others who were in the same position, if he could, and took part in counselling groups.

A lapsed Catholic, but still very much a *believer*, like myself, Manuel sought solace at St Michael's Uniting Church, where the executive minister was Dr Frank Macnab. In 1961, Macnab opened the Cairnmillar Institute, a clinical psychological centre; the largest in Australia, which was for some time the largest training body for psychologists and counsellors in the country. Dr Macnab was Executive Director until Professor Kathryn von Treuer, took over the reins in late 2015. (Coincidentally, this is the same Kathryn, or *Kate*, who was my girlfriend when I was at university!)

A few months after his initial diagnosis, Manuel's partner, who in her medical role had been so instrumental in saving his life, left him on Valentine's Day, and he has never heard from her in the years since.

Devastated, Manuel found solace and the internal strength to *carry on* from his yoga, and read many survival stories which encouraged him to keep on getting better. He had a great group of friends who rallied around him in those dark times.

Manuel was plagued by very dark dreams for several months, where he felt as though he was surrounded by *Demons with teeth*. When walking one night, he was inspired to take a new approach; he could mentally re-frame the *demons* as *smiling friends,* and when he started doing that his dark thoughts receded. These days, Manuel runs Imagine Business Consultancy in St Kilda, Melbourne, which he founded in 2013, several years after he was first diagnosed. He has a great group of friends, who are *there* for him, and he plans to be around for many years yet.

Keith and Manuel compare notes

CHAPTER 33

The Thin Edge of The Wedge

In a quaint, snug, and very ancient pub named *The Eagle and Child* on St Giles Road in Oxford, not too far from the wonderful Oxford University Museum of Natural History, members of Oxford University's *Inklings Club* used to meet to share their ideas and musings. This social and intellectual milieu over convivial pints bred such literary heavyweights as C.S. Lewis, and J.R.R. Tolkien, known now as the authors of The Chronicles of Narnia, and The Lord of the Rings, respectively. Both authors' books were made into monumental film successes in the last decade.

Professionally, both men were Oxford professors of literature; Lewis in the area of medieval romance and Tolkien in the area of Norse myth. These two men met in 1926 in an Oxford staff meeting, and struck a firm friendship where they shared their ideas of how to impart the great moral truths to children using myth and fantasy.

C.S. Lewis authored many books and articles, however the one I most relate to is *The Screwtape Letters*, which represents a series of letters from a major demon to a minor demon, on all the tricks and ruses to deploy to get a person derailed from his or her life calling. Lewis dedicated The Screwtape letters *To J.R.R. Tolkien*.

A major device Lewis alluded to in his other classic *Mere Christianity* is the use of the *thin edge of the wedge*. This idiom is very interesting in that during my constant struggle with my *little issue* I have repeatedly never let my guard down with the words I speak or the reinforcing of any negatives into my thought life.

Much as a well-placed wedge can cleave a block of granite apart with a focused blow, the metaphysical wedge is best neutralised by never being allowed to exist in one's thought life in the first place. Sheer bloody-minded denial is a healthy place to start from.

I maintain that if you deny something strongly enough, for long enough, you are empowering the opposite vision to the one that is being denied, and therefore you can form a rock-solid metaphysical platform of *absolute belief* in a positive future instead of an overwhelming vision of doom. One metaphysical and epigenetic platform switches on the genes enabling recovery, and the other switches on the downward metabolic spiral of neuronal dysfunction and programmed cell-death or apoptosis.

Sometimes even people who seem to have one's very best outcomes at heart give well-intended but defeatist advice. PREPARE YOURSELF.

One person very dear to me recently declared "You need to live in the here and now, Keith! Now! You're always making plans for the future, but you live *Now!*".

Though on the surface, this person was giving me very well-intended and pragmatic advice, it wasn't necessarily advice for me, as a person. If one is living in the present, and the *present* isn't quite what one would like it to be, then why not live in *hope*, and add to that by doing something constructive, in the present, towards a better outcome? This is what is known in psychology as '*forward-focussing*'; something that Victor Frankel really pioneered when he was in Auschwitz, when he envisaged himself describing his brutal beatings by Nazi guards to a future audience of psychology students, savouring the moment, but applying it to a future goal.

1. The "I know someone who thought that they could get better too" wedge.

Yet another person, an elderly neighbour, had lost a son to a brain tumour, and he enquired about my health. When I declared I was going very well and was very hopeful of a good long-term outcome, he looked at me pitifully, stating "my son thought that could happen, too…. but he was wrong!" I let it disband to the cosmos as he was obviously still deeply grieving.

2. The "You MUST see this health practitioner" wedge.

If the seat of your nervous energy has a major issue, it doesn't make much sense to chase practitioners and appointments here, there, and everywhere, no matter how good they may be. You've got to HOARD all the nervous energy you have. It's like a battery you need to re-charge, not discharge. Gratefully thank anyone who offers a suggestion though, because it is well-intended. I will, eventually, get to see most practitioners as I heal enough to cope.

3. The "You're in for the fight of your life" wedge.

I've heard that, yes. "Fighting for my life" sounds very stressful, however my body made this 'little issue' as a result of any number of varying stresses over the years. Am I going to heal best while calm, or while 'fighting'?

4. The "We're so sorry to hear your news" wedge.

There were many 'caring' people who came and said things to me like "We're so sorry to hear your news, Keith"…with empathic overtones akin to speaking to a man who was 'as good as gone', so I would always say "What news have you heard, that I don't know about? I'm feeling like a box of fluffy ducks at present, and getting better all the time!" (I probably looked grey/green at the time!)

Another corny but stock-standard reply I give to the regular "How are you?" question is "FANTASTIC!!!.... But I'm getting better all the time!"

5. The "I'm trying my best to tell you" wedge.
   (also known as the 'be sensible' wedge.)

Another man who I've known for years, phoned me up specially from interstate to ask me what my prognosis was. It went like this:
Friend: "What's your prognosis, then, Keith?
Keith: "My personal prognosis is *excellent*, but the medical prognosis is *appalling!*"
Friend: "I don't think you're taking this nearly seriously enough, Keith! These people are, after all, *specialists!*"
Keith: "Well, I'm the most-qualified specialist on Keith Livingstone I know, so my personal prognosis is the only one that counts", and so on.
I'm sure the poor guy thought I had *flipped my lid* totally, and he soon ended the call in a resigned and disappointed voice, saying
"Well, I don't agree, Keith, and I think you're being irresponsible and unrealistic by what you're saying. But I do wish you well… Bye!" (Translation: "well- I tried my best to tell you, but you won't listen!")

From my current perspective, I cannot fathom the underpinning psychology behind that conversation, however I am forced by self-preservation to consider him a friend I cannot associate with for now. What a shame.

6. For severe Cases (VERY RUDE PEOPLE)
Invoke 'The Cone of Silence' and just look at them this way.

Just as the thin end of a wedge can eventually cleave a block of granite in half, the trick is to never let that 'wedge insertion' occur in the first place. So I've treated this "terminal condition" as if it was the flu; something that's a nuisance but can't let one interfere with one's life. Not a big deal. A 'rough patch', that's all!

For anyone going through a rough patch, this idiom represents the philosophy I feel has been crucial in my strong survival to date. As far as I'm concerned, the 'thin edge of the wedge' takes a firm hold when one chooses to take personal ownership of a serious health issue. Just let the little issue have the right to exist as an entity that's separate from yours, and don't think about it. I live every day happily ignoring what many specialists consider to be a very 'serious' medical condition. Because I take no notice of it and just enjoy life, the 'bone-pointing' potential of the doom and gloom prognoses has no permanent effects on my outlook whatsoever.

I've 'brainwashed' myself into total denial that I am unwell. After my latest surgery a few months ago, I was half-convinced, (but apparently not quite fully), that my days might be numbered, and this was because I'd made the mistake of reading my discharge sheet. Reading that was enough to convince almost anyone that the patient was on 'borrowed time'.

I've heard it said that one of the original Middle-English meanings of *Belief* is *Be In Love With*. I am totally in love with the idea of reclaiming a good life.

This *Belief* powers my days with enthusiasm about my future. I couldn't readily deny *hard evidence* like 6 kilograms of muscle dropping off my already compact frame, and having to re-learn how to walk, jump, skip and throw; that *evidence* was absolutely apparent to me. But it was totally my choice to not let my situation depress me; it was totally *my responsibility* to pull myself back into my *Belief* state, while I focused only on eating well and getting better again once out of the hospital system. No-one was saying what they were probably thinking; that "Keith has very little time left." I was *too thick* and caught up in my own Belief to know that I was *as good as gone*. Since I've recovered nicely again after many weeks in a medical ward, all kinds of people have admitted they thought I was a *goner*, including my fantastic GP, Arvind, and even my brother.

Apparently I *did* come within a whisker of departing the planet, and everyone thought my time had come, but it didn't dawn on me personally at a deep enough level to shake me off my one single goal—to get as healthy as possible again; it amazes me what my brain and body chose to recover from, with pulmonary emboli (blood clots in my lungs) at multiple levels, infection of the brain that required antibiotic therapy, delirium with hallucinations, and the need for two months of daily 'Clexane' injections into my abdomen to dissolve the pulmonary blood clots and prevent them from travelling to my brain or lodging in my coronary arteries.

I was so medically sick, weak, and wasted that the staff in one medical ward thought I was unable to get up and walk. Apparently the night nursing staff freaked out when they saw me walking around in a reading room during a violent lightning storm that prevented me from sleeping.

I made a pact with myself to get better again, no matter what, and keep on going, regardless of what everyone around me at the time regarded as hard evidence. What they regarded as *hard evidence* I regarded only as *current information; liable to change for the better*. Now I am very much better, and my *vision* of an interesting future has come right back to the forefront of my thinking.

CHAPTER 34

Don't Take Ownership of Illness!

For instance, this has never been *my* very serious brain tumour. I don't have anything to do with it. *Tumour* just means *growth*. It's been just a brain *growth* which my body made under constant mental and financial and nutritional stress, with a prognosis that various experts have tried to convince me is dire and can recur at any time.

However in my view, with the right conditions, I can get back from this illness, and definitely contain and outlast it. The fact that the tumour mass may have been accelerated by woeful financial strains, and happens to look just like a known nasty type of brain tumour under the microscope, known as Grade IV Glioblastoma Multiforme, the 'brain cancer death sentence,' doesn't particularly perturb me. I just wake up each day and get on with it.

My Little Issue

I have so dissociated myself from my 'little issue' that when I hear of someone else coming down with any illness of similar 'seriousness', I think "Poor person! I hope he or she gets better!"

Right from the start, I have deliberately disempowered the fear-inducing influence of the medical diagnosis and prognosis associated by the tumour by referring to it as my *little* issue. That's a *small- L little*. Even if the boys from the funeral home are already measuring you up for your final flight back home, it's a very funny thing to do, so you might as well enjoy yourself by talking the issue down for as long as possible. (You'll only make people miserable by whining, anyhow!)

This is the great thing about having a strong faith or sense of unfulfilled life purpose. Love of God and family and a sense of unfulfilled life purpose are much more powerful than the small problem of a *terminal* brain tumour in the context of the vast and mysterious universe we live in.

CHAPTER 35

Dealing with Doubts and F.E.A.R.

To this day I have never really acknowledged or *owned* the *fact* that I have had a major health issue; even after a very recent recent episode with a third neurosurgery, where I came as close as it gets to *going down the gurgler* with paranoia and confusion swirling around me, and all the medical emergency activity going on, which by the look of the Discharge Notes was pretty major stuff.

The problems were all post-operative. I was hospitalized with pulmonary emboli: there were blood clots at multiple levels in both of my lungs, and I was *kept* in hospital as a *medical* patient under the care of a neurologist for 4 weeks as I settled down from active hallucinations, post-operative delirium, fever, and confusion. Significantly, as more or less a *prisoner* in the medical neurology system due to my surgically-induced delirium, I was deprived of my regular low-carbohydrate, moderate protein, high in vegetables and higher fat diet for over 6 weeks. After being kept inside for weeks on end, deprived of my preferred and proven nutritional support, I was in a position where no-one would tell me why I was really in hospital. It turned out that my family couldn't have me at home because my behavior was too erratic, and because I was delusional it was not possible for me to function normally within our family context.

A *slipping-anonymously-away, as-predicted* type of ending doesn't dovetail at all with the vision I have had for a full, long, useful, interesting and productive life, and I don't want to just be defined by surviving an illness —I still want the lot! When I do eventually meet My Maker, I'd rather let go in happy and fulfilled circumstances, ideally with family and friends nearby.

If I hear of someone else afflicted with a *cancer*, I still think the way I used to before I had my *little issue*; I feel a bit sorry for them and their family. *Cancer* is still something that happens to other people, but not to me. I've removed myself totally from that mindset of relating to cancer personally.

"For God gave us a spirit not of fear but of power and love and self-control." 2 Timothy 1:7

Absolutely the main thing I had going for me was a rock-solid basic Christian faith, and an absolute belief in the power of prayer. These days I just know that my Maker constantly meets my needs! We seem to have a really good friendship and I talk to Him all the time; especially when I'm out mountain biking and decide to have a crack at a challenging bush-track. One *trick* that works for me is to say *Thank You* in advance for the granting of a positive solution to whatever concerns me at the time, from a future-based or forward-focused stance.

I am always in a state of thanks, and even if I was to die today, I've had an incredibly fortunate and enjoyable life so far. No complaints whatsoever.

Even if I was feeling sub-par, which was most of the time in the early days, I was determined not to rain on anyone's parade. Whenever anyone asked how I was faring, I'd always say "Great!"

If you say it enough, and act that way enough, then it becomes part of you and you have changed the course of your illness. This also makes sense when we understand that the more we do of any one activity, the more normal it becomes neurologically, and that whatever is happening neurologically becomes whatever is happening physiologically.

I won't deny that I went through some very tough and upsetting times in all of this, but as far as I could I concentrated on my best possible outcome. So if you want to get better from a brain issue, keep acting the way you want to end up; in other words- keep *faking* till you get there. It worked for me.

This irreverent attitude to my *serious, life-threatening illness* didn't go down well with one specialist. She wrote in a note to the neurosurgeon that

"Mr Livingstone clearly hasn't embraced the seriousness of his condition".

She was absolutely correct in her assertion. Why on earth would I do a silly thing like that?

The Trick Is To Never Let the Evidence Overwhelm You!

F.E.A.R stands for *False Evidence Appearing Real*:

Your job is to find *facts* to explain the *false evidence*.

Fear is what kills people, I'm convinced. I'm not a fearful type, and have never had empathy with fearful people. We are not supposed to be fearful people.

I also believe "I can do all things through him who strengthens me", as the scripture goes. All my reading over the years has convinced me that once *fear* has a foothold, it is already *game over.*

For instance, I well-remember one of the many MRI scans coming back with a note from the radiologist saying that there appeared to be *sinister* shadows in one of the views. I was feeling OK at the time and trusted that I'd know about it well before the radiologist if something was afoot. I said to Joanne that he was probably going to be looking hard for anything to report because of the known aggression of this tumour type, and he therefore reported anything he could imagine might be the start of something.

Missing something on a report would not look good for a specialist radiologist, so naturally, every possible little shadow would get noted! Radiological reporting is still a very subjective science. So I didn't give it another thought. And nothing happened.

Another night, quite bizarrely, I woke up in the middle of the night not able to see, but also not able to control eye movements. I had to feel my way to the bathroom, not able to see anything. I closed the bathroom door and turned the light switch on and off, not seeing a thing. Clearly, this was a bit of a problem. My eyes felt as though the extra-ocular muscles were all *twisted* like a wound-up rubber band. I didn't bother waking Joanne or panicking her, but just said *"Thanks Lord for sorting this out for me- it's too big for me!"*, and went back to sleep. In the morning I could see again, but I couldn't get up and walk because the room was spinning constantly. It was OK if I lay on my left side, but it went out of control if I turned the other way. Obviously there was an inner ear or *oculovestibular* disturbance going on. A trip to the chiropractor for an upper-neck adjustment sorted that out in one go.

Imagine what a tailspin was possible if I had been an everyday bloke who'd never been to a chiropractor or learnt to *Trust God*.

The *Real Evidence* that I was going to make it all the way back to health was everywhere around me. I had card after card from old friends telling me I was strong. I claimed certain powerful words of scripture as my very own, and found real power in reciting my favourites throughout the day. I would say that off my own strength I'd have had a good chance of getting through, but by allying my resources with those of my Creator my *little issue* was dead in the water from the outset.

It just took quite some time for my body to catch up with my goals. Some days, I feel so strong again that I am almost certain that I have this thing *beaten*. Others, I know that I'm not quite all the way back yet, and have definitely taken quite a hiding. But with Patience, (my weakest link- but it's improving!) I think I can get there. I hardly ever have any of the severe seizures I once had, and if I ever do have a seizure, it's only mild and I know how to ride it out. I never a worry about things that haven't happened, or even things that have.

There were people praying for me or sending me good thoughts from all over the world. At a 20-year Chiropractic College reunion, in 2008, only one year into my recovery, my friend Bob Owens said "You're really going to beat this one, aren't you, Keith?" Obviously, something about my general demeanour at the time indicated that I was getting better, not worse. Every positive comment I took as an affirmation of my goal. But by far the biggest boost to my confidence came from my mother, Valerie, as soon as she saw me within hours of my first surgery. She took one long look at me and said "You're going to be just fine, Keith!"

Mothers know more than all the specialists and neurosurgeons in the world; and my mother had seen me bounce back as a tiny child from some very challenging things; one intestinal condition, intussusception, had been present for several months, with my having passed faecal blood after three haemmorhages over several months. These days, intussusception is described in the medical literature as being *uniformly fatal unless treated within 7 days*. Somehow, at a very young age, I'd soldiered through several months of the transient presentations, and duly recovered each time, until emergency surgery was finally necessary.

My list of good reasons for living was immensely more convincing and powerful than my list of reasons to die. In fact, I could not find one good reason to die other than it was an expected medical prognosis.

I did realize that things were going to be pretty tough for a while, though. Sometimes all you can do is hang in and keep showing up to get where you need to go.

At the back of my mind was that my childhood friend Grant Vesey had eventually died of a very similar tumour a few years earlier, and he was as tough as they come. He was a former New Zealand surf lifesaving champion. Grant was about 4 years older, and like me, he was only 48 when he was first struck down. His first symptom was complete loss of speech. It was an awful time, although his brother Greg says that Grant was peaceful and *ready to move on*, spiritually.

My first major achievable goal was to get through to the birth of my next child. I wanted to see and hold him or her, knowing that if I could do that, I'd have more reason to live again. Jo was only three months pregnant when I collapsed. At that stage, still unsure of what my immediate future held for me, and besieged by negativity on all fronts, I needed to get to the point where I could get a strong mental foothold on my climb above this thing. I knew if I could make it to the birth, that would be huge for me.

I looked back at the times as a tiny kid where'd I'd got through emergency abdominal surgeries. I looked at all the fights I'd had with would-be school bullies, and how none ever came back for *seconds*. I remembered things like a rusty nail going through my wrist; a date palm spike going right up my nose; being electrocuted; being stung by a whole nest of hornets; being kicked by a horse... bitten by a monkey, failing of bikes at full speed; even out of a moving car when I was little.

As an adult I've survived all kinds of idiotic scrapes. I was the fool who would climb in and out of car windows on the motorway, or go car to car through open windows. I've quite a collection of scars these days, and each one has a story. Then there were the wins; always testing my personal limits in training and competition. I can't recall how many running races I've won at different levels over the years, but a swag of yellowing newspaper clippings and a large jar full of medals in the shed tell me that it was quite a lot. I wasn't satisfied with just beating someone- I was more concerned with how far I could push myself. So on a mental and physical basis I was stronger than most, and I was pinning my hopes on this, plus my faith that God had a plan for my life that didn't include an early exit.

After continually awaking every day to find I was fine and still going OK, I became more and more used to the idea I was supposed to be here for some time, despite all the doubters. I had children to bring up, and an example to set them. I like to think I'm the great great grandfather of some remarkable descendants, and even if my name is forgotten in time, the *vibe* of my life will chime down the DNA. If, as the scriptures say, the *iniquities of the forefathers shall be visited to the fourth and fifth generations*, then why shouldn't the strengths of the forefathers be visited to the descendants in a similar manner? I have no intention of caving in and wimping out of the deal; not now I know that it's far more than my own life at stake here.

CHAPTER 36

The Five Stages of Grief

One thing I've never had time for is the almost universal acceptance of Dr Elisabeth Kübler-Ross's credo; *The Five Stages of Grief*. Probably this popular misunderstanding is *dumbed-down* considerably from Kübler-Ross's own deep understandings, as often happens with works of genius. However, the Five Stages of Grief as popularly adhered to are the *Highway to Hades* as far as I can see, for a number of very good reasons; only one stage- *the first*- is truly useful:

1. *Denial*; very, very useful
2. *Anger*: No good- produces destructive stress hormones
3. *Bargaining*; Becoming a 'beggar' isn't going to cut it. More Stress.
4. *Depression*: Be miserable yourself and make everyone else miserable too? Give me a break!
5. *Acceptance*; Just roll over and die???? You're joking, right?

My 'Five Stages of Healing' are Much Better, instead

1. *Flat out Denial*
2. *Denial* while still enjoying the good things in life (coffee!)
3. *Denial* while choosing to still be happy
4. *Denial* while choosing to still make life fun
5. *Denial* until you find the body's health returns all around you

My strategy was to do the exact opposite of what everyone else seemed to do, or expect of me, in this situation, which was panic in a frenzy of self-preoccupied new activities like juicing, fasting, going vegetarian, and meditating. Clearly, if most people who did that were dead after 18 months from the initial diagnosis, an entirely different approach was the way to go. So far, it has worked amazingly well.

There was quite a bit of potentially scary *evidence* that I was soon to depart the mortal coil. But at the end of the day, all of my dire prognoses were just a set of opinions, and if I took my thinking out to the biggest God's-eye level, my issues were very tiny ones to sort.

CHAPTER 37

Know Who You Are and Find Where You Come From

It pays to know exactly who you are, and where you come from when faced with a large challenge. It's only in the last 20 years that I've come to know more about my ancestry, and how my nature has been shaped not only by the genetic code, but by the gene-modifying epigenetics of the moral strengths visited down by two very interesting, very hardy family lines. When I visited the late Baron Alastair Livingstone, the head of my Scottish clan (the Clan MacLea / McLay are also Livingstones…long story!) on the Isle of Lismore, a number of years ago, he showed me possibly the oldest Christian relic in the United Kingdom outside of the British Museum. I was very privileged to see it: however, as I was a clansman who had made the long trip *home*, he let me hold it.

The small, very dark piece of timber (St Molaug's *crook*), was worn smooth with the touch of thousands of hands over the years since 564 AD when St Molaug had his apocryphal race with St Columba for the beautiful little isle that sits jauntily in Loch Lynne, with one end facing Northern Ireland, and the other towards Ben Nevis. Saint Columba had to settle for the more famous Iona, further up the Highlands coast, but the jewel of the Highlands was the Isle of Lismore.

It was there with Bachuil,(the name given to the Baron's traditional home, as well as to his position as clan chief), that I learnt of the real reason why the Livingstone clan have been people of high ideals, underlying a John Livingstone signing the American Proclamation of Independence in 1776, as well as giving a supportive lineage to the young David Livingstone, great explorer and Christian missionary, who in his search for the source of the River Nile managed to end the East African slave trade and do the observations and calculations for the transit of Venus on behalf of the Astronomer Royal.

In my research of my personal lineage, I have come to believe that Doctor David Livingstone was a first cousin of my ancestor John, both being listed in census documents as being woollen weavers in Blantyre. They shared common grandparents, and common kinsmen. There is something very decent, very ordinary, and very noble about the highland Scots that I have always felt attuned to. Some people say that our genes carry an affinity to people of similar *wave-length*. If that's the case, then I have always felt right at home with raw Scots humour like Billy Connolly's.

My paternal Y-DNA, the way things work in genetics, is highly likely to be exactly the same Y-DNA as David Livingstone's, and he was a bit of a hard nut to crack himself. In my mind, the *God-fearing* Highlander ancestry goes a long way to explaining my survival to date. That is *fear* in the sense of awe-struck and humbled, not craven or cowed. I've never seen God, but I've often felt *His* vast and peaceful presence, and I'm getting used to the subtleties of how He communicates with me.

Sometimes when I experience little roadblocks in what I'm doing, I've learnt to think about what I'm being told. If I do something that I really shouldn't be doing, He just lets things frustrate me until I work out where I went off track. My brother Colin eventually worked out a correlation between how much his big golden retriever dog *Stan* played up on him, as a reflection of how much he was doing exactly the same thing to his own *Master*.

CHAPTER 38

A Sense of Purpose

Finding one's life purpose is a very popular term these days. I think it's because *Life Purpose* is an extremely important factor in enjoyment of a long, happy, productive life.

I marvel at memories of how happy my father was to just potter around in his hobby-room, or when reading his books in the lounge-room. Often he had a mug of black coffee with far too many sugars, and a large purring black cat on his lap, with classical music on in the background, while he pored over books that were usually about vintage machinery or historic engineering feats. He had spent eight years doing that after he retired from the British High Commission in Auckland, where he ran the accounting affairs of Pitcairn Island, Britain's smallest protectorate.

I've never seen anyone happier in his own space. I very much doubt whether Dad was self-absorbed enough to actively identify and pursue his life purpose, but he didn't need to. He just lived it. The blessing of his contentment and gentle nature on our family and friends *was* his life-purpose, as well as the happiness his many magazine articles and three published books engendered with readers in his areas of influence.

At his funeral, in 1988, I was astonished to hear from Marie and Claire Murphy (the mother and older sister of my late school-friend John Murphy) that Dad had built a model railway for the kids in the renal dialysis unit rooms at Auckland Hospital, and visited for half an hour every Friday night. John's younger and only brother Martin Murphy had chronic kidney failure, and it was only dialysis that kept him alive. Dad *saw a need* and quietly went about filling it in his unique way. That's a story I'd not heard of, and neither had my brother or mother; there may be many more, but he really was an extraordinarily kind and self-contained man.

How kind and considerate could a man get? If a spider or an insect fell into a bath, and was struggling with all its might to get out, Dad would go out of his way to fish it out and deliver it to the garden, simply because it was *having a go*. That behavior is something I've taken on too, and maybe it goes back many more generations before him.

I'm not at all like my father, but I marvel at him, and anyone else who can find true joy and contentment in simple activities, without fanfare or the need to be lauded or recognized.

Somewhere on life's journey I went from being a kid who was fascinated by art, archaeology and anthropology to a teenager who needed to beat everyone at everything, especially if it was physical. Testosterone could have been a major cause of this change in direction, but I relate it to having spent too many weeks as a boy in hospital wards. I didn't need to prove to myself that I was *clever*, but becoming as strong and fit as possible was very attractive, especially in sports-mad New Zealand.

The Assistant High Commissioner at the British High Commission in Auckland, Gordon Morris, who also had two sons at Sacred Heart College, told Dad that the *Leading Sportsman* prize was much better currency than *dux* at a boys' school. I'm not sure if that gelled with my Dad's thoughts, but he mentioned it to me in passing, and seemed quite chuffed about Gordon's comments.

When I understood more about how the world works, the self-absorption gave way to the pleasure of contributing to causes higher than my own; being a valued member of a family or *tribe*. The highest cause for my altruism is the long-term happiness and well-being of my wife and children, and by extension the well-being of my children's children, and so on, all of whom I'm planning to inspire or meet, and encourage, in my healthy, active future.

Among possibly hundreds of books devoted to *finding purpose*, apart from Victor Frankel's all-time classic *Man's Search for Meaning*, my favourite is *Life on Purpose: How Living for What Matters Most Changes Everything* by Victor Strecher.

Victor Strecher is the type of guy I'd love to have a beer with. He's a serious academic with a great sense of humour that is inescapable in his writing, and he's an ardent respecter of the spiritual or vitalistic health philosophies that are no longer politically correct in health research circles. Not only can he *talk the talk*, but he's *walked the walk*. A PhD research scientist, he's a professor at the University of Michigan's School of Public Health and its Director for Innovation and Social Entrepreneurship. He has peer-reviewed published research on *Purpose in Life* and its effects on healthy living and longevity.

Strecher's epiphany about life purpose occurred after losing his 19-year old daughter Julia to heart failure. Julia had endured several heart transplants since the age of two, and, knowing their time together was likely going to be short, it became Strecher's life purpose to give Julia a *big life*. They adventured everywhere together.

Julia died in her sleep while on a family holiday in the tropics, on a night when she had announced at a family dinner a few hours earlier "I'm so happy I feel I could die".

When Julia died, her father's life purpose died too.

The following paragraphs are excerpts from an interview with Strecher in Michigan University's online magazine *michigantoday.com*, by writer Julie Halpert.

'Three months after she passed away, he retreated, alone, to his Northern Michigan home. "I just didn't care about living at all," he says. "I'd lost my way."

'At 5 a.m. one morning, after seeing Julia in a dream, Strecher began kayaking, surrounded by nothing but water and the rising sun.

"I just started sobbing out there and I felt Julia come into me," he recalls. "She said, 'You've got to move forward, Dad.'" Later, he realized this occurred on Father's Day.

'At that moment, Strecher decided to help others find a purpose and meaning he finds lacking in a self-centered society that celebrates overconsumption and excessive vanity.

"I'm a scientist, so I made it a point to learn more about the process I was going through. I tried to become more resilient as a result of this traumatic event," Strecher says.

He spent six months reading books by philosophers. He pored over more than 200 scientific journals. There he found many compelling studies demonstrating that those living with a stronger purpose are better able to change unhealthy behaviors, allowing them to lead a higher quality existence.

Strecher's eyes light up, childlike wonder and enthusiasm brimming in his voice, as he discusses research he discovered that showed a link between having a purpose and reductions in risks for strokes and heart attacks. One study found that people with a strong purpose in life were 2.4 times less likely to get Alzheimer's disease in their later years.

…"Rather than anchoring for changing our motivation around death and disease, we should anchor it around a *purpose in life*," he says.'

There are several more fantastic researchers and authors making their presence felt who I'd love to share with you. As you'll find, I appreciate academics who've experienced raw life from outside their ivory towers the most; life experience is the philosophical conduit which brings theory into the *here and now*.

Perhaps the most interesting voice for me is that of *Professor Amy Cuddy*, a PhD researcher in social psychology whose own story is one of survival and breakthrough against massive, debilitating odds. If I was 30 years younger, I'd be sitting in one of her classes at Princeton.

Amy Cuddy suffered an appalling brain injury when she was a student at the University of Colorado. She was thrown, while asleep in a sleeping bag, through the windscreen of a car in an accident on the way home from a seminar on social psychology interstate, where she and her two co-attendees shared the driving home on a massive trip across several states.

Cuddy's brain must've been slammed hard in its cranium with massive impact; she suffered a *Diffuse Axonal Injury,* (DAI) which meant that many of the neurons in her brain had been stretched or sheared apart. After months of rehabilitation, she wanted to resume her graduate course, but her former level of functioning was greatly decreased. Her IQ dropped by 30 points, meaning that the Harvard PhD which had looked so imminent months before was now out of her reach.

Cuddy persisted for years, which is why I'm a big fan, gradually making herself whole again, honing her theories on the links between habitual postures and psychological outlooks. She gave the second most popular TED talk ever, with over 47,000,000 views, citing her research outcomes on *Power Posing,* with common postures like *hands on hips* being renamed *Wonder Woman.*

Cuddy suggested that our body language governs how we think and *feel* about ourselves, and thus, how we hold our bodies can have an impact on our minds. In other words, by commanding a powerful stance, we can make ourselves actually *feel* more powerful. The evidence of *power posing* came from a study that Cuddy completed while at Harvard University, where participants sat in either a high-power pose (expansive posture) or low-power pose (leaning inward, legs crossed) for two minutes. Cuddy found that those who sat in the high-power pose *felt more powerful* and *performed better* in mock interviews than those who had not.

With all the media buzz this generated came controversy, with some of Cuddy's claims about possible changes in hormonal expression being called into question, but a further paper published in March 2018 in *Psychological Science* seems to have put the question of the links between expansive postures and feelings of power to rest; expansive postures *do* make people *feel* more powerful. The postures are now referred to in the science as *postural feedback.*

Suggested reading: *Presence: Bringing Your Boldest Self to Your Biggest Challenges, by Amy Cuddy*

CHAPTER 39

Nutritional and Lifestyle Support for Brain Function

Current neuroscience research indicates that it is entirely possible to build new cortical mass through healthy lifestyle and nutritional choices rather than through drug therapies. Although I have been greatly helped by drug therapies in terms of seizure prevention, they come at a cost. It's safe to say there are no drugs without long-term side-effects, however *small*.

It's useful to look at the spate of *metabolic* illnesses such as diabetes, obesity, and dementia as having a common underlying cause.

To me, the brain is already running into trouble metabolically before it gets to the threshold where a diagnosable tumour presents itself. The mitochondria in the brain's neurones can get exposed to constantly high levels of blood glucose if we have a diet that's too high in carbohydrates, and because of this constant high presence of glucose, insulin floods the brain, much as it can in the muscular system of the body, causing what is now called *brain diabetes* or *diabetes type III*, or *early dementia*. The brain that has had to cope with metabolic or pre-diabetic syndromes is predisposed to accumulation of *AGE* by-products; very poorly metabolised, toffee-like *Advanced Glycation End-Products* that sit amongst the neuronal circuitry and glial structures in the brain.

I think it's certainly possible to protect my brain from seizures without taking anti-seizure drugs, long-term, however I'd like to heal my brain more fully for another year or so before going down that path. I currently have a new anti-seizure medication called *Keppra* (Leviteracetam) that replaces my previous medication that I was on for a decade: I was formerly on Dilantin (phenytoin) each day to prevent seizures, however long-term use of this drug can impair renal and liver function, and deplete stores of minerals and vitamins, as well as set one up for periodontal problems like gingivitis and receding gums. After ten years of excellent diet and weekly chiropractic care, none of these issues have surfaced in my case.

The low-carbohydrate, moderate protein, high-fat *ketogenic diet* has been used successfully for over 90 years with epileptics. A seizure needs a ready source of high-energy fuel to act itself out, and by limiting that fuel source (carbohydrate) markedly, the likelihood of a seizure occurring is lessened.

I effectively am a high-functioning epileptic now, after the scarring from the surgeries, the chemotherapy, and the intense radiation therapy.

Another non-drug alternative I've researched is the amino-acid *L-carnosine*, which has anti-seizure properties, and supplementing with coconut oil, which is showing huge promise in the treatment of neurodegenerative disorders like Parkinson's disease and Alzheimer's Disease, amongst others. The medium-chain triglycerides (MCTs) in coconut oil are rapidly processed by the liver into ketones, which are an alternative energy source for the brain, with 15% higher energy yield than glucose. Ketones can be described as *water-soluble fatty acids*, and ketone metabolism is very easy on the mitochondrial machinery.

In a recent assessment by a *neuropsychiatrist*, she was surprised by how high-functioning I still am on cognitive function tests, scoring 30/30 and 97% on two standard tests, better than most *normally healthy* people tested without my issues. She was surprised as the latest MRI studies confirmed that the cortical density in my parietal lobes was about 30% lower than expected for a man of my age. Perhaps some of the seizures I've had over the years *fried* my parietal neurons into cell-death.

That finding, plus the history of long-term medication, ionizing radiation, and chemotherapy indicate I am at a *significantly higher risk* than most to suffer dementia or neurodegenerative problems in the future. In out-living my prognosis, there's a new raft of *problems* to overcome in the near–future. Because so few people survive well, for long, there's little information around on coping with the long-term effects of the *treatment*.

Am I particularly worried? No. Obviously what's in the cortical mass that's still remaining is still humming along quite nicely, and is likely to be *very well-connected*, and *improving*, with all the specific dementia-prevention work I've been doing.

You don't need a lot of brain *mass* to perform complicated functions exquisitely. Look at what a peregrine falcon can do with a brain the size of a large pea; able to reach 240 km/hour in a dive, and capable of more complex avionics and motor coordination at breathtaking speeds than any other creature.

My aim is to rebuild cortical mass with evidence-based non-drug, lifestyle and nutritional strategies that I will share with you. Wouldn't that be exciting when I get re-examined at some stage and have been successful in increasing my cortical neuronal mass again? It's certainly possible.

The glial cells give metabolic support to the actual neurones of the brain. The tumour was made up of of these metabolic support cells, not the neurones that were being supported. If I could restore full health to the surrounding tissues, perhaps the diseased cells could be placed in a better position to heal.

The main idea is to make the brain structures around the tumour as healthy and well-nourished as possible; it's hard to imagine diseased cells continuing to be malnourished and dysfunctional, while resting in a matrix of well-nourished healthy glial cells.

CHAPTER 40

The Best Possible Diet for someone with a brain issue

1. Doesn't Over-excite the Brain's Neurones

Neurologist Russell Blaylock has written an excellent book, 'Excitotoxins, The Taste that Kills'- How Monosodium Glutamate, Aspartame (Nutrasweet), and similar substances can cause harm to the brain and nervous system, and their relationship to neurodegenerative diseases such as Alzheimer's, Lou Gehrig's Disease (ALS) and Others'.

Upon reading this, it is evident that we must avoid MSG and any of its similarly derived chemical analogues due to the very harmful excitotoxic effects like brain cell death that they can cause when taken in even tiny amounts.(In my opinion, if enough brain cells die at once, you'll usually have a seizure to announce it, but below a certain threshold, apart from feeling a bit 'hyped', you may not realise what damage is being done.)

According to chiropractic educator extraordinaire Dr Dan Murphy, the worst possible offering to fry your neurones is one of those packets of instant noodles or instant soups that are so popular with those who rush their food. Close on the heels of the noodles are a huge array of supermarket bakery products. There are more three-digit numbers on the ingredients lists than actual fresh whole-food ingredients. If in doubt, search the many online sources of information about excitotoxins or glutamates in your food.
In Other Words–Just Eat Fresh Food!

2. Calms the brain

Magnesium calms the brain. There is much evidence that magnesium supplementation is neuro-protective in cases of brain trauma and depression. Case studies of supplementation with 125-300mg magnesium glycinate or magnesium taurinate, for instance, cleared major depression within 7 days in a 2006 study.

Omega-3 fatty acids calm the brain. Fatty Acids such as docosahexanoic acid (DHA), obtained most preferably from Krill Oil supplements, have important structural and functional roles in the brain, with established clinical benefits for supporting brain development and cognitive function throughout life. Consistent with these critical roles of DHA in the brain, accumulating evidence suggests that DHA may act as a promising recovery aid, or possibly as a prophylactic nutritional measure, for Mild Traumatic Brain Injury (mTBI).

3. Keeps Brain Energy High without raising blood sugar

The application of ketogenic dietary principles (keeping carbohydrate intake as low as possible, and relying on higher-fat foods like cheeses to provide energy) will ensure that the brain's energy levels are maintained with a 15% higher energy production by the mitochondria with energy sourced from ketone metabolism being superior to that of glucose metabolism. There is less oxidative damage to the brain neurones' mitochondria from ketone metabolism, as opposed to glucose.

To achieve this ketogenic state, you keep your intake of carbohydrate as low as you can, while you are free to enjoy as much higher-fat food as you like. (I will often eat small slabs of cream cheese during the day to maintain good brain energy, or I'll have a tablespoon of coconut oil. Often, I'm not truly hungry till about 3pm if I've been eating ketogenically)

4. Avoids Refined Carbohydrates

Refined Carbohydrates like white rice or white flour tend to raise blood glucose levels quickly, invoking an insulin response in the body as well as the BRAIN. Raised blood glucose in the brain tends to accelerate the formation of 'AGEs' (Advanced Glycation End-Products).

Under the microscope at an autopsy, these 'AGEs' are clumps of sticky toffee-like substances: an end-result of what is now being described as *Diabetes Type III* from too much glucose! Refined carbohydrates will elevate your triglyceride levels and get deposited as body fat, whereas fats will just get metabolised as the fatty acids they are and will power you around all day.

5. Maintains High Levels of Coloured Vegetables

The coloured vegetables, especially the brassicas like Broccoli, Brussels sprouts, and Cauliflower, are high in glucosinolates, which have anticarcinogenic properties. The green leafy vegetables like spinach and kale have high levels of magnesium and chlorophyll; when lightly simmered in something like butter, high in butyric acid and saturated fats, these vegetables' fat-soluble nutrients like vitamins A, K, D and E become far more bio-available. Butter also has the miraculous ability to make even a Brussels Sprout taste 'yummy'.

All the orange and red vegetables will have varying amounts of the many hundreds of carotenoids, which have anti-oxidant and neuro-protective properties related to their provitamin A content.

If you can obtain traditional yellow, red, or orange sauces or spices from a wholefood market, they're usually tasty condiments that are loaded with brain-protecting nutrients. Ideally, you'd live next to an Indian restaurant and order a different type of orange, yellow, or red spice-based sauce each day to go with brain-maker vegetables simmered in coconut oil or butter.

6. *Maintains a Healthy Microbiome.*

One of the new breed of nutrition-conscious neurologists worth reading is Dr David Perlmutter, the neurologist who wrote 'Brain Maker'-The Power of Gut Microbes to Heal and Protect Your Brain-for Life'.

Dr Perlmutter advocates a diet high in the probiotic foods like cultured yoghurts and sour creams, as well as prebiotic foods high in largely indigestible plant fibres (or 'roughage') which enable healthy bacterial colonization of the gut.

He is particulary keen on fermented foods in the diet, and there appear to be many types of fermented foods from many different cultures that will enable a healthy microbiome. From fermented fish to fermented eggs, these days there's a vast variety of fermented foods that you can buy at a wholefoods store, or even your more enlightened supermarket. You can brew your own if you've a spare cellar.

There's impressive research that has been done in Australia by gastroenterologist Professor Thomas Borody of the Centre for Digestive Diseases, in Sydney, that has clearly demonstrated the ability of a *new, healthy microbiome* to heal chronic bowel diseases that till recently have defied most interventions. The process can be breathtakingly simple, relying on the microbiome's own inherent ability to balance itself out and kill off harmful bowel pathogens, when a transfusion (or *transpoosion*) of a healthy bowel microbiome is undertaken from a healthy donor. Even the notoriously persistent antibiotic-resistant pathogen *clostridium difficile* can be brought under control in a matter of weeks, apparently, when the healthy introduced bacteria start proliferating very quickly.

It doesn't really matter if you can't have every type of fermented food from *a to z*; what's important is being consistent with your intake. I enjoy several glasses of a fermented Indonesian tea drink called *kombucha*; my favourite kombucha base is fermented from tea, with a ginger and turmeric base. If the drink is a bit cloudy, you will find it's well-fermented and full of carbon dioxide, which gives it its *spritz* or *fizz*.

One thing I like about Perlmutter's book is that he's uncovered some good evidence for benefits from drinking coffee. He cites a Finnish study published recently in the Journal of Alzheimer's Disease, which found that older people who'd drunk 3 to 5 cups of coffee a day (a *moderate* intake) in midlife showed an incredible 65% decreased risk of developing Alzheimer's compared to low-intake coffee drinkers. There were not enough people in the sample to make statistical claims about higher intakes of coffee, except that there were still benefits from higher than moderate intakes of coffee that were apparent.

7. Maintains a Healthy Omega 3:Omega 6 Fatty Acid Ratio

Ideally, the ratio of these two types of fats should be 1:1. That ratio is what our paleolithic ancestors' diets are estimated to have hovered around. We should avoid many of the cheap seed-based cooking oils that are high in omega 6 fats, as explored elsewhere in this book. The worst source of omega-6 oils will unfortunately be those your fish and chips usually get cooked in; those oils are often re-heated several times over, ensuring that they become rancid and oxidised, and dangerous to your neurology, in short order. It's best to bake your own chips in an oven, with perhaps a light coating of coconut oil for flavour. The saturated fat in the coconut oil is ideal to intensify the flavour of whatever it is cooked with, and will release fat-soluble nutrients in the meal.

In Summary:

Keith's Brain-Protecting Diet is an Inclusive, Nutrient-Dense, Traditional Foods Diet which is Delicious AND Evidence-Based.

I eat as many green, orange, or red vegetables as I like, and because they're so nutrient-dense and so low on calories, I have no worries about putting on excess weight. The indigestible plant fibres in my butter-simmered greens provide an ideal *prebiotic* base for my *probiotic* bacteria (sourced from yoghurt, kombucha, or sour cream) to breed up in. Virtually every day for the last ten years I've eaten a *brunch* of two or three lightly poached eggs on toasted heavily buttered sourdough bread*, with smashed avocado and feta cheese, with a sprinkling of pink Himalayan salt (very high in trace elements) or Celtic sea salt (also high in trace elements, but not as pretty.)

*(Sourdough bread is a fermented *wild yeast* bread in which most of the gluten proteins in normal wheat flours are broken down enzymatically. The yeast spores are airborne, and the flour dough is seeded with yeasts naturally by being left in an open container outside. The yeast *mother* is very valuable, and can last for many years)

Now and again, I might vary the theme with a slice of broccoli that's been lightly glazed in butter, or add some mushrooms in butter.

My egg and avocado brunch is made perfect if I have some butter-sizzled plain bacon, without nitrites, as well as a strong flat white coffee as per the Finnish coffee research findings discussed by Dr Perlmutter.

If I have a cross code clue book puzzle to work on, my morning is made even more perfect if I can complete a difficult puzzle, starting with only one clue, during the course of a still-hot cup of coffee. This serves as a sort of a test for how rested my brain is.

Before: beautiful full cup of coffee: untouched single-clue *cross code* puzzle

CHAPTER 41

The Best Exercise For Your Brain

Is Exercise. Huff n' Puff Physical Exercise

There are some very simple activities and nutritional habits that are proven to build new neurons and neuronal connections in the brain. These activities and habits can promote the release of *brain-derived neurotrophic factor, (BDNF)* which stimulates new neuronal growth in the brain in people of any age.

1. Regular exercise of any kind, including resistance training with weights, can promote BDNF in the body, as does

2. Reducing calorie intake, with periodic fasting every few days

3. Avoiding sugar, as it is heavily implicated in neuro-degenerative processes across the board. Sugar ingestion results in increased accumulation of toffee-like AGE (Advanced glycation end-product) substances within brain tissue. Metabolically, these AGE substances function just like toffee; they are sticky and gummy, and slow brain metabolism immensely.

4. Getting out <u>into</u> the sun, not out of the sun! A few minutes of exposure to the sun results in the natural production of vitamin D3 by the skin, which is actually best-absorbed by not washing it off. So if you get out into the sun and your skin breaks a sweat, don't shower immediately; let your skin reabsorb the vitamin D3 it has produced.

5. Having turmeric-rich foods like curries (the active ingredient in turmeric is curcumin). It's thought that curcumin may increase BDNF production in the hippocampus especially among those with brain injuries.
*I love having *turmeric lattes*; these can be bought in powder sachet mixes from most good wholefood outlets, and are often enhanced with coconut milk powder and stevia for sweetening. Turmeric powder is incredibly cheap for its benefits; it acts as an antioxidant and an anti-inflammatory once inside your body, as well as its scientifically proven brain-building payback!

6. Drinking Green Tea – When researchers were looking at the effects of green tea they trialed it on people with neurodegenerative diseases. These individuals typically have low levels of BDNF. Remarkably they found an increase in BDNF levels after drinking green tea. This is significant, as extremely low levels of the polyphenols were believed to reach the brain after drinking green tea.

CHAPTER 42

My Lifestyle Routine

It is extremely important that I always get a good night's sleep. Most of the time, I try to get up with the rest of the household around 7:30 am, and be in bed by about 10:00 pm. It doesn't always work out this way, but most of the time I get ample sleep for my needs.

During the morning and afternoon I usually put in a few hours writing or editing at the computer, if I'm not doing rehabilitation exercises at our local hospital or the gym.

Every day I will try to get in an ideal meal for my brain health, before 2pm; this often includes poached or scrambled eggs on sourdough toast with lots of butter, with smashed avocado or a salad as a side. Because I eat ketogenically, and don't rely on blood sugar from carbohydrates for my satiety, I often don't feel true hunger for hours into the day. To stave off the need for quick-energy carbohydrate snacks I will often eat small slabs of cream cheese every few hours. A good strong coffee always goes down well at some stage of the morning. Some people following ketogenic principles put a spoon of butter in their morning coffee. I try to get a couple of tablespoons of coconut oil down the hatch most days, just for the beneficial effect of the ketones on my brain function. Coconut oil can be mixed in with any salad too.

During an ideal day I will do some form of brain training or balance training; the brain training will often involve a crossword, or online games with a brain training site like lumosity. com. The balance training is just an intense short stimulus to get the best response; sometimes standing on a *bosu* ball while I try to trace set patterns on a wall-chart with a small laser headlight. I never spend more than 5 minutes in a row on the balance, as I've found that it's quite easy for me to overdo things there. Daily spurts of *maintenance* for a few minutes seem to keep me where I need to be.

Every night, after I've completed most of my writing for the day, I go for a short and very hilly walk of up to 5 kilometres, often with the resident hound and a son. Lately, as it's wintry and wet, we just do a short hilly loop, with the hills giving me enough *work* to maintain my basic health. As the days get longer and my health returns to its best, I'll reintroduce the mountain bike, and daily gym sessions.

The main purpose of my evening walk is to exercise *and* give thanks at the same time. I feel these *ritual walks* are pivotal for me. I never fail to give thanks for my health during these walks, and I pray silently if I have company. My favourite bushland circuit near my house takes about 30 minutes to amble around, and has lots of short steep hills.

The circuit at one stages circles around a large fenced paddock which has a large dam in the middle, and sits below a small hill, so I make it resemble parts of the Twenty-third psalm, which I *always* recite from heart.

The Twenty-third psalm is one I find very comforting, so I start to recite that sacred ancient scripture at the start of about 300 metres of walking *through the valley of the shadow of death,* which is in reality quite a pretty glade of native bushland in the lee of the hillside that eventually opens up to the scene below.

The Twenty-third Psalm goes as follows

The Lord is my shepherd; I shall not want. He makes me lie down in green pastures.
He leads me beside still waters.
He restores my soul.
He leads me in paths of righteousness for his name's sake.

STARING DOWN THE BEAST

Even though I walk through the valley of the shadow of death,
I will fear no evil,
for you are with me;
your rod and your staff,
they comfort me.

You prepare a table before me
in the presence of my enemies;
you anoint my head with oil;
my cup overflows.
Surely goodness and mercy shall follow me
all the days of my life,
and I shall dwell in the house of the Lord forever.

My Daily *Ritual Walk*

Depending on the season, the scenery is either dry or very green, so I use my imagination to act out the scripture as I walk around that part of the circuit. If it's summer, as it was when the previous picture was taken, you'll see that there is still sufficient water in the dam to describe it as *still water*, but I have to imagine the pasture is green. You will even be able to see a few sheep under the trees to remind you of the Good Shepherd. Sometimes there are kangaroos in there as well as sheep, but I don't think it affects the power of the ritual.

Walking on my circuit with Henry a couple of summers ago. This is on an imaginary path of righteousness just before the large paddock with the still water and sheep. Henry is now my height, at only 14!

CHAPTER 43

More On Mental and Physical Exercise Increasing Brain Density

Deliberate Practice

Prolonged periods of concentration, bordering on frustration, while trying to master a particular skill can be called *deliberate practice,* a term coined by neuroscientist Anders Erricson.

In essence, the more hours at the task, the higher the likelihood of achieving *mastery,* which eventually results in such a rapid flow of information along just a few select neuronal circuits that they are stimulated to *myelinate. Myelin* is the white cholesterol-based substance that can *insulate* the neurons on *very high traffic* pathways to speed up information transfer by a huge amount, much as plastic around a wire is used in electrical cabling.

The *ten-thousand-hour rule* coined by writer Daniel Coyle in his great book *The Talent Code* is a rough approximation of Erricson's research outcomes.

Blogger Coert Visser says it succinctly:

"Anders Ericsson's body of work has demonstrated through research that building top expertise is more than a matter of raw talent: it is a matter of long and repeated deliberate practice."

Deliberate practice is an *effortful activity* designed to improve individual target performance and it consists of the following four elements:

1) It's designed specifically to improve performance,
2) It is repeated a lot,
3) Feedback on results is continuously available,
4) It's highly demanding mentally, and not necessarily particularly enjoyable because it means you are focusing on improving areas in your performance that are not satisfactory. Thus, *it stretches you.*

One very well-known thinker seemed to have employed Deep Practice habits: Albert Einstein apparently maintained that it was his ability to simply stick with a problem longer than most people that enabled him to solve complex problems.

If you're able to undertake deliberate practice, you'll benefit by becoming better, especially if you're able to keep it up for extremely long periods of time. Top performance in a wide array of fields is always based on an extreme amount of deliberate practice. Researchers estimate that a minimum of 10,000 hours is required to take a person from an average level to an elite level. This equates to 40 hours a week for 5 years.

Recommendations: To build a Healthy New Brain– Exercise the Brain Like a Muscle

Structure periods of *deliberate practice* into your daily life. I will often do *Code word* (or *Cross Code*) puzzles, where one has to piece together complete words assigned by specific series of numbers, starting with one to three of the 26 letters in the Alphabet.

These puzzles involve a lot of tenacity, and often quite a lot of heavy correction and changes, to get them out. However, when done several times a day, one reaches a level where it's possible to complete a whole puzzle during the duration of drinking a cup of freshly brewed coffee– maybe 5 minutes– with ease. I have comparisons of *tired brain* and *fresh brain* outcomes, where a fresh brain has very little correction, and a *tired brain* has had numerous corrections and over-writing to get the answers out.

On a *tired brain* attempt, where nothing appears obvious after several minutes, I may resort to a *peek* at the correct puzzle answer––just one completed word usually––and then proceed from that to solve the complete puzzle. If I have *peeked* in the attempt, I give myself one tick. If I have flown through the whole puzzle without resorting to peeking at any clues, I give myself two ticks. If I can do that on a one-letter *code word*, I know my brain is in good shape in that department.

I attempt to grind out every puzzle, no matter how long it takes, as I feel it is this intense thought that achieves the *ignition* of myelin sheath formation referred to by Daniel Coyle.

In fact, prolonged attempts to master any new mental or physical activity can be successful in *re-mapping* the injured brain with new neurons.

Another fun and *addictive* hobby that can measurably increase performances in several types of *intelligence* is online brain-training. I was lucky to be directed straight to one of the original online neuroscience-based brain training sites, *lumosity.com* early after my first collapse in 2007, by Dr Steven Sexton, a chiropractor with a PhD in neuroscience.

The *lumosity* brain-training approach is through a series of games and puzzles, where an algorithm behind the games assesses one's achieved outcome relative to a massive and ever-growing database.

When I first started on *lumosity* I felt that I was initially reacting during games like *greased lightning*, however the overall BPI (Brain Performance Index) scores were woeful—at kindergarten level—when compared with scores achieved within a few months. The games move one along imperceptibly to continually higher levels of performance, without really realizing one's subtle improvements because it's all done in a fun and challenging environment.

A performance index of 1000 in each of the mental areas of *Speed, Memory, Attention, Flexibility,* and *Problem Solving* is regarded as being a good achievable result for most participants in the statistical bell curve with due training.

I cannot presently access my initial BPI score from August 2007, but across these domains of intelligence, when I thought I was doing very well, the truth was a woeful BPI score of 367, from memory. That was way less than half of a good score for the population median on the site, due to all the swelling and inflammation and trauma. The score started to climb very quickly, finding me spending several hours a day in total mastering the games, with short walk breaks around the park in between sessions. That first progress graph looked like the ascent of an escalator till I finally cracked the 1000 BPI, with an overall score of 1050, sometime in 2008.

Despite my injured brain having been very challenged early on, the overall BPI increased with a period of many more hours of constant *deep practice* several years ago, to 1424, nearly four times the initially achieved level. That was in the top percentile for my age group.

Like physical fitness training, it's best to train harder and longer when the brain is well-rested, and the similarities don't end there. As with physical fitness training, the amount of work required to maintain a high achieved BPI is far less than the amount required to gradually get there. A bit of practice here and there every few weeks can maintain the BPI at a high enough level to be more than adequate for any of the normal challenges of a normal life.

Kangaroo brain or Clydesdale Brain?

A kangaroo can hop anywhere it cares to go, clearing unbelievable obstacles, bounding over large areas of fenced paddocks, and taking it all in, in a fraction of the time a big, blinkered, steady Clydesdale draught horse could walk the length of its paddock. A *Clydesdale brain* is fantastically adapted for accepting and applying conventional wisdom, without the benefit of seeing outside the blinkers. A *kangaroo brain* is what I have. It's unfortunately not the type of brain that leads to academic achievement in a conventional setting, because it is continually analyzing and thinking things through from other perspectives. In a black and white *right / wrong* academic scenario, that doesn't help at all.

After a good year or so without any online brain training, I trained intermittently for several weeks early last year (2017) and achieved a score of 1301; still nearly four times better than my initial untrained brain performance, and better than most people's using the site. In fact, my individual scores in the domains of *flexibility* and *problem solving* are in the top percentiles of the whole database, more than competitive with brain trainers in any age-group. This acquired skill could be the current re-firing of a *kangaroo-brain* neurology shaped by the early stimulus of a fascinating childhood with loving, creative parents, as opposed to a blinkered Clydesdale upbringing in one sheltered environment.

A lady neuropsychiatrist was very puzzled recently as to how I was able to score 30/30 and 97/100 on cognition tests, when my brain scans indicated a loss of bilateral parietal lobe density of 30% compared to men in my age-group. She asked "Have you had a very high level of education?" I said "I suppose so," in response, but really I think my very early upbringing did most of the initial wiring for my kangaroo brain. Obviously, there's far more to brain function than mere cortical density. *Connectivity* of the neurons matters most. There are cases in the literature of people functioning well with half a brain, or even a brain turned to gel, in the case of an air force test-pilot who experienced huge g-forces and survived, fully functionally, neurologically.

CHAPTER 44

Feeding the Brain

Current neuroscience nutritional research shows that there's *no drug* that is as effective as several common spices and herbs, a readily available cooking oil, and basic healthy lifestyle approaches, to establish new neuronal mass. Thank goodness! About time!

There is every sign that many currently promoted medical paradigms are seriously questionable and unviable for brain health, such as the lemming-like fad to put older people on cholesterol-lowering drugs, despite the *lipid hypothesis* having been fully debunked for many years now. There is *no evidence* that lowering cholesterol promotes good health outcomes in older age. In fact, the opposite has been proven time and again; older people with higher levels of cholesterol live longer and have better cognitive function than those whose cholesterol levels have been lowered artificially.

In fact, low cholesterol levels in the elderly are associated with a higher morbidity, or higher chance of death. Dr. Harlan Krumholz of the Department of Cardiovascular Medicine at Yale University, reported in 1994 that old people with low cholesterol died twice as often from a heart attack as did old people with a high cholesterol.[1]

There is even good evidence that high blood cholesterol levels protect against bacterial infection.[2]

"To be more specific, most studies of old people have shown that high cholesterol is not a risk factor for coronary heart disease. This was the result of my search in the Medline database for studies addressing that question" says cardiology researcher and writer Uffe Ravnskov, MD, PhD.[2]

1). Krumholz, H.M. et.al. "Lack of association between cholesterol andcoronary heart disease mortality and morbidity and all-cause mortality in persons older than 70 years." Journal of the American Medical Association272,1335-1340,1990.

(2) Ravnskov, U. "High cholesterol may protect against infections and atherosclerosis." Quarterly Journal of Medicine 96,927-934,2003.

There are Oils... and then there are Other Oils

Omega 3 oils and Omega 6 oils are both necessary for human health. They should IDEALLY be ingested in even quantities, or a ratio of 1:1. Omega 6 oils help mediate the immune response. However, if the ratio of omega 6 oils to omega 3 oils increases a great deal past the 'IDEAL' 1:1 ratio, there is an inflammatory cascade in the body that is thought to predispose to many of the degenerative diseases and cancers that the Western World suffers from.

Ischaemic heart disease was virtually unknown until earlier last century when American-grown vegetable and seed oils high in omega-6 fatty acids flooded the markets, after the traditional supply of coconut oil and palm oil from the Western Pacific and South East Asia was disrupted by the Japanese during World War Two. Some oils were hydrogenated to create margarine. Margarine's biologically useless trans-fats and omega 6 oils compete with essential omega 3 fatty acids for receptor sites in our brain and nervous system, and can muck things right up hormonally and in the expression of gene pathways in cells. These are the nasty fats in your favourite packet of salt and vinegar potato crisps, unfortunately, or in your battered fish with chips. If I ever munch on some, (they are unfortunately *very* tasty!) I immediately dose up on fish oil capsules, high in omega-3 fatty acids, to redress the ratio.

CHAPTER 45

The Heuristic Theory of Everything

At a seminar in Melbourne in 2016, Dr Dan Murphy, a brilliant chiropractic research presenter, and a popular professor at Life Chiropractic College West in San Francisco, outlined his method of keeping the wholism of good nutrition at the forefront with his undergraduate students, with what he termed his *Heuristic Theory of Everything* teaching method. (*heuristic | adjective: enabling a person to discover or learn something for themselves: a *hands-on* or *interactive heuristic approach to learning.*)

Instead of talking about these nutritional theories, he gets his students to assay changes in their lipid profiles with pin-prick sampling of their blood every couple of weeks, over several months. They experience for themselves how different ratios of omega 3 to omega 6 fats affect their health and energy status, and by gradually implementing strategies to normalize those levels, they *live* the lesson.

The SAD Diet

The *Standard American Diet* and its copycat, the *Standard Australian Diet*, are way out of control as far as the ideal ratios for good health are concerned. Dr Murphy expressed his shock that in the cohort of health-conscious undergraduate health practitioners he was teaching, one female participant's levels had blown out to as much as 1:70, and several more students were at the levels that are typical of many modern Americans; around 1:15 to 1:30! Dr Murphy mentioned that most of the cohort *appeared* to be fit and healthy, even if their ratios vastly exceeded the *healthy* range.

Who would know what *irreversible* processes had been started, especially in the girl who had the 1:70 ratio?

Finding how otherwise *normal* American kids could have such terrible levels of omega 6 in their bodies is not hard; *vegetable oils* are in virtually every packaged food product.

Often, they're not even oils sourced from *vegetables*, but processed from *seeds* that would otherwise be *left-overs* after processing in commercial food production. Why chuck something out when you can make a profit from it? Unfortunately, these oils are often heated and reheated to levels of rancidity in fast food outlets.

Elevated levels of vegetable oil omega 6 fats in the body cause an elevated inflammatory response, and current scientific thinking implicates *inflammation* as a root cause of many degenerative conditions.

I find it useful to picture the two necessary types of essential fatty acids, omega 3 and omega 6, as entering two parallel and inter-related metabolic cycles, each with its own desirable outcome. If there is an imbalance in the *desired* 1:1 ratio, (mostly with an excess of omega 6 fatty acids due to the prevalence of vegetable and seed oils in the SAD diet) then more and more omega 6 will pile into the omega 3 cycle, reducing the metabolic benefits in proportion to the omega 3: omega 6 ratio, and increasing the inflammatory cascade similarly, in inverse proportion.

C-REACTIVE PROTEIN

Is an enzyme produced by the liver in the presence of acute inflammation that can occur anywhere in the body, however it is also highly correlated with risk of atherosclerotic heart disease. It is a good idea to keep your levels of C-reactive protein down as far as possible. The most accurate test for C-reactive protein levels is the HS-CRP test (High sensitivity C-Reactive Protein test).

CHAPTER 46

Keep those Cholesterol Levels Up

Some of what I'll share here could be quite alarming, but it's very well backed-up by recent research. In my personal research of the *cholesterol myths* over the years, I'm at the stage now where I don't worry one iota about cholesterol; what I do try to control is lifestyle stress and inflammation or oxidation of fatty acids in the body. Inflammatory hot-beds in the lining of arteries tend to oxidize circulating lipids into calcific atherogenic plaques. Elevated saturated fat intake has *not* been demonstrated to have an association with heart disease, despite every attempt by major vested-interest groups to demonize what was always part of a healthy diet until the 1950s.

What if the total cholesterol in my bloodstream is a bit higher than currently suggested good levels for health? That's fine, my brain absolutely needs it to function at 100%. Every cell membrane in the body incorporates cholesterol, including the brain.

In my extended family, we witnessed first-hand the harmful effects of cholesterol-lowering medication on my wife's mother, *Lalli*, who was turned from a healthy, active woman in her early 70s, who exercised in dance classes with her friends several times a week, to someone so weak she could not climb the steps in her pantry or even hold her hair-dryer up for more than a minute or so. As a very healthy and high-functioning post-polio survivor, she should never have been placed on cholesterol-lowering medication, however, for some reason she was seen by a lady doctor who routinely prescribed her a statin drug, *Lipitor*.

When *Lalli* started to feel unwell and *out of sorts* on her medication, she advised her doctor, whose response was "Oh! Well if you don't lower your cholesterol, you won't live very long then!"

It took many months of supplementation with Coenzyme Q10, the mitochondrial enzyme that statin drugs are notorious for depleting, and chiropractic adjustments to re-stimulate her central nervous system, to get *Lalli* back on track.

What about the *clogging of arteries* in the heart? Yes... what about that emotively-termed myth? Ingestion of saturated fats such as those found in organic butter and grass-fed beef *normalizes* blood lipid profiles to healthy levels; saturated fats *haven't* been proven to raise risk of heart disease at all.

Eating simple carbohydrates and grain cereals, however, *will* create the inflammation necessary to drive up low density lipids and the formation of atherosclerotic plaques in coronary arteries, *not* eating fats! Stay off grain cereals and *white anything* (rice/ bread/ sugar) and your inflammatory load will lighten straight away.

Getting off simple carbohydrates and elevating your omega 3 fish oil intake will lower your triglyceride levels nicely. To raise your HDL (High Density Lipid) to desired levels you need to exercise steadily on several days a week, for periods of at least 30 minutes. Walking *ticks the box* there nicely– preferably in a park or bushland setting, getting in contact with nature.

If you can also walk barefoot for half an hour or so, that could be very good, as there is a new body of research into the positive effects of *grounding* or *earthing* the body with the constant electron-rich surface of our planet. You literally *plug into* the biggest source of antioxidant electrons available. Direct contact with the earth's field of electrons can explain why we usually feel so enervated after walking on the beach and diving into the surf. By the seaside, you are benefitting from masses of *negative ions* generated by the action of the wind on the surf, and by diving into the surf, one is literally immersed in a *sea of electrons*. A similar effect is reported near waterfalls and running rivers.

Earthing mats that hook into the *earth* wires of normal homes have been available online for several years. It is possible to sleep overnight with one's bare feet resting on cotton pads with highly conductive micro-thin silver strands woven in. Because no other current is involved, it is totally safe. The same effect could be obtained by connecting any type of conductive foil to a wire that is attached to a tent peg in the garden. (No! Not a plastic tent-peg!).

You could simply sit with bare feet on your back lawn for half an hour to receive the suggested benefits, while getting a bit of sun on your arms and legs; the surest way to stimulate your body's own production of vitamin D3.

CHAPTER 47

When Is a Vitamin No Longer just a Vitamin?

Vitamin D3 is a cholesterol-based steroid hormone that until recent years was relegated to the sidelines as a vitamin involved in the normal clotting of blood, and in the prevention of the bone-softening disease, rickets. However, in the last two decades much research has come to the fore that suggests that vitamin D deficiency is extremely common, even in active people who spend a lot of time outdoors.

I considerably annoyed my naturopath early on with my *little issue* when I queried why I needed to have my blood levels of vitamin D tested when I was outside in the sun on a mountain bike most days. It turned out that she knew far more than me about the subject, and in the 20 years since I had studied clinical nutrition, vitamin D had been moved to the front of the queue in terms of *importance*, and was now described as a valid steroid hormone. It had acquired a dirty big US Government-funded Not-for-Profit Group, the *Vitamin D Council*, such was its rapid elevation.

Guess which vital substance is depleted by the anti-seizure medication I had been on for a decade, before it was changed to a much-better medication, this year? Phenytoin, or *Dilantin*, induces deficiency in calcium, and vitamin B12, as well as vitamin D. For the last thirty years I have usually eaten several free-range eggs a day, lots of baked or roasted coloured vegetables, lots of cheese, and lots of fresh green salads.

Fresh lightly-braised salmon is a favourite, along with mashed avocado, feta cheese, and broccoli. Himalayan rock salt, loaded with over 80 trace minerals, is superb on eggs, along with black pepper. Eggs are rich in Vitamin D, and are good sources of Vitamin B12, Omega-3 fatty acids, calcium, and zinc, as well as other vitamins, minerals, and carotenoids (precursors of vitamin A). The egg is a powerhouse of disease-fighting nutrients like lutein and zeaxanthin as well.

While vitamin K1 is preferentially used by the liver to activate blood clotting proteins, vitamin K2 is preferentially used by other tissues to *deposit calcium* in *appropriate* locations, such as in the bones and teeth, and *prevent* it from depositing in locations where it does not belong, such as in the soft tissues and arterial walls.

Fresh dark leafy green salad leaves are a rich source of vitamin K1. These are also sources of phytic acid, which actively inhibits absorption of minerals like iron and magnesium, so it's best to break down the phytates by cooking or simmering on a low heat. To access the fat-soluble vitamins, which include vitamins A, K, D, and E, it is best to cook with a healthy source of saturated fat like *grass-fed* butter or cold-pressed olive or coconut oil. Amongst the dark leafy green vegetables, the one with the highest source of vitamin K1 is *kale,* a form of spinach.

The richest sources of vitamin K2 are in goose liver pâté or traditionally fermented cheeses. The delicatessen or whole food store is the best place to source your vitamin K2 naturally. Since researching this, my opinion of people who regularly fare on pâté and cheese has increased hugely. At one time years ago, a potential girlfriend was wooed away by a suitor who invited her to have some pâté at a café, earning himself the jealous moniker 'Pâté' from me. He not only got the girl, but he probably has great bone structure and cardiac health now, too.

CHAPTER 48

Getting off the Anti-Seizure Drugs with Nutrients

Unfortunately, I am currently on these drugs to prevent seizures with *100% certainty*. I hate the idea of being on any drugs, and my aim eventually is to reach healthy, fully-functional advanced age without being on any medications whatsoever. To ensure this, I have to make sure that I don't have any more major seizures, as well. This is entirely possible if I remove myself from stressful situations and stick to the proven drug regime for now. It's a matter of submerging my ambition to be totally drug-free for a few more years, while at the same time propping up my neurological health with an abundance of neuro-supportive nutrient-dense foods and minerals.

I definitely never have seizures if I eat and sleep well, go for my daily walks, and take my anti-seizure medication every morning and evening. However, I have found myself hours from home, having forgotten my medication on several occasions, with no access to my prescription, and I got around OK for a few days on large amounts of fish oil and magnesium supplementation from the supermarket, with no sign of a seizure. This is promising.

With another year totally free from seizures and their neuro-excitatory damage, while I build up my neuronal mass with the nutritional and lifestyle strategies I described earlier in this chapter, I believe it's possible to slowly wean myself off anti-seizure medication and replace it with omega-3 fish oil, magnesium, coconut oil, and the amino-acid L-carnosine. These have all shown to be neuro-protective and seizure-preventive to varying extents.

I read recently that if one limits one's carbohydrate intake per day to 25gms or less, then the blood glucose levels will be far too low to fire a seizure. *Even though blood glucose levels will be on the lower side, overall brain energy and mitochondrial energy output can still be maintained at a high level with ketone bodies.* When the body has adapted to fats and is manufacturing sufficient ketones, this is known as *ketosis*, or the *ketogenic state*.

A great way to raise your beneficial HDL levels is to use coconut oil regularly as a condiment. Coconut oil is anti-inflammatory by nature, and is rich in lauric acid, a medium-chain triglyceride fatty acid (MCT) that is particularly amenable to human metabolism. MCTs get rapidly metabolized by the liver into water-soluble variants of fatty acids called ketones which as well as giving richer energy yields than glucose, have the benefits of far less free radical formation within the *energy furnace* cells of the body, the mitochondria.

If one induces ketosis with the ketogenic low carbohydrate/higher fat diet, then the brain can still get its energy requirements from the ketones, once the system has become fat-adapted. If you're still in the process of getting fat-adapted, ketone production will be sluggish and intermittent. Getting fat-adapted with your diet takes about three weeks, whereby one gradually introduces higher-fat foods while progressively limiting carbohydrates.

Ketosis is not to be confused with *keto-acidosis*, which is a symptom of diabetes and renal failure, where the breath smells of acetone. Medical doctors, who don't study nutrition, may confuse ketosis with *keto-acidosis*, which could explain why healthy fat-adapted eating is seen as a fad.

During the fat-adaptation phase, while you are aiming to be in ketosis, you can supplement with coconut oil, which will ensure a good level of ketones is available for brain energy.100ml of coconut oil, or a couple of tablespoons that can be spread over a salad or mixed in with your meal, will do the job. If you haven't had much coconut oil before, you may find that it is an excellent laxative; just a warning before you put on your tight-waisted white bell-bottomed stretch-polyester trousers for a night at the disco.

I don't envisage a calcium or vitamin D3 deficiency, or a K2 deficiency from the years of anti-seizure medication I have had already, as I eat such large amounts of all the right foods.

With neurodegenerative conditions, which are often coined *Type III Diabetes*, or *Brain Diabetes* there is insulin resistance in the brain, thereby starving the brain of its glucose uptake. *However*, it has been shown that the brain can metabolize ketones derived from the MCTs in coconut oil for energy, bypassing the need for insulin uptake. Not only that, the energy yield from ketones is higher than for glucose, and it is likely that the metabolism of ketones within the mitochondria does not produce the same degree of harmful Random Oxygen Species as glucose metabolism would. In essence, there is a net anti-inflammatory effect from ketone metabolism as compared to glucose metabolism, and ketones are said to be very *clean* fuels for the body.

It could well be that the use of coconut oil early in the treatment of brain tumours could feed the healthy brain cells while depriving the tumour cells of the only source of rapid energy they can process: glucose. Certainly there is some evidence that coconut oil can induce *apoptosis* or *cell death* in bowel cancer.

What interests me personally is that this ketogenic approach to diet has been successfully used for over 90 years in the treatment of epilepsy and type two diabetes, and has been shown to be very effective in preventing seizures in epileptics. However, it is not in the interests of the large carbohydrate producers (*Big Grain*) who dictate a great deal of nutritional science these days.

Nutritional science is as bad as any other science in terms of being personality-driven, industry-driven and populist-driven. The power of *orthodox* nutrition to skew us away from our best health outcomes is exemplified by the recent very public trial of the much-published Dr Tim Noakes, in South Africa. Dr Noakes *was* the doyen of carbohydrate proponents, and a world leader in research into carbohydrate use in endurance sports.

Dr Noakes started to suffer Type II diabetes complications a few years ago. His father and a brother had succumbed to the condition previously, so he decided to embark on a ketogenic approach to his personal nutrition and lost 44 pounds (20 kg) in the process, reversing his Type II Diabetes, while returning to good enough shape to run again. He then *back-flipped* from his carbohydrate diet tenets established over a lifetime career in research, and went in another direction altogether.

The backlash to his newly affirmed dietary position was vicious, with high-profile *colleagues* and former acolytes in the nutritional research world going as far as saying he'd "lost his mind". He was reported to the health practitioners' registration board in South Africa by a hospital dietician who got very upset with a non-dietician advising people on nutrition apparently. He won his case at the highest level in the court system in South Africa, however the remarks on his case were that his views were *not orthodox,* or *not in keeping with the majority viewpoint.*

It could be many years before the *majority viewpoint* is allowed to *catch up with the times* without getting practitioners deregistered.

There is obviously a great deal more to the reason why divergence from the accepted norms of the SAD diet will invoke the wrath of registration bodies. Apart from the obvious challenge to the existing nutritional paradigms, upon which many academic reputations and huge corporate fortunes have been made, I'd say that large vested-interest groups in the food industry have a big say *behind the scenes,* just as the pharmaceutical giants who manufacture statin drugs and sponsor many medical conferences and University Chairs have a large say in the amazing denial of recent science that debunks their views. It's all at the expense of the public's long-term physical and cognitive health.

To me, it is absolutely unacceptable that publicly-funded agencies like the Heart Foundations continue to promote an outdated paradigm like the lipid hypothesis of heart disease. It is *outrageous* that the paradigm is still believed, over 20 years after having been debunked in peer-reviewed studies, and it is even more outrageous that the statin drugs are still on the market.

If It Walks Like a Duck and Talks Like a Duck.

It probably is. The very nutrients which have been demonstrated by peer-reviewed research to have a positive effect on reversing atherogenic plaques are criticized in carefully-placed off-hand comments by the American Heart Association. Red palm oil is one of the richest sources of two of the most powerful forms of vitamin-E and vitamin-A antioxidants in nature: the tocotrienols and the carotenoids.

Tucked away on one of the American Heart Association web pages under the helpful title *About Cholesterol* is the following comment, handily placed to throw just enough caution into the mix about these healthy non-drug alternatives:

Some tropical oils, such as palm oil, palm kernel oil and coconut oil, also can trigger your liver to make more cholesterol. These oils are often found in baked goods.

That's what your liver *should* be doing with saturated fats; making more cholesterol! The more the better! No mention is made of the far more harmful grain and seed oils (often labelled as *vegetable oils*) that are in packaged baked goods, with their inflammatory loads of omega-6 oils, and added sugars. The *only* oils mentioned are the two oils that have been shown by recent research to have a *beneficial* effect on atherosclerosis (ie: they *lessen* atherosclerotic plaque formation). If these oils are taken with fats sourced from cream cheese or tasty cheese, or even goose fat, all rich in vitamin K2, then the atherosclerotic plaque will be reversed.

What needs to be looked at a little closer is *why*, from all food sources, these particular beneficial tropical oils have deserved special mention. That's the subject of a whole book, which has probably already been written by several people with more expertise in the politics of nutrition than me.

CHAPTER 49

What do shoe-laces and chromosomes have in common?

Meet Your Telomeres!

Melbourne University was the top-ranked university in Australia in 2015. One of the oldest Halls of Residence at Melbourne University is Janet Clarke Hall, where my scholarship-winning oldest daughter Annabel resided until recently. (As a very proud Dad I just had to put that in there!)

Janet Clarke Hall was where a Hobart-raised girl named Elizabeth Blackburn studied in the early 1960s. Elizabeth Blackburn won the 2009 Nobel Prize for Medicine and Physiology for her work on the chromosomal replenishment enzyme *telomerase*, and *telomeres*, the protein complexes which function much like the *aglets* on the ends of our shoelaces that prevent them from fraying.

The 'Shoelace-based Science of Chromosomal Breakdown'

'Healthy Telomere': good levels of 'telomerase' present.

'Unhealthy Telomere': about to shorten, affecting chromosomal longevity and gene expression.

Telomeres apparently unwind and shorten with aging and high *stress* levels. The genetic material at the ends of the chromosomes is replenished by the enzyme *telomerase*. Low telomerase levels are associated with 6 markers for heart disease.

How we eat, move, think and feel can either help keep our cells healthy or put them into early retirement, according to a growing body of research cited in Blackburn's new book, co-authored by Elissa Eppel, PhD, *The Telomere Effect: A Revolutionary Approach to Living Younger, Healthier, Longer.*

According to an online article by Adriana Barton of The Globe and Mail, Toronto, there are five main recommendations to draw from Professor Blackburn's research.

1. Telomeres Respond to two types of *Aerobic* Exercise

In a German study published in 2015, resistance exercise, such as weightlifting, had little effect on telomerase, the enzyme that replenishes telomeres. This is a different outcome to the production of BDNF, which is increased with resistance-training as well as aerobic exercise like walking, cycling or running.

But over a six-month period, two forms of 'aerobic' exercise increased telomerase activity twofold. One was moderate exercise, such as light jogging or fast walking, performed three times a week for at least 45 minutes. The other telomerase-friendly workout, also performed three times a week, was high-intensity interval training, consisting of a 10-minute warm-up, four alternating intervals of fast and easy running (at three minutes each) and a 10-minute cooldown.

(*Speaking as a long-time endurance athlete and coach, I would go for the low-intensity type first, as high-intensity intervals that last 3 minutes can take your system into moderate acidosis and immune-suppression if done too regularly. However, if you're fit and well, and still want to protect your telomeres, alternate the higher-intensity exercise with moderate aerobic recovery days, or do the 'intervals' one day a week. This is sufficient to promote the desired physiological response without 'frying' your aerobic system.)

2. Excess Sugar means ANY simple sugar.

Excess sugar consumption shortens lives.

In a 2014 study of 5,000 Americans, people who drank 590 millilitres of sugary pop a day had the equivalent of 4.6 extra years of biological aging (as measured by telomere shortness) compared with those who did not. Americans who drank 237 milliliters of pop daily had telomeres the equivalent of two years older. The link remained even after researchers ruled out other factors, including diet, smoking, income, age and body-mass index.

3. Telomeres thrive on fish, seaweeds and flaxseed oil

All are sources of omega-3 essential fatty acids, linked to longer telomeres. In a 2010 study, researchers from the University of California, San Francisco, tested blood levels of omega-3s in 608 middle-aged patients with heart disease. The higher their blood levels of omega-3s, the less their telomeres shortened over the next five years. Of those who had telomere shortening, 39 per cent died in the next four years, according to a follow-up report. Of those whose telomeres appeared to have lengthened, 12 per cent died – a significant difference considering that all participants had heart disease.

(*If you're a male wanting to increase your natural free testosterone levels, obtain your omega-3 fatty acids from fish oil, and avoid flax seed oil. Flax seed oil contains an excessive amount of lignans, plant compounds which annihilate free testosterone and can be considered a way to *biologically castrate* a male).

If you're worried about possible mercury contamination in fish oil sourced from larger fish higher up in the food chain, this can be achieved by using oil sourced from marine creatures at the bottom of the food chain: krill, or shrimp, which are not only the main source of nutrition for the blue whale, but also one of nature's richest sources of omega-3 fatty acids, with the benefit of having high levels of the powerful neuro-protective antioxidant and carotenoid, astaxanthin, which gives krill oil its distinctive dark purple-red colour.

4. Depression and anxiety deplete telomeres

In a 2015 study of nearly 12,000 Chinese women, depressed women had significantly shorter telomeres than women who weren't depressed. Chronic depression appears to be the most harmful. In a 2014 study of nearly 3,000 Dutch people, researchers found that the longer and more severe the depression, the shorter the telomeres.

Anxiety, pessimism, hostility, mind wandering and rumination have also been linked to shorter telomeres. Fortunately, practices known to help us break these mental habits may help lengthen telomeres. (My personal way of countering those tendencies is to recite the 'Fruits of the Spirit' and The 23rd Psalm each evening on my peaceful 35-minute bush-walk).

In a 2012 study, researchers divided 64 people with chronic-fatigue syndrome into a control group and a group who learned *qigong*, a Chinese practice that emphasizes meditative movements and breathing. After four months, participants who practiced *qigong* had significantly greater increases in telomerase activity, and reductions in fatigue, than those not doing *qigong*.

5. No Yo-Yo Dieting and No Sugar

Repeated weight loss and weight gain (yo-yo dieting) appears to shorten telomeres. Instead of focusing on the numbers on the scale, the authors write, we should take steps to reduce excess belly fat (as opposed to fat on the hips and thighs) and improve our metabolic health.

One way is to lower our sugar intake.

While the war on sugar is nothing new, Telomere science quantifies the degree to which excess sugar consumption shortens lives.

In a 2014 study of 5,000 Americans, people who drank 590 millilitres of sugary pop a day (1 standard bottle) had the equivalent of 4.6 extra years of biological aging (as measured by telomere shortness) compared with those who did not. Americans who drank 237 millilitres of pop daily had telomeres the equivalent of two years older. The link remained even after researchers ruled out other factors, including diet, smoking, income, age and body-mass index.

Further Suggested Reading

These books are thoroughly recommended for everyone who wishes to improve with brain health and nutrition.

Brain Maker–The Power of Gut Microbes to Heal and Protect Your Brain–for Life. Dr David Perlmutter with Kristin Loberg

10% Human: How Your Body's Microbes Hold the Key to Health and Happiness. Alanna Cohen (This is a comprehensive book from a microbiologist who has been studying the microbiome of the gut for decades)

Excitotoxins The Taste that Kills Russell L. Blaylock, M.D.

Stop Alzheimer's Now! Bruce Fife, N.D. Foreword by Russell L. Blaylock, M.D. (A great, highly referenced book that is extremely high on detail; it's a 'classic' in the new field of metabolic nutrition)

The BIG FAT SURPRISE Why Butter, Meat & Cheese Belong in a Healthy Diet Nina Teicholz (Nine years of research by a journalist and New York Times best-selling author)

Primal Endurance Mark Sisson and Brad Kearns. (When 60 year olds look like these guys, sit up and take notice!)

21 Day Total Body Transformation Mark Sisson (This book explains how to transition your diet into a primal, ketogenic diet in three weeks).

Keto Clarity Your Definitive Guide to the Benefits of a Low-Carb, High-Fat Diet Jimmy Moore with Eric C.Westman, MD, and a panel of 22 experts

Presence: Bringing Your Boldest Self to Your Biggest Challenges by Amy Cuddy

Life on Purpose: How Living for What Matters Most Changes Everything by Victor Strecher

Man's Search for Meaning by Victor E Frankl

The Telomere Effect: A Revolutionary Approach to Living Younger, Healthier, Longer Elissa Eppel PhD, Elizabeth Blackburn PhD.

CHAPTER 50

Winding Things Up for Now

This has never been *my* very serious brain tumour: it's simply been just *a* brain tumour which my body made; a greatly-exaggerated *little issue* with a prognosis that various experts have tried to convince me is dire and can recur at any time. Aside from that, I have very little to do with it.

In my view, with the right conditions, I can get back from this *illness*. The fact that the tumour mass may have been accelerated by woeful financial strains, and happens to look just like a known nasty type of brain tumour under the microscope, known as grade IV Glioblastoma Multiforme, the *brain cancer death sentence*, doesn't particularly perturb me. I just wake up each day and get on with it.

This is the great thing about having a strong faith or sense of unfulfilled life purpose. Love of family and sense of unfulfilled life purpose are much more powerful than the small problem of a *terminal* brain tumour affecting one man on planet Earth, in the context of the vast and mysterious universe we live in, and the *Mind behinds all Minds* that permeates it.

Psalm 46:10 says "Be still, and know that I am GOD".

Another meaning is "Stop striving, and know that I am GOD".

In that sense, I've learnt to *not believe* the *reality* around me when it comes to being supposedly very sick, and I've had to learn to *let all concerns go*, however *convincing*. Some people can't relate to my Christian fervour, however they are just as happy to recognise the Deity as *The Universe*, or *Source*, or *The Great White Spirit* or *The Great Mystery* as some Native American peoples call HIM.

My convictions are of the Christian persuasion, because that is the culture and the upbringing I grew up with. For me, it totally works. The broad principles of darkness and light, evil and good, are themes that have been recognized by every people group on earth, whether Christianised or not. It has been said that there is a place in the hearts of all men that understands the basic mores of right actions and wrong actions, and their consequences.

I've waged my own personal war of light upon dark, good versus evil, in the broadest sense. I'm finding out who I am the older I get, and it has a great deal to do with responsibility to my children, and their children, and those that come after. And we all know children like FUN.

"You don't stop laughing when you grow old, you grow old when you stop laughing." — George Bernard Shaw

EPILOGUE

The Good Book says somewhere that the iniquities of the fathers shall be visited to the fourth and fifth generations;(OK-in Leviticus 26:40); this is another way of saying what modern psychology confirms; familial traits of hopelessness, dependency, substance abuse and family violence are learnt when very young, and familial traits of loving successful families are also visited by the same process. So it's just an ancient but pragmatic observation of familial psychologies, not necessarily a *curse*, but the outcomes can appear accursed *if you buy into them*.

After all is said and done, I am very proud of my family, and that together with the Good Lord, we have made sure that we have been able to make it so far in good shape. Things have not been easy for any of us, but at this stage Joanne and I have reared five healthy intelligent children who are ready for whatever challenges come their way. We've done this despite me being supposedly *terminally ill*.

I always get fully cheered up by the following scripture when I start to think too deeply and darkly about things:

Finally, brothers and sisters, whatever is true, whatever is noble, whatever is right, whatever is pure, whatever is lovely, whatever is admirable--if anything is excellent or praiseworthy--think about such things. Phillipians 4:8

There's only one more quote I think I need to finish this book:

"You are not beaten, until you admit it!" General George S Patton.

ABOUT THE AUTHOR

When former elite athlete, successful chiropractor, and father of five Dr Keith Livingstone suddenly collapsed with an aggressive *terminal* brain tumour, his happy, positive world was thrown into a dark maelstrom of despair. There were no known long-term survivors of glioblastoma multiforme anywhere in the world at that time. No medical specialist could advise him on ways to get better, or on a proven path to follow, so he found his own way, based on the latest natural health and medical knowledge he could find. He decided to ignore the *hopelessness* of his situation, and get on with the job of living, *enjoying* himself and making light of the situation, and slowly and steadily he has regained his health, with a couple of relatively minor setbacks that were possibly to be expected. Keith chose to *ignore* the *hard evidence* around him that he had a terminal condition, re-labelling it as *current information only—liable to change for the better.* This is an optimistic, extremely useful, fast-paced romp written in a light-hearted *stream of consciousness* style, where Keith shares about his early life, friends, and family as well as the philosophy, exercise routine and nutritional science that he feels will allow him to *outlast the process,* (*God willing!*)

When not writing, Keith enjoys family life and exercise. Keith is a life-long learner who loves meeting up with friends at cafes, and reading about health, history, nutrition, and exercise science. He enjoys drawing and painting as a hobby.

Printed in the United States
By Bookmasters